EXPLORING CHILDHC AND YOUTH

This exciting new book illustrates and analyses the complexities of children's and young people's everyday lived experiences throughout childhood. Taking an interdisciplinary approach, it provides theoretical frameworks and case studies to critically examine assumptions in the field and explore emerging perspectives. Considering different stages throughout childhood and youth, chapters cover key topics such as eating practices, gender, play, digital media and the environment.

Drawing upon insights from cultural studies, sociology, social anthropology, psychology, health and education, this book focuses on four key areas:

- Bodies and minds
- Space, place and belonging
- Inequalities and inclusion
- Childhood in the past, present and future

Essential reading for students on childhood and youth studies and education courses studies courses, *Exploring Childhood and Youth* is an important resource for practitioners working with children and young people, and for parents, communities and legislators who have influence over children's and young people's lives.

Victoria Cooper is Senior Lecturer in Childhood and Youth Studies at The Open University, UK and is former Co-Director of the Children's Research Centre. She is particularly interested in issues of identity, research methods, and children and young people's experiences living with a family health crisis.

Naomi Holford is Lecturer in Childhood and Youth Studies at The Open University, UK, and specialises in the area of gender, sexuality and class in childhood and youth.

EXPLORING CHILDHOOD AND YOUTH

This book forms part of the module 'Exploring childhood and youth' (E232), an inter-disciplinary module which develops theoretical knowledge about children and young people across the world. This is a key module in the Open University BA (Hons) in Childhood and Youth Studies qualification, a leading interdisciplinary programme, which offers a range of critical perspectives on children's and young people's lives in the twenty-first century. It is designed for anyone working with children and young people or with a general interest in the field.

Details of this and other Open University modules can be obtained from Student Recruitment, The Open University, PO Box 197, Milton Keynes MK7 6BJ, United Kingdom (tel. +44(0)3003035303; email general-enquiries@open.ac.uk). www.open.ac.uk.

EXPLORING CHILDHOOD AND YOUTH

Edited by
Victoria Cooper and
Naomi Holford

Routledge
Taylor & Francis Group

LONDON AND NEW YORK

The Open
University

First edition published 2021
by Routledge
2 Park Square, Milton Park, Abingdon, Oxon OX14 4RN

in association with
The Open University, Walton Hall, Milton Keynes MK7 6AA, United Kingdom,
www.open.ac.uk

and by Routledge
52 Vanderbilt Avenue, New York, NY 10017

Routledge is an imprint of the Taylor & Francis Group, an informa business

British Library Cataloguing-in-Publication Data
A catalogue record for this book is available from the British Library

Library of Congress Cataloging-in-Publication Data
A catalog record has been requested for this book

ISBN: 978-0-367-48543-6 (hbk)
ISBN: 978-0-367-48544-3 (pbk)
ISBN: 978-1-003-04157-3 (ebk)

Typeset in News Gothic
by Wearset Ltd, Boldon, Tyne and Wear

Printed in Great Britain by Bell and Bain Ltd, Glasgow

CONTENTS

EDITORS' ACKNOWLEDGEMENTS

Many colleagues within and beyond the Open University contributed to the production of this book. We are appreciative of all the authors for their contributions and for responding with patience to our editorial changes. We would also like to thank other colleagues at the Open University who contributed vital feedback and support: Sheila Curran as a member of the module team, and Kate Breeze, Sara Clayson, Jennifer Colloby and Stephen Harrison as critical readers. Gill Gowans was instrumental to this book's production. We are indebted to Sarah Richards (University of Suffolk), our external assessor, for her insightful and constructive feedback on drafts throughout.

In particular, we would like to thank Sally Black, our curriculum manager, for invaluable support throughout, ensuring production ran smoothly.

We are also grateful to Annamarie Kino and Alex Butterworth at Routledge for all their work and support.

Victoria Cooper and Naomi Holford, July 2020

CONTRIBUTORS

Jiniya Afroze's PhD research with The Open University explored children's experiences of everyday violence in the intersections of education, work, and generational and gendered inequalities across social spaces in an Urdu-speaking Bihari camp in Dhaka, Bangladesh. She is currently working as the Country Coordinator with Terre des hommes Foundation in Bangladesh for a DFID funded project – Child Labour: Action-Research-Innovation in South and South-Eastern Asia (CLARISSA) – led by the Institute of Development Studies (IDS) and implemented by a consortium which includes Terre des hommes, ChildHope UK and Consortium for Street Children. She is interested in learning from children and combining her research with action on issues related to children's everyday lives.

Victoria Cooper is a Senior Lecturer in Childhood and Youth Studies at The Open University and is former Co-Director of the Children's Research Centre. She has published articles and book chapters on a wide range of topics, with a specific focus on issues of identity, research methods, and children and young people's experiences living with a family health crisis. She has recently written a new book on parenting with Heather Montgomery and Kieron Sheehy entitled *Parenting the First Twelve Years: What the Evidence Tells Us* (Pelican, 2018). Before joining The Open University, she worked in a variety of education roles spanning early years teaching, further and higher education, and professional development.

Karen Douthwaite was a Lecturer in Early Childhood at The Open University at the time of writing and continues her association with the University as an Associate Lecturer, teaching on early childhood modules. Her research interests focus on the professional development experiences of early years educators. She has also written about the merits of using participatory methodologies to engage with young children's perspectives and has a keen interest in the value of young children's drawings, photography and stories to connect with their ideas. She has a considerable career history working with young children and their families, most notably as a Sure Start Children's Centre Manager, in which she used participatory approaches to develop responsive services for, and with, the community.

Naomi Holford is a Lecturer in Childhood and Youth Studies at The Open University. She specialises in the area of gender, sexuality and class in childhood and youth across different age ranges from the early years to teenagers and has written broadly in this area. She teaches across the childhood and youth undergraduate programme at The Open University and is currently involved in research focusing on children's rights with The Open University Children's Research Centre.

Lucinda Kerawalla was a Senior Lecturer in Childhood and Youth Studies at The Open University at the time of writing. Her research interests include investigating the experiences of young researchers and the development and evaluation of software to support argumentation in the classroom. She now works as an Education Consultant.

Peter Kraftl is Professor of Human Geography at the University of Birmingham, UK. He is also Honorary Professor of Education at RMIT, Melbourne. His research interests include children's geographies, childhood studies and geographies of education. He has published eight books, including *Geographies of Alternative Education* (Policy Press, 2013) and *After Childhood* (Routledge, 2020). He has been Editor of the journals *Children's Geographies* and *Area* and was a founding member of the Geographies of Childhood, Youth and Families Research Group of the Royal Geographical Society (with IBG).

Brenda A. LeFrançois is a Professor at Memorial University of Newfoundland in Canada. Her teaching, scholarship and activism focus on children's psychiatrization, sanism and anti-sanist praxis, from mad studies, sociology of childhood and critical children's rights perspectives. She has edited and authored many books, special volumes and journal articles on these issues. Her most notable contributions include the anthology *Mad Matters* and edited volumes in *Children & Society* and *Intersectionalities*.

Heather Montgomery is a Professor of Anthropology and Childhood at The Open University. She is a social anthropologist interested in ideas of childhood and cross-cultural parenting, and also of children's rights. She is the author of *Modern Babylon? Prostituting Children in Thailand* (Berghahn, 2001) and *An Introduction to Childhood: Anthropological Perspectives of Children's Lives* (Blackwell, 2008), co-author (with Victoria Cooper and Kieron Sheehy) of *Parenting the First Twelve Years: What the Evidence Tells Us* (Pelican, 2018) and co-editor (with Martin Robb) of *Children and Young People's Worlds* (Policy Press, 2018), and (with Martin Robb and Rachel Thomson) of *Critical Practice with Children and Young People* (Policy Press, 2019).

Fiona Reeve is a Senior Lecturer in Lifelong Learning at The Open University. Current research interests include higher education provision within both Further Education and Higher Education institutions, and the implications for learners. She co-edited (with Jim Gallacher) *New Frontiers for College Education: International Perspectives* (Routledge, 2019). She teaches on the Childhood and Youth degree programme at The Open University.

Jonathan Rix is Professor of Participation and Learning Support at The Open University and at the Inland Norway University of Applied Sciences. He teaches on courses dealing with inclusion, early years and special educational needs. He has worked in education in many different settings. He spent 13 years as a support teacher in a Hackney secondary school in inner London, as well as working in a wide variety of other community settings. His research interests focus on policies, practices and language that facilitate inclusion within the mainstream; capturing diverse perspectives; and developing models to facilitate our thinking about the form and function of education. He has a strong and broad interest in issues relating to learning difficulties and issues of equality and participation. His book, *Must Inclusion Be Special? Rethinking Educational Support within a Community of Provision* (Routledge, 2015), brings together the range of research he has undertaken since 2002, identifying the challenges inherent in the predominant educational systems and possible tools for moving beyond these.

Kieron Sheehy is Professor of Education (Innovation Pedagogies) at The Open University. His teaching and research interests are within the broad field of inclusive and special education, often focusing on how teaching approaches or services can be developed to successfully support diverse groups of learners. He has a particular interest in addressing issues for those who might be stigmatised and excluded within educational systems.

Mimi Tatlow-Golden is Lecturer in Developmental Psychology and Childhood and Co-Director of the Centre for Children and Young People's Wellbeing at The Open University (UK). Through the lenses of topics such as food, digital media, self-concept and fun, she examines how children and young people's experiences and subjectivities interact with, are constructed by, or resist, systems and expectations that the adult world devises. She also has a particular interest in digital marketing/data ecosystems and their implications for children's rights. She collaborates globally with academics in food marketing, law, rights and public health, and with agencies such as the World Health Organization, UNICEF and the European Commission.

Gavin Williams is an academic in the School of Education, Childhood, Youth and Sport based at The Open University in Wales, where he has worked since 2014. Prior to this he worked for ten years in the voluntary sector where he managed a range of services for children and young people with disabilities followed by a role as a National Young Person's Lead for a mental health charity. His current research interests centre on social inequalities and education, and promoting children's and young people's voices and rights through participatory methods.

Introduction

Victoria Cooper and Naomi Holford

In this book we explore the complex, multi-faceted, but often taken-for-granted lived experiences of children and young people. Childhood and youth studies is now a firmly established academic field, with university courses continuing to grow in popularity, and many publications bringing children's and young people's experiences to an adult audience. The idea that children's and young people's lives and perspectives should be taken seriously is now itself taken seriously.

Many of the core assumptions at the heart of childhood and youth studies retain the power to surprise and disturb, challenging ideas about childhood that are deeply embedded in the UK and the Global North more broadly. Teaching Open University students, who bring a wealth of experience and expertise from their own backgrounds, we find they are still intrigued and compelled to discover a subject that considers the world from a child's and young person's perspective. As such, this book is designed to introduce new audiences to key founding themes of childhood and youth studies: the idea that children and young people are active agents in shaping their own lives, that childhood is socially constructed, that children's and young people's perspectives are worthy of study in their own right (James and Prout, 1997), and that their rights are important and require respect. At the same time, we aim to reflect the broadening of contemporary childhood and youth studies, critically examining assumptions of the field and exploring emerging areas and perspectives. This book is designed primarily for a mid-level undergraduate audience with an interest in children and young people, including (but not limited to) those currently working in different areas of childhood and youth services or with a desire to do so in the future, as well as parents, grand-parents and relatives. It has been designed to explore a range of themes pertinent to the lives of children and young people within a UK context, complemented by an analysis of international childhood experiences, covering the age range from early years to young adulthood (0–23 years).

One key aim in this volume is to foreground the everyday – those aspects of children's and young people's lives and contexts that might otherwise go unexamined, be overlooked or taken for granted – the material things, such as games, pictures and toys which furnish their lives, the food they routinely eat, digital media they engage with, how they play and their relationships with the environment – and how close inspection of these everyday experiences can provide rich insights into the interplay between adult power, children and young people's rights and their own personal agency. Of course, what is everyday to one child is not to another. The experience of institutionalisation as a psychiatric inpatient is everyday life to 15-year-old Andrew (Chapter 13), just as using his dad's computer is to six-year-old Bernie (Chapter 1) and avoiding violence from her supervisor in a small hand embroidery workshop is to 12-year-old Rima (Chapter 5). In all these examples, everyday experiences are shaped by an array of social, cultural, political and economic factors around the individual child.

These intertwining influences mean that in order to understand any child or young person's life we need to adopt an interdisciplinary approach. The authors come from a range of backgrounds in the social sciences, with some drawing upon the more familiar disciplines within childhood and youth studies, such as anthropology and sociology. Others draw upon newer disciplines, like 'mad studies' (a relatively new field of academic study focused on making overtly visible the violence experienced by people deemed mad). Many authors incorporate insights from children's geographies, which has produced so much of the influential work in recent childhood and youth studies. In addition, several authors work with psychology. Childhood studies and psychology have not always sat comfortably together; indeed, early work in childhood studies (e.g. James *et al.* 1998) was often explicitly framed as a rejection of developmental psychology, and what was seen as its tendency to consider childhood as a series of universal stages, establishing norms of development from which deviation is considered a problem. While we share some of these critiques of certain forms of developmental psychology and continue to emphasise the importance of the cultural shaping of childhood, we also consider psychology as a wide and varied field and value its insights into childhood as well as its critiques from within (Montgomery and Tatlow-Golden, 2020). Through the chapters in this book there is also a focus on embodiment, recognising the importance of the body and biological factors in shaping (and being shaped by) childhood. Indeed, Peter Kraftl argues in our final chapter that childhood and youth studies may need to look further than the social sciences, with contemporary and future childhoods profoundly and inescapably affected by climate change.

As we adopt an interdisciplinary approach, bringing different disciplines together, so we aim to look at childhood through an intersectional lens, understanding how different aspects of children's and young people's identity come together – how they intersect – and what that means. Crucially, intersectionality (a term introduced by the black feminist Kimberlé Crenshaw in 1989) emphasises inequalities between and among different groups; it is not interested just in describing differences but in examining relations of power between people. Discussing the impact of her theory over 20 years, Crenshaw described intersectionality as:

> a lens through which you can see where power comes and collides, where it interlocks and intersects. It's not simply that there's a race problem here, a gender problem here, and a class or LBGTQ problem there. Many times that framework erases what happens to people who are subject to all of these things.
>
> (Columbia Law School, 2017)

Childhood and youth studies has always been concerned with power and difference; perhaps most fundamentally with considering the power differentials and relationships between children and adults. Outlining the key founding concepts of childhood studies, Allison James and Alan Prout included the principle that childhood is not a 'single and universal phenomenon' (1997, p. 8), but is one aspect of social analysis that cannot be entirely separated from other categories like class, gender or ethnicity. Taking an intersectional approach to childhood and youth studies requires recognition and analysis of the complex inequalities that shape children's lives. As Konstantoni and Emejulu (2017) argue, ' "being a child" and "having a childhood" mean different things to different children by virtue of their race, class, gender and geographical location' (p. 17). As explored throughout this volume, geographical location or place influences children's and young people's experiences greatly. One key axis of power/difference is divisions between the Global North – high-income, Western countries like the USA, UK, Australia, New Zealand and Europe; and the Global South – low- or middle-income countries like many African countries. Although it is important to stress that there are vast differences within these regions as well (there is significant poverty and inequality in the Global North, and significant wealth in the Global South), the power relations between these regions generally favour the North at the expense of the South. Throughout this book, we aim to take seriously the broader factors that shape children's and young people's everyday lives and identities, and to focus on those who are marginalised. Nevertheless, we recognise that we, and the contributors to this volume, are primarily situated in the Global North, and that our interpretations are inevitably shaped and limited by this.

The year 2019 saw the thirtieth anniversary of the United Nations Convention on the Rights of the Child – the human rights treaty ratified by all UN member states except the USA, which outlines the rights to which all children across the world are entitled. Children's rights have become widely accepted and embedded in politics and society – at least in theory. Of course, for many children and young people throughout the world their rights are challenged on many levels. Poverty, disability, mental health issues, complex gender identities and violence can challenge everyday experiences and in this book we explore these themes in relation to children's and young people's learning and schooling, play, access to further and higher education and their sense of self. In situating children's and young people's everyday experiences at the heart of this book we recognise their fundamental right to share their views on matters which impact upon their lives. Furthermore, this recognises that although children's and young people's lived experiences are shaped to a greater or lesser extent by social and cultural forces such as policies, legal frameworks and political ideals – which are examined in this book – children and young people have agency and the capacity to steer and influence their own lives.

The authors in this volume are thus committed to children's rights to provision, protection and participation, and to foregrounding children's and young people's voices. However, we also recognise the tensions and challenges of children's rights. These arise both practically: for instance, how should rights be implemented, and what does it mean to champion children's rights when so many children still lack those rights and there may be little practical recourse; and theoretically: how might rights be in tension?

For instance, might a child's right to protection from harm come into conflict with their right to participation, to make a decision over their own medical care? Can we acknowledge children's and young people's rights to expression, information and participation in the digital sphere, while also upholding their right to protection from harm that may come their way online? At the same time, children's rights may sit uneasily with the rights of adults; for instance, the particularly complex and controversial question of considering where the right to life begins, in the context of a pregnant person's right to control their own body. Similarly, we recognise the limitations of listening to children: whose voices are speaking; whose voices are being heard; and what difference does that make? While throughout this volume we draw upon research carried out with children and young people, and some research that is led by children and young people, we have not included contributions from authors who are children or young people themselves; we must acknowledge that our childhood and youth studies is shaped by adults.

In compiling this volume authors were provided with a broad brief, and this is reflected in the distinct styles of writing and diverse voices presented here. In a number of chapters authors take a very distinct approach in an attempt to convey a particular argument or point of view. Some of these views may challenge your own thinking and experiences and you may disagree with some of the material presented – indeed, some authors within our collection might disagree with others on certain points. All of our authors draw upon contemporary and emerging research with children and young people to theorise lives and experiences, and questions may be raised that are not fully answered; the aim here is to encourage deep thinking, reflection and debate, inviting readers to critically analyse children and childhoods.

Despite the stylistic differences between chapters, this book has been organised around four core themes, namely to explore *bodies and minds*; *places, spaces and belonging*, issues around *inequality, diversity and inclusion*, and *childhoods: past, present and future*.

The chapters

The first four chapters draw upon contemporary research examining children's and young people's identities questioning when a child is recognised as a child, how they define their sense of self, how they are seen by others and how identities are connected to the everyday themes of food, materials and bodies. With a shared focus on identity, each chapter looks at different aspects of children's and young people's emerging sense of self. The opening chapter by Victoria Cooper looks at identity formation as a dynamic process in which children construct multiple identities throughout their lives and how material things, such as toys and pictures, provide a medium through which to understand how identities are shaped by intersecting social and cultural systems and how children shape their unique sense of self. But when does childhood begin? This is a challenging question central to Chapter 2. Here Heather Montgomery focuses on the infant body and looks at how different cultures understand the beginning of life. This chapter questions how children become socially recognised as human beings and how it is intertwined with their biological development before and after birth. While recognising the multifaceted and complex nature of childhood identity, in Chapter 3 Naomi Holford concentrates on one aspect: gender. This chapter explores what we mean by gender, how young people experience and construct masculinities and femininities in physical and digital spaces, and how ideas about gender are changing in contemporary societies. The social construction of childhood identities is expanded in Chapter 4 where Mimi Tatlow-Golden considers food as one of the ways in which children, young people and families express their belonging to groups. It examines ways in which food in children's and young people's lives articulates identities relating to family, culture and class, moral and ethical views of the world, as well as generation and gender.

Children's and young people's experiences do not occur within a vacuum and are shaped in part as they move between different places and everyday spaces such as home, community, pre-school and school, and forge a sense of belonging. The next section of the book looks at the complex relationship between social structures, adult power and children's and young people's own personal agency and rights in these everyday spaces. In Chapter 5 Jiniya Afroze draws upon her own international research to consider how children and young people understand and negotiate the accepted and somewhat routine violence experienced in a Bangladesh camp, including violence shaped by gender and age. The intersection between children's lived experiences, and broader social structures and policies, is a core theme of Chapter 6 which focuses on the early years and how children's play and learning relationships are influenced by the places they are in as well as their 'place' in policy provision and thinking. Here Karen Douthwaite explores a range of historical, political and theoretical perspectives on the purpose of early years provisions and their relevance to young children's play and learning relationships. Chapter 7 by Lucinda Kerawalla adopts a critical stance in considering children's views and experiences of school in the UK – a space where children spend so much of their time. The chapter considers the value of listening to children's and young people's perspectives on their experiences of life in their classrooms but questions the extent to which their right to be heard and listened to is put into practice.

In the next section of the book the chapters examine issues around inequalities, inclusion and diversity. In Chapter 8 Gavin Williams considers the relationship between poverty, place and learning. Focusing on his own research in the south Wales valleys, he explores the importance of place and belonging and how it shapes children's learning experiences in an underprivileged area, through a Bourdieusian lens. In Chapter 9, Fiona Reeve extends this use of Bourdieu, asking some important questions about inequalities and access to further and higher education in the UK and other Global North countries, such as why some young people transition seamlessly into higher education and others do not consider this as a possible future, and whether certain forms of education are more highly valued by society. In Chapter 10, Jonathan Rix considers inclusive professional practice from a broad perspective, looking at the tension between individual and collective solutions to supporting children and young people considered disabled, and asking how we can change the way we think about practices. Interactions between advantage and disadvantage are examined in Chapter 11 by Heather Montgomery, where she explores the growing trend in volunteer tourism among young Westerners – often on gap years – working as volunteers in orphanages.

Here she considers the intercultural contacts between young Westerners and children overseas and the impacts these contacts have on both groups of children and young people, raising important questions about power imbalances and the role of good intentions in improving vulnerable children's welfare.

The remaining four chapters are grouped around the core theme of *childhoods: past, present and future*, and look at how ideas, attitudes, policies and practices about childhood have shifted and sometimes changed in a range of areas, including mental health, disability, the environment and digital media. Indirectly or directly, the authors are all concerned with how different ideas and understandings affect the lives and experiences of children and young people. In Chapter 12 Kieron Sheehy addresses the highly sensitive topic – the history of disability and particularly the way of thinking known as eugenics, which made judgements about the worth of disabled children and how they should be treated. These decisions included the enforced segregation and long-term incarceration of children, involuntary sterilisation of young people, the withholding of life-saving care from infants and even, in some countries, a targeted extermination of disabled children. In Chapter 13 Brenda LeFrançois examines another sensitive and challenging topic of childhood mental health and particularly the dominance of medical models in diagnosis and treatment, which she presents as forms of oppression and marginalisation. In Chapter 14 Mimi Tatlow-Golden looks at how children's and young people's lives changed dramatically in the late twentieth and early twenty-first century with the expansion in digital media; she explores the nature and extent of technological surveillance, and how privacy works for children and young people in online spaces. Finally, in Chapter 15 Peter Kraftl discusses childhood and youth studies in the context of changing environmental conditions, considering ways in which childhood and nature are entwined, and exploring children's agency in climate protests. He argues that the complex and interconnected nature of today's challenges requires complex, interdisciplinary approaches for understanding childhood and children's lives; a call that reflects our intention and focus across the book as a whole.

References

Columbia Law School (2017) *Kimberlé Crenshaw on Intersectionality, More than Two Decades Later* [Online]. Available at www.law.columbia.edu/pt-br/news/2017/06/kimberle-crenshaw-intersectionality (accessed 5 August 2019).

Crenshaw, K. (1989) 'Demarginalizing the Intersection of Race and Sex: A Black Feminist Critique or Antidiscrimination Doctrine, Feminist Theory and Antiracist Politics', *University of Chicago Legal Forum*, vol. 1989, no. 1 [Online]. Available at https://archive.org/stream/Demarginalizing TheIntersectionOfRaceAndSexABlackFeminis/Demarginalizing+the+Intersection+of+Race+and +Sex_+A+Black+Feminis_djvu.txt (accessed 5 August 2019).

James, A. and Prout, A. (1997) *Constructing and Reconstructing Childhood: Contemporary Issues in the Sociological Study of Childhood*. Abingdon: Routledge.

James, A., Jenks, C. and Prout, A. (1998) *Theorizing Childhood*. Cambridge: Polity Press.

Konstantoni, K. and Emejulu, A. (2017) 'When Intersectionality Met Childhood Studies: The Dilemmas of a Travelling Concept', *Children's Geographies*, vol. 15, no. 1, pp. 6–22 [Online]. DOI: 10.1080/14733285.2016.1249824.

Montgomery, H. and Tatlow-Golden, M. (2020) 'Childhood Studies and child psychology: Disciplines in dialogue?', *Children and Society* [Online]. DOI: https://doi.org/10.1111/chso.12384.

1 Childhood identities and materiality

Victoria Cooper

Introduction

A well-worn blanket that has lived with a child since birth; an ageing teddy-bear which arrived as a gift and continues to remind a growing child of home; a wooden box full of 'stuff', including pictures, a party invitation, letters, doodles, photographs and drawings – are these things important? If so, how – and what might they reveal, if anything, about childhood identity?

Identity is not fixed or singular but fluid and multifaceted, and reflects a range of social, cultural, economic and political influences. Identity formation is recognised as a dynamic process in which children negotiate, construct and reconstruct multiple identities throughout their lives (Cooper and Collins, 2008). Some aspects of children's identities reflect distinct social markers, such as age, gender and ethnicity and family and group membership. Yet there is more to identity, which appreciates the dynamic and fluid quality of children's everyday lives, including how they play, places they go and how they engage with the material world. A growing body of research calls for a broad understanding of identity which considers how children interact with physical, material things (Cross, 2004; Horton and Kraftl, 2006; Horton, 2008; Jones, 2008; Grube, 2017) to communicate aspects of self. Materials not only leave traces of where children go, the people and places that are part and parcel of their lives – but also the things they enjoy and produce, as well as how they project their own unique identities. However, the materiality of childhood has been somewhat overlooked and is a relatively recent focus of research across childhood studies and children's geographies (Edwards and Hart, 2004; Jones, MacLure *et al.*, 2012; Cooper, 2017). These research developments recognise that material things not only take on social meanings, but that humans interact with and use materials in a variety of ways which provide order, structure, meaning and a sense of self.

This chapter is structured to look, first, at identity and what this concept means, before introducing ideas about materiality. The remaining sections discuss how materiality is a useful medium for exploring childhood identity; first, in relation to how objects such as toys, games and pictures are marketed, selected and often used in ways which reveal how childhood identities are shaped within social and cultural systems; and second, how children themselves engage with and use material things to narrate their individual and unique sense of self.

What does the concept of identity mean?

When we talk about identity, what exactly do we mean? Is identity an 'it' – something that can be located, grasped and easily understood?

Identity is a complex term, synonymous with notions of *self*, *me*, *I*, *self-image* and *self-concept* (Harter, 1999; Sani and Bennett, 2004; Guerin and Tatlow-Golden, 2019). It is infinitely nuanced and subjective due to its 'slippery, blurred and confusing' features (Wetherell, 2010, p. 3). Concepts of identity in relation to childhood hover around subjective ideas about who children are and how they feel about *self*, as much as how they relate to and are seen by others as part of communities, societies and cultural groups.

In a small-scale research project I carried out with a colleague, a group of 18 children (eight boys aged between five and 11 and ten girls aged between four and 11) were asked during focus groups to talk about identity: what it means and the different ways to describe who they are. The children talked about many different aspects, for example:

> 'It's about who you are.'
> 'It's what makes us different.'
> 'Our attitudes and behaviour.'
> 'How you think.'
> 'We can be different at school and different at home.'
> 'Your feelings about yourself.'
> 'We do change as we get older.'
> 'I am more confident.'
>
> (Cooper and Collins, 2008, p. 12)

While the descriptions here are different, they each offer some insight into the intricacy of identity. In the extracts above the children focused on the uniqueness of a person's identity and the potential difference between how children think about self and how they behave and are seen by others. The emphasis on difference presents further complexity, as it places the child within a social arena where comparisons can be made, and indicates how aspects of identity can change, not only in response to a space or setting but also as children mature. Identity can therefore be seen as *socially contingent*. Social contingency refers to the way in which social behaviour occurs through intersecting relationships between individuals and contexts and is a central theme within *symbolic interactionism*. Associated with the work of American sociologist George Herbert Mead (1863–1931), *symbolic interactionism* is a theory which focuses on the relationships among individuals and explores the distinct way in which people make sense of their social worlds.

When talking about identity children draw upon socially constructed definitions of themselves – they use language, images and behaviour that reflect the social norms rooted within any given culture. When asked 'Who are you' children typically describe themselves in relation to others, particularly their family and friends, and use markers such as age, ability, likes and dislikes to communicate aspects of self (Cooper and Collins, 2008, pp. 14–15), as the following extracts from the same focus group illustrate:

> I am Amy. I am a girl. I am me. I like playgroup. My friend is Chantelle. She plays duck, duck goose. I have long hair. Chantelle is pretty.
>
> (Amy, aged 4)

> I am Berty. I am a boy. I like Pokemon. I play with Joseph, Edward and Aiden. I like running. I like jumping. I like climbing. My brother makes dens. I do karate. I am good at maths. I live in my house. I live in Stroud.
>
> (Berty, aged 5)

> I am Layla. I am a girl. I have a pink room. I squabble with my brother. I play with him as well. I am a human. My teacher is called Miss Sullivan. She teaches us and me as well. I help my Mum cook. Berty is my little brother. I live with him. I love him. We live happy in this house. Josie is my best friend. I play with her a lot.
>
> (Layla, aged 6)

These extracts show how notions of self are relational, insofar as they reflect the social relationships that are important to children. Furthermore, they reveal how descriptions of self are often 'tied to bodies' (Weigert *et al.*, 1986, p. 93) and draw upon physical aspects of identity, including gender and ethnicity (Harter, 1999) as well as ideas about perceived attractiveness (Weedon, 2004). It follows, therefore, that a child's identity derives in part from these socially constructed meanings (Weigert *et al.*, 1986) and attributed labels (Hudak, 2001; Hudak and Kihn, 2001). Throughout this chapter the self is not viewed as a concrete, static form but as an ever-changing, fluid, multi-dimensional representation that weaves in and out of social life (Cooper, 2017). This emphasis on fluidity is important. Researchers have explored how identity is constantly evolving (Kelleher and Leavey, 2004; Layder, 2004). This is not to suggest that children are continually revising their sense of self but implies that changes can and do occur through the interaction of social circumstances, life events and an individual's reactions to them.

William James (1890, 1893), a late nineteenth- and early twentieth- century psychologist, first distinguished between *I* and *me* as aspects of identity, reflecting the contrast between how children view themselves as individuals – *I* – and in relation to others – *me* – and further reflects the distinct aspects of childhood identity: the *individual* and *social*. Children are born into families, communities and societies as *embodied* beings, with a physical sense of self which develops, grows and changes throughout life and within a social context. Embodied identities can fuse a host of markers, including age, gender and skin colour as well as gait, physicality and ideas about beauty (Robinson and Jones Diaz, 2016). Thus, while many of these markers can be bestowed through biology, they can also be enhanced and modified. Children can make decisions as to how they choose to represent their gender, for example, which may be in contrast to their biological sex (Capous Desyllus and Barron, 2017) – this is covered in more detail in Chapter 3. How children relate to their embodied self, which will develop and change to some extent throughout life, owes much to how they feel about themselves at particular points in time and reflects how children become who they are through their relationships with others; their emotional and social experiences (Bion, 1952) and affective qualities, such as their motivations and interests as well as their aversions. The concept of identity therefore incorporates many different aspects which are embodied, affective (a term that means relating to moods, feelings or emotions) and socially contingent. Clearly, the concept of identity can mean many different things and, as a consequence, is notoriously difficult to research.

The various ways to describe children in research have often drawn upon well-versed conceptualisations typically used by adults, which mark transitions, developmental milestones and categorisations. These describe, for example, the *infant*, *young child* and *adolescent* – as well as qualities such as confident, shy, sporty and clever, which can be used to identify children at particular points in their lives (Cooper and Collins, 2008). Much of identity research has characteristically used observational studies of how children behave within the social world, and also self-reported accounts where children are asked to define and describe themselves and how these accounts change over time in a developmental sequence (Harter, 1999; Sani and Bennett, 2004). Psychologists have also applied attitudinal scales in an attempt to locate traits and characteristics children use to describe themselves in comparison with others. However, not only have observational accounts of children been critiqued for their capacity to only gauge a small aspect of identity, namely that which is social and observable (Cooper, 2014), but children's descriptions of self, much like adults' descriptions, are limited (Thrift, 2005). Erving Goffman (1959), a Canadian-American sociologist and social psychologist, addresses such limitations and has argued that there are many parts of identity. He highlights the difference between what he termed *performed self* – the 'on-stage' self that people present to others – and *private self*, which children, much like adults, may prefer (consciously or unconsciously) to keep hidden. Goffman uses the analogy of the theatre performance to explore how human beings present themselves to the world, much like an actor on stage presenting a role to an audience.

The vast majority of developmental theories about childhood identity within child psychology have drawn heavily upon adult interpretations (Brooks, 2006). Work in some other social sciences has promoted participatory approaches which acknowledge the value of children as collaborators within research (Christensen and Prout, 2005; Kellett, 2009; Clark, 2011) who can provide insight into the complex worlds they inhabit. So, rather than rely on adult versions of 'knowing and telling' (Jones, 2008, p. 199), participatory studies provide opportunities for children to share their views, contribute to, and in some cases take a leading role in research about their lives. Participatory studies have utilised multi-modal methods,[1] including pictures, photographs and map making, for example, as research methods which enable children to collaborate, and include research which examines how children come and go, play and relate to people, places and things (Einarsdottir, 2005; Flewitt, 2008; Plowman and Stevenson, 2012; Kullman, 2012; Cooper, 2014, 2017). Horton and Kraftl (2006) focus on how meaning is communicated through the material things that children choose, such as preferred toys and clothes along with a variety of artefacts such as bags and pictures, looking at how things hold affective connotations and may trigger strong feelings and emotions which can reveal different aspects of identity. The focus on materiality in shaping children's social experiences and contributing to their developing identity has recently been examined in a variety of different ways from exploring the materials that children select and interact with daily (Jones, 2008); how children learn from and with materials within the home and school (Jones *et al.*, 2012) and how children choose different material objects to talk about and so narrate their identities (Cooper, 2014, 2017).

Materiality

Material objects matter to children in so many different ways. Not simply 'the stuff of the world' (Law and Hetherington, 2000, p. 52), materials are imbued with memory, imagination, language and culture (Dale and Burrell, 2008) and as Latour (2005, p. 20) states, 'consider things and you will have humans'. And yet materials have so often been overlooked. Law and Hetherington (2000) describe how materials have typically been thought of as fairly meaningless inert stuff, taken for granted and regarded as somewhat incidental to what is really going on in one's social life. Dale and Burrell (2008) note how this is further reflected across academic disciplines where the study of materiality has traditionally been positioned within the natural and physical sciences, leaving the study of social life within the realms of social science and most notably psychology, sociology and social anthropology. In part, they suggest that this is due to the tendency across these academic disciplines to separate the materiality of the social world from the thinking, human mind. Such dualism reflects the philosophical premise of the *Cartesian split*, most famously associated with the French philosopher and scientist René Descartes (1596–1650). Descartes argued that the mind and body are quite distinct and separable. Furthermore, he asserted that the mind controls the body and how we use our bodies to interact within the social world. The prevalence of this view may explain the extent to which so much of identity research has relied on self-reported accounts – favouring the rational thinking mind – where children are asked to describe themselves with less emphasis on embodied, everyday experiences.

There has been an increasing focus on materiality in social sciences over the past 30 years, and its significance in understanding childhood not only mirrors developments within the field of childhood studies, particularly children's geographies, but is also marked by a much broader awareness of everyday experience and mirrors debates on what is termed the *material turn* (Rose and Tolia-Kelly, 2012) in social science (Urry, 2000). This approach recognises how materials can carry part of a person with them (Law and Hetherington, 2000) as much as they link up to events and contexts and can also retrieve something that may have been lost or forgotten (Harper, 2002). A material approach considers how objects are enmeshed with meanings that cross boundaries and carry with them the ordinary qualities of life; as such, materiality can provide a different approach through which to examine the fine nuances of childhood (Jones, 2008). There are things children do and feel that are part and parcel of everyday life, which often go unnoticed yet may provide rich insights into children's sense of self. Engaging with and listening to the views of children includes the rich multi-modal experiences that make up children's lives and so reflects how they play and interact with friends, family and *things* (Cooper, 2014).

There are different ways of applying the concept of materiality to explore childhood identity. Here I look, first, at how objects, things and artefacts generally such as books, toys and pictures provide a useful medium to explore ideas and representations of childhood within broad social systems. I then look at how children interact with and use toys, games and personal things to communicate personal, subjective ideas about self. These different ways of exploring childhood identity – the *social* and the *individual* – are not necessarily in opposition, although they are quite distinct but intersect in many ways, thus revealing the complexity of identity.

Materiality: constructing views about childhood

Children are born into societies and cultures where the quality or properties of a material object define its use, or at least suggest how it can or should be used. Not just the back-drop to children's lives, material things are deeply entwined with how childhood is represented and understood. Indeed, as will be explored in Chapter 2, childhood is con-structed through materiality even before a child is born. Ideas about childhood have been explored and represented through art, photography, music, literature and commer-cial products such as toys. Through the examination of a wide range of pictures of chil-dren from the sixteenth century up until today, for instance, Higonnet (1998) examines how children are portrayed in distinct ways; as the romanticized child depicted during the sixteenth century to the savvy and knowing child evident in more contemporary visual images. Similarly, toys and games are marketed commercially to represent ideas about children and how they might play. Some toys might represent ideas of children as 'cute and innocent' while other games and toys might align to ideas about children as 'cool and depraved' (Cross, 2004) – think, for instance, about debates over toy guns, or what kinds of dolls are appropriate for young children.

Artefacts have the capacity to 'embody and invoke' descriptions of childhood, argue Jones and colleagues, and so have strong social and cultural links with what is deemed right or wrong and 'whilst dummies might be for babies, the lip-gloss pens might signal age-inappropriateness of the opposite valance – as being too mature' (Jones *et al.*, 2012, p. 55). Many material things are also infused with commercialism (Bucking-ham, 2000; Jones *et al.*, 2012) and marketed in ways which promote ideas about how children should behave, when and with whom. The soft toy and carry-cot; the swing and paddling pool; the bike and scooter; the school bag and iPhone – such objects can denote a particular stage within childhood and the types of materials deemed socially acceptable. Similarly, toys, clothes and other items are often linked closely with gen-dered identities through marketing as well as adults' and children's attitudes (dis-cussed further in Chapter 3). Materials also have the capacity to connect historically to

Figure 1.1 Children's toys can be seen as a representation of childhood.

a particular period of time; from childhood games and toys, such as spinning-tops, skipping ropes and marbles of a childhood past, to the smartphones, tablets and electronic devices of twenty-first-century childhood. Materials connect to the experience of *being* a child and thus provide insights into the much broader understandings and representations of childhood across time and space.

The work of the French philosopher and sociologist Henri Lefebvre (1991) is significant in connecting two important aspects of materiality. As Dale and Burrell (2008) note, Lefebvre clearly differentiates between physicality – what marks out a material as an object or thing – and the imaginary aspect of materiality which conveys meaning, place and memory. Toys, games and stuff generally, like much of the physical and material world, have a trajectory and what Thrift describes as an 'afterlife' (2008) invested with values and power (Tagg, 1988; Legene, 2004; Cooper, 2017). Materials have the capacity to rouse, to evoke memories and to unveil a whole host of feelings for children and adults, from nostalgia, desire and jealousy to frustration, aversion and repulsion:

> An object may be a danger to self or others; or a distraction from the serious business of learning; or an incitement to inappropriate social behaviour, such as coercion or theft. It may stir up unwanted affect, such as anxiety if lost or stolen; or annoyance or complaint from parents. Expensive objects may encourage undesirable tendencies such as bragging or ostentatious display and, correspondingly, feelings of envy or exclusion on the part of children who could not hope to possess them.
>
> (Jones *et al.*, 2012, p. 54)

In researching how children interact with materials at home and school, Jones *et al.* (2012, p. 52) note how a variety of things such as security blankets, teddy bears and dolls are all objects which carry with them a set of social and culturally derived beliefs, and often customs. In observing a three-year-old child, for example, Alisha, they note that when separated from her parents at the start of school Alisha was inseparable from her toy which she brought with her from home – Brown Dog. They describe how for Alisha her relationship with Brown Dog carries almost 'magical qualities' where Brown Dog has the capacity to soothe and comfort and so relieve her trauma of being separated from home and her carers. Thus there is a sense in which materials evoke meanings within contexts. But they can also cut across boundaries with children as they move in and out of different spaces and places. While children can and do interact with objects such as soft toys to pacify and console them as they move between places, my own research reveals how the domain of home may impress its own set of rules about what can and cannot cross boundaries to be revealed to the outside (Cooper, 2017). Certain items of clothing such as underwear and dressing-gowns, for example, are regarded as private, and certain toys labelled within certain domains, such as bedtime toys, and as such recognised as things not to be shared outside the home. Similarly, Jones *et al.* (2012) indicate that schools can also set expectations and boundaries as to those materials that are acceptable and those that are not; thus controlling the types of objects, toys and games such as toy weapons that are allowed (or not) to be brought into school from home. Children's perspectives on their emotional experiences in school will be explored further in Chapter 6.

The process of selecting, using and interacting with materials denotes a practice in which social structures have the capacity to impose values and where adults often wield most power. Learning equipment, household artefacts such as pictures and ornaments, as well as clothes and toys, for example, are often subject to interventions by adults. They are chosen, purchased and gifted by adults to create spaces for children to sleep and play, to confer gender identity and to provide sources of comfort and reassurance, such as cuddly toys and comfort blankets. At the same time, materials can also be policed, removed and vetoed by adults according to their social acceptability and general desirability. Guns, weapons and certain kinds of dolls, such as Bratz dolls, have been labelled as unacceptable and undesirable by many parents for different reasons (Jones *et al.*, 2012). Materials therefore provide a focus through which the interplay between social and cultural values and the child can be explored. As Allison James (1993, p. 107) argues, the complex 'historiography of childhood' provides a clear message in how ideas, values and representations of children can shape children's experiences of growing up.

Although materials are useful in exploring how ideas about childhood can be constructed through things such as toys, games and pictures, this assumes that children share a common identity and are in some respects a *homogeneous* group as James suggests:

> the TV programmes children watched, the books they read and the toys they played with present a culture of childhood based on regularities, generalities and uniformities.
>
> (1993, p. 107)

Materials are never neutral but are imbued with expectations and ideals, and so provide a medium to consider the complex power relations in which childhood identities are to some degree shaped and often bounded by adult interventions within broad social and cultural systems. And yet conversely it is important to recognise that children, while sharing a great deal, will also have very different experiences growing up and are not a *homogeneous* group. Children have what sociologists term *agency* – that is, personal autonomy, and the ability to affect their lives and make choices for themselves. Childhood identities are not just something children slot into or have thrust upon them by their families, culture and wider society. As Steven Pinker, the Canadian-American psychologist (2002, p. 399), suggests, it is often easy 'to think of children as lumps of putty to be shaped' rather than agents within dynamic relationships, societies and cultures. The idea of agency challenges the belief of children as passive travellers in the world, framing them instead as protagonists of their own learning and lives (Grube, 2017).

Materiality: children's own constructions of self

Children connect to things within their material world (Horton and Kraftl, 2006). How they play, the toys and games they interact with, and how they create private spaces furnished with artefacts are linked to subjective experiences as well as to friends, family, people and places. From the pictures they produce and the clothes they wear, materials reflect the different elements of self across public and private spheres. In research with children and young people, material objects can often act as triggers which can stimulate children to reflect upon and talk about their own identity and sense of self. In my own research exploring how children interact with materials to talk about self, children aged between 4 and 8 years were each given a digital camera to take home and were encouraged to take photographs of things during their leisure time and within their local communities to build up pictures 'all about me' (Cooper, 2014, 2017). The children were then asked to select their favourite pictures of things and these were used to build identity narratives through individual interviews.

Photographs of toys and equipment were frequently taken during play and as part of a game. Pictures also referenced to equipment used as part of a journey or routine activity such as travelling to and from school on a scooter. There is a mobile quality to these pictures and their accompanying narratives which reveals the dynamic practices of childhood identity such as play, hanging about and visiting different places.

In the following extract, Bernie (aged six years) talks about some of the things he has photographed:

> I like my 3DS. It's my favourite thing. I play on it all the time at home. I like the computer. It's my dad's but I have my own account. I go on Amazon. I am good on the computer. Do you know that's Homer Simpson. I painted that. I love the Simpsons. When I get my own. I can't have a room of my own yet. Cos. Well, it will be a Simpson room I think. And at night I always have my night time water. See. My name's on it. It helps me sleep. I know it's time for bedtime.
>
> (Cooper, 2014, p. 10)

It is interesting to note how Bernie selected things to signpost a selection of features not only about himself and the things he liked but also his achievements and pleasures as well as the everyday routines within his social life, such as bed and leisure time. My data indicates that children can use artefacts to communicate a subjective, individual view of themselves and to depict personal preferences and social networks such as family and friends; to document their achievements, such as sporting successes or personal artwork as well as their likes and dislikes (the work of Guerin and Tatlow-Golden (2019) found similar results). All the children also took photographs of things which made explicit connections to their domestic habits, including pictures of chairs, cupboards, shelves and bedrooms. Sally (aged seven years) selected a picture

Figures 1.2a, 1.2b and 1.2c Children can use pictures of things to narrate their identities.

of her family cereal cupboard to talk about everyday domestic routines, as indicated in the following extract.

> On Saturday we can choose cereal. Special cereal [pointing to the picture of cereal boxes]. I like Krave ... I love chocolate [laughs]. I am not allowed it on school days. I have Weetabix. Me and Philip [Sally's brother] eat in the TV room.

These pictures, while relatively meaningless to me as the researcher, clearly connected to the traditions and patterns unique to each child and revealed how identities are tied to habits of everyday living. These everyday experiences may be considered quite mundane, but for a child growing up they provide a sense of home, their place within it and what this might mean to them. By talking about material things, children offered a glimpse into the complex web of identity connections within contexts such as the family, including how they routinely come, go and play alongside family members, pets and friends, and further afield to include other contexts such as schools and clubs. Such discussions provided rich opportunities for me to listen to the children; to engage with different aspects of their lives reflected in their pictures, and to gain some insight into the things they liked and disliked, and the fine nuances about their lives which often sit outside conventional research agendas. Bruner (1990) argues that in exploring who children are, it is important to consider the meanings, cultures, contexts and social practices of their daily life. Materials play an important part within this process.

It is important however to acknowledge that images are not 'records of reality' (Liebenberg, 2009, p. 445). Meanings always depend on when, how and where the images were constructed, as well as by whom and in what way the images are interpreted. The emphasis on meaning-making here is important. Not only does this acknowledge research as a process in which knowledge is produced but it recognises children's role in contributing to this process. In this sense, data is not extracted by the researcher to be represented elsewhere, but that research as a process is able to capture how meaning is constructed. As tools for navigation in my own research, material things forged useful connections which allowed me to explore children's daily routines, unique experiences and identity connections. The order of the day and what marks out the

Figures 1.3a and 1.3b Pictures of things can connect to everyday routine aspects of children's identities.

weekend – mealtimes, family practices of what children do, when and how – these all provide childhood with structure and meaning and make useful connections to child-hood identities. As Law (1994, 143) argues, 'modes of ordering' are impossible to step out of. They provide cultural pathways (Plowman and Stevenson, 2012) through which children construct and reconstruct 'maps' which can provide meaning and, as Iovina and Opperman (2014, p. 3076) suggest, 'the amalgamation of self and materials is the source of life's narrative'.

Concluding thoughts

Developments within social science have taught us a great deal in terms of recognising the complexity of children's identity as embodied, affective, socially and culturally con-structed (Cooper, 2014). Identity is not a *thing* but a dynamic process in which chil-dren negotiate, construct and reconstruct multiple identities throughout their lives (Durand, 2010; Cooper and Collins, 2008; Cooper, 2014, 2017). Thus while the notion of childhood identity sits alongside well-established and adult constructed ideas of stages and categories, other ways of looking can also provide a different lens through which to appreciate childhood identity as nonlinear and fluid. Identity is continually constructed through everyday practices and connections between people, places and things (Butler, 2003, p. 129). Horton and Kraftl (2006, p. 71) argue that meaning is often lost or hidden in the taken-for-granted ways of understanding the world, and urge researchers to consider some of the hidden and seemingly mundane aspects of child-hood which contribute to a child's constantly evolving identity. As Grube (2017) sug-gests, material things not only 'juxtapose the past with the present' but can be a 'bridge, a common stomping ground' (p. 3075) that connects to childhood. So, if researchers are to examine how children give meaning to themselves it is important to locate and examine the complex meanings into which the individual is born and raised.

Note

1 Multi-modal research methods typically incorporate both language-based and nonverbal com-munication to explore key areas.

References

Bion, W. R. (1952) Group dynamics: a review. *International Journal of Psycho-Analysis*, 33. Reprinted in M. Klein, P. Heimann and R. Money-Kyrle (eds) *New Directions in Psychoanalysis*. London: Tavistock Publications, 1955, pp. 440–477.

Brooks, L. (2006) The Story of Childhood: Growing up in Modern Britain. London: Bloomsbury.

Bruner, J. (1990) *Acts of Meaning*. Cambridge, MA: Harvard University Press.

Buckingham, D. (2000) *After the Death of Childhood: Growing Up in the Age of Electronic Media*. Cambridge: Polity Press.

Butler, J. (2003) Identity, deconstruction and politics. In M. Gergen and K. J. Gergen (eds) *Social Construction. A Reader*. London: Sage, pp. 129–131.

Capous Desyllas, M. and Barron, C. (2017) Identifying and navigating social and institutional challenges of transgender children and families. *Child and Adolescent Social Work Journal*, 34(6), 527–542.

Christensen, P. and Prout, A. (2005) Anthropological and sociological perspectives on the study of children. In S. Greene and D. Hogan (eds) *Researching Children's Experiences: Approaches and Methods*. London: Sage, pp. 42–60.

Clark, A. (2011) Multi-modal map making with young children: exploring ethnographic and participatory methods. *Qualitative Research*, 11(3), 311–330.

Cooper, V. L. and Collins, J. (2008) Children and identity. In J. Collins and P. Foley (eds) *Promoting Children's Wellbeing: Policy and Practice*. Bristol: The Policy Press, pp. 9–40.

Cooper, V. L. (2014) Children's developing identity. In M. Reed and R. Walker (eds) *A Critical Companion to Early Childhood*. London: Sage, pp. 281–295.

Cooper, V. L. (2017) Lost in translation: exploring childhood identity using photo-elicitation. *Children's Geographies*, 15(6), 625–637.

Cross, G. (2004) *Cute and Cool: Wondrous Innocence and Modern American Children's Culture*. Oxford: Oxford University Press.

Dale, K. and Burrell, G. (2008) *The Spaces of Organisation and the Organisation of Space. Power, Identity and Materiality at Work.* Basingstoke: Palgrave Macmillan.

Durand, T. M. (2010) Celebrating diversity in early care and education settings: moving beyond the margins. *Early Child Development and Care*, 180(7), 835–848.

Edwards, E. and Hart, J. (2004) *Photographs Objects Histories. On the Materiality of Images*. London: Routledge.

Einarsdottir, J. (2005) Playschool in pictures: children's photographs as a research method. *Early Child Development and Care*, 175(6), 523–541.

Flewitt, R. (2008) Multimodal literacies. In J. Marsh and E. Hallett (eds) *Desirable Literacies. Approaches to Language and Literacy in the Early Years.* London: Sage, pp. 122–139.

Goffman, E. (1959) *The Presentation of Self in Everyday Life*. New York: Doubleday.

Grube, V. J. (2017) Material forms: What is really going on? Shaping who we are and what we do. *The Qualitative Report*, 22(11), Article 13, 3075–3087.

Guerin, S. and Tatlow-Golden, M. (2019) How valid are measures of children's self-concept/self-esteem? Factors and content validity in three widely used scales. *Child Indicators Research* (Early Access).

Harper, D. (2002) Talking about pictures: a case for photo elicitation. *Visual Studies*, 17 (1), pp. 13–26.

Harter, S. (1999) *The Construction of Self: A Developmental Perspective*. New York: Guilford Press.

Higonnet, A. (1998) *Pictures of Innocence: The History and Crisis of Ideal Childhood*. London: Thames & Hudson.

Horton, J. (2008) A 'sense of failure'? Everydayness and research ethics. *Children's Geographies*, 6(4), 363–383.

Horton, J. and Kraftl, P. (2006) What else? Some more ways of thinking and doing 'children's geographies'. *Children's Geographies*, 4(1), 69–95.

Hudak, G. (2001) On what is labeled 'playing': locating the 'true' in education. In G. Hudak and P. Kihn, (eds) *Labelling: Politics and Pedagogy*. London: Falmer Press, pp. 9–25.

Hudak, G. and Kihn, P. (eds) (2001) *Labelling: Politics and Pedagogy*. London: Falmer Press.

Iovina, S. and Opperman, S. (eds) (2014) *Material Ecocriticism*. Indiana: Indiana University Press.

James, A. (1993) *Childhood Identities: Self and Social Relationships in the Experience of the Child*. Edinburgh: Edinburgh University Press.

James, W. (1890) *Principles of Psychology*. New York: Holt.

James, W. (1893) The stream of consciousness. In *Psychology*. New York: H. Holt and Company.

Jones, L., MacLure, M., Holmes, R. and MacRae, C. (2012) Children and objects: affection and infection. *Early Years*, 32(1), 49–60.

Jones, O. (2008) 'True geography quickly forgotten, giving away to an adult-imagined universe'. Approaching the otherness of childhood. *Children's Geographies*, 6(2), 195–212.

Kelleher, D. and Leavey, G. (eds) (2004) *Identity and Health*. London:Taylor & Francis.

Kellett, M. (2009) Children as researchers: what can we learn from them about the impact of poverty on literacy opportunities? *International Journal of Inclusive Education*, 13(4), 395–408.

Kullman, K. (2012) Experiments with moving children and digital cameras. *Children's Geographies*, 10(1), 1–16.

Latour, B. (2005) *Reassembling the Social. An Introduction to Actor-Network-Theory*. Oxford: Oxford University Press.

Law, J. (1994) *Organizing Modernity: Social Ordering and Social Theory*. Oxford: Blackwell.

Law, J. and Hetherington, K. (2000) Materialities, spatialities, globalities. in J. Bryson, P. Daniels, N. Henry and J. Pollard (eds) *Knowledge, Space, Economy*. London: Routledge, pp. 34–49.

Layder, D. (2004) *Social and Personal Identity: Understanding Yourself*. London: Sage Publications.

Lefebvre, H. (1991) *The Production of Space*. Oxford: Blackwell.

Legene, S. (2004) Photographic playing cards and the colonial metaphor. Teaching the Dutch colonial culture. In E. Edwards and J. Hart (eds) *Photographs Objects Histories. On the Materiality of Images*. London: Routledge, pp. 96–112.

Liebenberg, L. (2009) The visual image as discussion point: increasing validity in boundary crossing research.*Qualitative Research*, 9, 441–467.

Pinker, S. (2002) *The Blank Slate*. New York: Viking.

Plowman, L. and Stevenson, O. (2012) Using mobile phone diaries to explore children's everyday lives. *Childhood*, 19(4), 539–553.

Robinson, K. H. and Jones Diaz, C. (2016) *Diversity and Difference in Childhood. Issues for Theory and Practice* (2nd edn). London: Open University Press.

Rose, G. and Tolia-Kelly, D. P. (eds) (2012) *Visuality/Materiality: Images, Objects and Practices*. Farnham: Ashgate.

Sani, F. and Bennett, M. (2004) Developmental aspects of social identity. In M. Bennett and F. Sani (eds) *The Development of the Social Self*. Hove: Taylor & Francis.

Tagg, J. (1988) *The Burden of Representation: Essays on Photographies and Histories*. London: Macmillan.

Thrift, N. (2008) *Non-representational Theory. Space, Politics, Affect*. London: Routledge.

Urry, J. (2000) *Sociology Beyond Societies: Mobilities for the Twenty-first Century*. London: Routledge.

Weedon, C. (2004) *Identity and Culture. Narratives of Difference and Belonging*. Berkshire: Open University Press.

Weigert, A. J., Smith Teitge, J. and Teitge, D. W. (1986) *Society and Identity: Toward a Sociological Psychology*. Cambridge: Cambridge University Press.

Wetherell, M. (2010) The field of identity studies. In M. Wetherell and C. Mohanty (eds) *The Sage Handbook of Identities*. London: Sage, pp. 3–26.

2 Becoming a child

Heather Montgomery

Introduction

Childhood and youth studies (CYS) is an interdisciplinary field, drawing upon sociology, legal studies, anthropology, history, psychology and many others. It has explored the social meanings given to childhood, the influence of wider social, cultural, political and economic factors on these meanings and the impacts that different understandings have on children's and young people's lives. More recently scholars have also begun to look at childhood as a biological phenomenon characterised by bodily and psychological change, and based on an acknowledgement that children's bodies are small, fragile, vulnerable and often in need of adult protection. A new strand of work in CYS has, therefore, emphasised childhood's 'hybrid character, part biological and part social' (Prout, 2011, p. 7) focusing both on 'embodiment' and the ways that children's and young people's bodies develop as well as the social meanings given to them.

Despite this interest in theorising bodies, one group of children has been almost entirely overlooked in CYS – infants, neonatal and unborn children. There are many reasons for this – not least because they raise often uncomfortable and highly politicised issues over when life starts, when childhood begins, whether the unborn are biological entities or the youngest members of society and whether they have – should have – rights and what implications this might have for the rights of others. Such discussions are emotionally and politically fraught, bound up in disputes about reproductive rights, personal experiences, and religious and ideological values. To discuss childhood in relation to the unborn is to be immediately positioned on one side or the other of these acrimonious disputes and it is hard to discuss without borrowing the language, imagery and implied ideology of one side or the other. This chapter does not seek to take sides on these debates (although it cannot ignore them either); rather it aims to draw infant and neonatal children into discussions about the nature of childhood and to look at how different disciplinary perspectives (and different scholars within those disciplines) have analysed childhood in very different ways, asking similar questions but presenting diverse, and sometimes conflicting, answers.

Cultural constructions of the unborn

It may be easier to start with the unfamiliar in order to show the differences in how distinct societies, and people within those societies, think about and give meaning to unborn and neonatal children. There are large cross-cultural differences in when the foetus becomes seen as human and a brief examination of some non-Western societies suggests that there are highly variant understandings of when a child becomes a fully recognised social person (Montgomery, 2009). In large parts of the world, as this chapter will go on to discuss, this recognition is assigned at fixed points in the life cycle such as conception, viability or birth (although when this point should be has led to highly emotive and contentious debates). However, in some cultures, children become people much more gradually and recognition as fully human members of society comes progressively, sometimes not until several days or months after birth, making the divisions between foetus/child and between the unborn and born much more fluid. The Waiwai of the Amazonian rainforest, for example, express great doubt about the nature of very young children and refer to new-borns as *okopuchi*, or 'little corpses' until they are around two weeks old, while the Huaorani of Ecuador have only one word – translated as 'in the process of being born' for foetus, new-born and infant. Similar ambiguity about the difference between a foetus and an infant can also be seen among the Aboriginal group, the Murngin, who use the same term for foetus and new-born and only use the word child after the baby smiles at about six weeks (Montgomery, 2009).

Whether or not the newly born are fully human and have full social recognition has important impacts on how they are treated, especially in situations of poverty and social vulnerability. Nancy Scheper-Hughes (1992) whose account of infant death and child neglect in the *favelas* [slums] of north-eastern Brazil details with much sympathy how, in times of scarcity and places of poverty, or when children are unwanted or sickly, there is likely to be a waiting period after birth before infants are acknowledged as full members of society. She identifies great ambivalence about infants among such poor mothers, noting that they do not 'trust' those that seem passive or weak to survive and therefore do not give them medicine (and usually cannot afford to) and treat their deaths with indifference and resignation. Mothers in the *favelas* do not recognise or acknowledge individual personhood, reusing the same name several times over for successive siblings and it is only when children show signs of being active, of having the will to survive, or when they are older and therefore worth investing in emotionally, that mothers acknowledge them as fully human.

Thinking about the personhood of the unborn emphasises the fluidity, complexity and diversity of ideas around the very youngest and their relationships to others. A further example of this comes in anthropological accounts of 'spirit children' who stretch the category of 'the unborn' to the furthest extreme. These are children who are believed to exist in the supernatural spiritual world, waiting to be born as embodied children. Their existence is recognised in diverse communities including those of Aboriginal Australia, West Africa and East Asia, and in these places the links between neonatal and unborn children and the spirit world are so strong that it is impossible to study the former without reference to the latter.

Some of the best ethnographies of this phenomenon have come from work carried out in West Africa and describe children who live fully consciously in a spirit world before being born into the bodies of human babies (Gottlieb, 2004). The Beng of the Cote d'Ivoire believe in a spirit world, *wrugbe*, where children exist before they are born and where people go after their deaths. Although *wrugbe* is reachable by some adults, especially through dreams, it is children who are closest to it and to whom it is most accessible. Indeed, young children are seen as having only partially emerged from *wrugbe* and are in constant contact with it for several years after they are born. A new-born child belongs completely to the spirit world and, until

> the umbilical stump falls off, the new-born is not considered to have emerged from *wrugbe* at all, and the tiny creature is not seen as a person. Hence if the new-born should die during those first few days, there is no funeral, and the fact is not announced publicly. In this case the infant's passing is not conceived as a death, just a return in bodily form to the space that the infant was still psychically inhabiting.
>
> (Gottlieb, 1998, p. 124)

After the stump has fallen off the child begins a slow process, which takes several years, of leaving the spirit world behind and becoming more firmly attached to its earthly life.

The Beng believe that both adults and children can live in *wrugbe* and that a child has both spiritual and earthly parents. *Wrugbe* parents are believed to get angry if the baby is not being properly looked after in its earthly life. If a child is being abused or neglected, not fed when crying or comforted when in distress, his or her spiritual parents may decide to take the child back into the spirit world and keep him or her there until better parents are found and the child can be reborn into a different family. In other instances, spirit children are thought to be malicious or malevolent, deciding how long they will live with their earthly parents or whether they will return to their spirit companions, leaving their earthly parents heartbroken.

Such accounts are thought-provoking partly because they have wider implications, and ideas about spirit children have been used to explain many phenomena in West African societies. One approach has been to analyse spirit children beliefs as a way of coping with the high infant mortality of the region and as an adaptive parental response to the ever-present threat of losing several children. Although beliefs in spirit children are changing, recent research shows that a significant number of women still believe in them and use these beliefs to make treatment decisions when their children are ill, an important consideration when it has also been suggested that such children show many symptoms associated with sickle-cell diseases or certain forms of mental illness. Beliefs in spirit children act therefore as metaphysical explanations of per-ceived physical or mental imperfections (Montgomery, 2009).

In both Japan and Taiwan there is a belief in 'ghost' or 'haunting' foetuses – those that have been aborted but come back to haunt their mothers – and there has been a recent rise in shrines and temples dedicated to the spirits of these foetuses (La Fleur,

Figure 2.1 Jizo (Ksitigarbha bodhisattva) statues in Zojo-ji Temple in Tokyo, Japan. Jizo is a guardian of aborted and premature children.

1992; Hardacre, 1997; Moskowitz, 2001). Women who have had abortions report a variety of symptoms for some time afterwards, including illness, the inability to eat, fatigue and the sense that there is a watching presence nearby. Foetuses are thought to grow into small children in the afterlife and some women report hearing babies or young children laughing. In Japan, such foetuses are referred to as *mizuko* or water-children, and are seen as having the potential to return to the same family, or to travel to the land of the gods, or to return to another family; meaning that abortion delays, rather than prevents, their births. Although they are occasionally benevolent, ghost foetuses often cause distress and are assumed to be dangerous and need to be placated though spiritual means. The only way to get rid of these hauntings is to pay substantial amounts of money to certain temples that will perform exorcisms to placate them (Moskowitz, 2001). Again, this can be analysed in multiple ways. Although not a politicised issue in either Japan or Taiwan, Buddhist values suggest that abortion is morally wrong and women who do terminate their pregnancies should suffer spiritually. Therefore, the ambivalence many feel about abortion may indicate that the upsurge in the numbers of women who talk of experiencing such ghosts or haunting can be understood as a means of coming to terms with abortion in culturally acceptable ways. More cynically it might be seen as the commercialisation of guilt and distress and the financial associations – which are another way of exploiting vulnerable women.

Sociological perspectives

Children are born as embodied beings which develop, grow and change throughout life, and this biological and bodily development occurs from conception. Children are also born as social beings, arriving into a web of relationships that begin long before birth. They exemplify therefore the hybridity of childhood as something both biological and social. In terms of the unborn and newly born however this hybridity is extremely fragile and, even more than the infant or the child, the foetus, unborn or neonatal child alerts us to the necessity to look at interconnectedness – not just the interconnectedness of the foetus to a woman's body (and vice versa) but also to wider social relationships which develop in the womb – a process Deborah Lupton has described as 'interembodiment' (2013, p. 37).

It is this interembodiment that makes the unborn so problematic. They have no physical independence from their mothers but are claimed by some (for example, devout contemporary Catholics and evangelical Christians) as divinely created persons from the moment of conception entitled to special protections – even against the will or indeed the well-being of the person without whose body they cannot survive. Historically, this has not always been the case however and other denominations of Christianity and some Islamic traditions have seen 'quickening' (when a woman first feels foetal movement) as the beginning of life and the moment when the soul of a person enters the body of a child in the womb. It is written in the *Hadith* (the sayings and actions of the Prophet Muhammad) that:

> Each of you is constituted in your mother's womb for forty days as a *nutfa* [semen], then it becomes a *'alaqa* [blood-like clot] for an equal period, then a *mudgha* [lump of flesh] for another equal period, then the angel is sent, and he breathes the soul into it.
>
> (Mussallam, 1990, pp. 38–39)

Some Islamic scholars have used this passage to argue that the first stage of development, when the foetus is simply a drop of fluid, lasts 40 days; the second stage, when the foetus is 'clot' shaped and clinging also lasts 40 days; as does the third stage, when the foetus becomes 'a lump of flesh'. It is only after this process, at 120 days of gestation, that the soul enters the foetus and it becomes possible to talk about the beginnings of life and a recognisable human child (Mussallam, 1990; Saadat, 2009).

In other communities also, it is the moving body of the foetus which indicates the beginning of new life and the moment a child's soul enters its body and it becomes a human being (Dunstan, 1988). Quickening therefore represents the fusing of the spiritual and the physical. In rural North India women distinguish clearly between a delayed period and the point, approximately three months later, when the baby is said to have 'rooted' itself in the womb (Jeffry and Jeffry, 1996). Women here deny the physical development of the foetus and any claims to humanity before three or four months of gestation, saying, 'there was no pregnancy', merely a 'blob of flesh'. Women only talk of a baby (*bachā*) after they have felt movement, claiming the baby has now 'adhered.' This is the time when the life or spirit (*jān*) enters the baby, its body parts begin developing and its sex is settled. Thereafter, vaginal bleeding is called a 'baby falling' (Jeffry and Jeffry, 1996, p. 24).

While religious and cultural beliefs are clearly very important, advances in medicine and technology have had extremely influential impacts on how ideas about how the earliest stages in pregnancy are understood and have meant that foetuses can be assigned the status of children and potential people at significantly earlier stages of gestation than has been previously possible. Whereas once the recognition of life was a woman's alone and she was the one who first felt foetal movement, such knowledge and confirmation of potential life is now supplanted by medical technology. The routine use of scans for Western women in pregnancy gives them an external view of the foetus and a visual representation of it long before they can feel it, supporting, or possibly supplanting, women's own sensations and recognition of new life. Technology has also allowed for images of the individual foetal body to become visible and represented as increasingly childlike and, indeed, as a separate physical entity from its mother who is presented only as a disembodied womb carrying this proto-human being. Ultrasound images of the foetus are thus a way of visually claiming personhood for the unborn – a point which has not gone unnoticed by the pro-life lobby in the USA. Indeed, several states mandate that any woman undergoing an abortion must look at an ultrasound image of the foetus before she is allowed to terminate.

Ultrasound technology has also allowed the body of the foetus to become a marketable commodity. The images it produces are no longer used only for medical and diagnostic purposes but are produced commercially in high-definition colour and in 3D supposedly showing foetuses 'walking in the womb' and offer parents-to-be the opportunity to 'capture precious moments' when their baby may be 'smiling, yawning, blinking, scratching their nose and sucking their fingers' in the womb (Kehily, 2010, p. 181). Yet such scans have also generated unease, and the way in which a medical, diagnostic tool has been turned into a form of entertainment and a commercial opportunity has also been questioned (Kehily, 2010). While companies claim to offer scans for 'bonding, reassurance and foetal well-being' there is little evidence that they do achieve this. Assigning personhood to foetuses by these commercial companies becomes less concerned with a social recognition of humanity and more a way of increasing consumer opportunities which play on parents' desire to start accruing (or buying) educational or social advantage for their children. Indeed, attempts to promote learning and education pre-birth, as if the foetus was sentient, have backfired. Anthropologist David Lancy has written about the deliberate blurring of the lines between foetus, infant and child by American corporations in their attempts to create a market of the unborn. He cites the example of the Walt Disney Corporation who had to refund the millions of parents who had bought 'Baby Einstein' videos which the company claimed (without any evidence at all) could boost foetal intelligence (Lancy, 2010).

Against a backdrop of religious belief and technological and commercial advance, however, the bestowal of personhood on a foetus (or not) remains a very personal one which varies according to individuals and their circumstances. A child that is wanted may be viewed in terms of his or her humanity from a very early stage and many

Figure 2.2 Parents prepare for their babies before birth.

women with a wanted pregnancy assign individuality and personhood to their baby long before it is born: few refer to it as a foetus (Layne, 2000). Miscarriages are rarely viewed with equanimity by parents and the medical terminology (foetus, or 'products of conception') contradicts and undermines the very real sense of personhood the parents had invested in a child and can be profoundly painful. In contrast a foetus that will be terminated may be talked about and understood very differently although, conversely of course, anti-abortion campaigners will talk about foetuses that have been or will be terminated as 'babies', which can also be very painful, illustrating how ideology is never far away from discussions about the foetus, as the final section of this chapter will go on to discuss.

This pre-natal creation of personhood has been the focus of sociologist Linda Layne's work (2000) on miscarriage and stillbirth in America. She examines how insistent many women are on the continuing humanity and personhood of their children, even if they are never born, and how distressing it is for them when others deny their child's existence.

Women now may begin to actively construct personhood of their wished-for child from the moment they do a home pregnancy test.... Their friends, neighbors, and colleagues may also have begun to participate in the social construction of the expected baby by asking the mother how it is doing, speculating on its sex and personality, buying presents for it, and putting on a baby shower.... When the pregnancy ends without a baby to bring home, the very people who have encour-aged the mother-in-the-making to take on this role and may have participated with her in the social construction of her 'baby' often withdraw their support ... and act as if nothing of any significance took place. The cultural denial of pregnancy loss challenges the validity of the cultural and biological work already undertaken in constructing that child and belittles the importance of that loss.

(Layne, 2000, p. 323)

A similar bolstering of claims to personhood and being a 'real' baby has been found in ethnographic work on premature babies. In her work on the material culture of incuba-tors, Kyra Landzelius discusses similar processes by which women understand and construct the foetal, stillborn and very sick body as 'real', thereby bridging the nature–culture divide. She writes about how mothers were determined to create childlike bed-rooms and nurseries, placing teddy-bears and toys in the incubators to try and mask some of the medical technology keeping the children alive; making 'the ambiguous figure of the preterm infant culturally-intelligible as well as biologically viable (Landzelius, 2001, p. 323).

The question of boundaries between a child and a foetus and between life and non-life has also been discussed by sociologists who have looked at the question of whether very premature babies do in fact have rights and whether they are recognised as social and legal persons. Nicole Isaacson (2002) describes those born at 24 or 25 weeks as 'unfinished infants'; children who are physically not yet finished and whose lungs are weak and cannot work on their own, whose eyes may be fused together and whose bodies are extraordinarily fragile. Outside the womb they can only survive with intense medical technological support, and yet parents are determined to 'finish' the unfin-ished infant through cultural and social means, claiming recognition of their humanity through both material culture (the teddy-bears in the incubator) and claims of individu-ality and distinctiveness.

Evidence of this was provided by Priscilla Alderson and her colleagues Joanna Haw-thorn and Margaret Killen (2005) in their ethnographic work in four neonatal intensive care units during 2002 to 2004 which looked at how premature babies were conceptu-alised by those looking after them and how decisions about their treatment and care were based on their quality of life and, crucially, their ability to communicate. Through detailed, and highly empathetic, observation of these babies and by focusing on the tiny cues they gave out, Alderson and her colleagues argue that these children did communicate (a view supported by parents and doctors) and were able to express par-ticular likes and dislikes. One baby, for example, did not like his feet being touched; another responded differently to different doctors and nurses and seemingly expressed a preference for one nurse over others. The authors found that both parents and paedi-atricians saw these babies as responsive, independent, autonomous *people* who appeared to fight and cling to life against sometimes overwhelming odds. 'Many parents and practitioners ... gave examples of babies continuing to survive against all expectations, or sometimes unexpectedly "giving up" as if, in some ways, the babies had the final say in whether they lived or died' (Alderson *et al.*, 2005, p. 39). In similar work on premature babies and their parents in Iceland, Jónína Einarsdóttir also found that the ability to communicate was central to ideas of personhood and decisions about treatment were made on this basis. She found that, except for one father, all parents agreed that it was justifiable to withhold treatment and hasten death for pre-mature babies when a severe disability was predicted (see Sheehy, Chapter 12, this volume). The decision about whether or not to treat rested not on biological viability or life itself but on the quality of life and, for the majority of parents, this came down to whether or not the child would be able to communicate (Einarsdóttir, 2008).

Legal and rights-based perspectives

There is no doubt that the question of when childhood begins is a complex and often very emotive subject. In the field of law it might be hoped to find some clear-cut answers but, as this section will examine, while the law in different countries sets legal boundaries and definitions, these are dependent on wider ideological, political and reli-gious beliefs, which are contested within and between societies (Greasley, 2017). Med-ically, conception is defined as being when the egg is fertilised and starts to divide, this then turns into an embryo (the stage of life from conception to eight weeks old), then a foetus (from eight weeks until birth), and then infant (from birth to one year), although these may be given very different meanings and usage in everyday life. Legally, there are different protections at different stages of gestation. In the UK, the Human Fertilisation and Embryology Act 1990 (amended in 2008) allows for the cre-ation, keeping and use of embryos for research or assisted reproduction purposes but forbids placing human embryos in any other animal. There is also a strict limit of 14 days' gestation for the use of embryos, chosen as the cut-off point because it is the earliest manifestation of a nervous system. Even at this early stage of gestation however, this limit was much debated and 14 days was a compromise between those who believed that life begins at conception and those who felt that an embryo was simply biological matter and that 14 days was an arbitrary bureaucratic boundary with little basis in science.

Within English law the foetus has no legal rights. It is not recognised as a child and does not have a legal personality until it is born and has an independent existence from its mother. In practice this means that it is legal to abort a foetus up to 24 weeks' gestation (or up to birth in the case of severe foetal abnormality). This limit of 24 weeks was set in 1990 on the grounds of foetal viability – it is the point where a foetus could survive outside the womb – but this leaves a large grey area in English law and the exact status of a foetus between 24 and 40 weeks gestation is unclear; it has some legal protections but it is not a legally recognised person. This ambivalence can be seen in the case of stillbirths and miscarriages. The existence of a child who is born after twenty-four weeks of pregnancy, but shows no signs of life, is officially recoded on the stillbirth register (not the standard register for births), suggesting some official and legal recognition of this child's existence. In contrast a child born before 24 weeks is medically referred to as a miscarriage or medical abortion and there is no need for

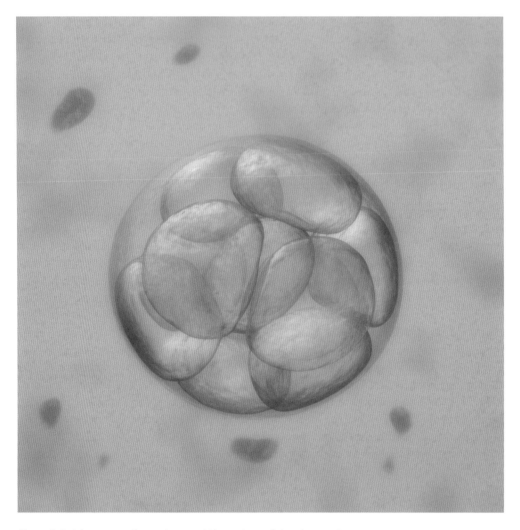

Figure 2.3 A human embryo at around three days of development.

official registry – although many NHS hospital trusts are trying to develop commemorative certifications for foetuses that are not classified as stillbirths. These aim to provide parents with some form of public recognition of a foetus which has no existence in law but, as the following section of this chapter will argue, is likely to have been socially and personally understood as a child by its parents and family (Layne, 2000; Miscarriage Association, 2017).

In the UK, birth is the moment when a child becomes an official, legal person with rights – but this is controversial and by no means universal. At an international legal level the definition of who is a child and when childhood begins is highly ambiguous. Article 2(1) of the European Convention on Human Rights guarantees that 'everyone's right to life shall be protected by law' but fails to define either 'everyone' or 'life' and in other rulings has specifically declared that there is no right to life for a foetus under the European Convention of Human Rights (Freeman, 1994). The Universal Declaration of Human Rights states that everyone is 'born free and equal', thereby implicitly excluding the unborn from its provisions. The United Nations Convention on the Rights of the Child (UNCRC) is more circumspect, stating that a child is 'a person below the age of 18' but saying nothing about when a child becomes a person or when childhood is seen to begin. It does however state in the preamble that 'the child, by reason of his physical and mental immaturity, needs special safeguards and care, including appropriate legal protection, *before* as well as after birth' (emphasis added). Article 6 of the Convention also sets out that all children have an 'inherent right to life' and that 'States Parties shall ensure to the maximum extent possible the survival and development of the child'. Yet there are no further clarifications and only four countries have unambiguously defined childhood in terms of when it begins. Two countries, China and the United Kingdom, have stated that they interpret the Convention as applicable only following a live birth, while Argentina and Guatemala have declared that Article One 'must be interpreted to the effect that a child means every human being from the moment of conception up to the age of eighteen'.

Such legal statements and definitions of when personhood begins have profound consequences not only for the right to life of the unborn but also for the rights of women and children already born. As Beth Conklin and Lynn Morgan (1996, p. 660) have argued, legal arguments on when childhood begins pivot on 'fixed, structural markers of personhood' such as conception, viability or birth. They go on to claim that the

> fixed, irreversible nature of such criteria makes fetal personhood an either/or, all-or-nothing proposition: once a fetus is deemed to be a minimal person, it is held to have individual rights (except for age-contingent rights) on a par with those of its mother. Consequently, most contemporary thinking about pregnant women and fetuses has been framed by an assumption of 'maternal–fetal conflict'.
>
> (Conklin and Morgan, 1996, p. 660)

Indeed, it is hard to see legal debates about the status of the unborn in anything other than these binary terms which can put women's (and children's) rights in opposition to foetal rights. Legislation which demands that foetuses are human from the moment of conception means that women die, children are forced to bear children, and women may be criminalised for miscarriage and forced to bear children when raped. Thus El Salvador which bans all abortion in all cases has recently prosecuted a woman for trying to abort the child she conceived after her stepfather had raped her for seven years. While in 2019 the authorities in northern Argentina denied access to abortion for an 11-year-old raped by her step-grandfather, forcing through a series of delays, against her own wishes and those of her mother, until an emergency caesarean was performed which the child did not survive (Politi, 2019). In Europe too, claims of in-utero personhood mean that abortion is forbidden absolutely in Malta and Northern Ireland. In 2019, the US states of Missouri and Alabama brought in laws to ban all forms of abortion at all stages (while Georgia forbids it after a foetal heartbeat has been detected, usually at around six weeks), although in order to defuse criticisms of criminalising vulnerable women, Alabama legislators claim that no woman will be prosecuted for having an abortion, only those who carry out the procedure. This however still leaves the possibility open for prosecuting women who miscarry if it can be shown that their actions, such as alcohol or drug use, had an impact on their pregnancy.

In contrast to those jurisdictions which attempt to legislate for foetal personhood, in England, Scotland and Wales it is birth which is the 'fixed, structural marker of personhood' (Conklin and Morgan, 1996, p. 660). This means that in terms of rights, the UK privileges the rights of women over those of the foetus and, should there be a conflict between the two, the woman's take absolute priority. It is a recognised principle of English law that a competent adult has a right to self-determination over their body. Legally, the foetus has no separate status and is seen as nothing more than part of a woman's body until it is born, at which time it becomes independent: until the moment of birth the woman's consent alone is sufficient for treatment to her and also to the foetus: her refusal is decisive for both of them. She cannot be compelled to accept treatment that is either for her benefit or for the benefit of her unborn child. For example, where a caesarean section is medically necessary to protect or preserve the well-being of the foetus, the mother may refuse the procedure, regardless of the impact on the foetus. Following a period of apparent uncertainty in the late 1990s, when competent women were being compelled to undergo caesareans against their wishes, the law was clarified and, today, where the pregnant woman is competent, she has an absolute right to refuse a caesarean, even if this is harmful or potentially fatal to her child. Medics cannot impose a caesarean upon her and even the father of the child has no say in the matter (Cornock and Montgomery, 2010, p. 6). Similarly, there is no way in English law to prevent a mother from taking actions which might be seen as damaging the health and well-being of the foetus, such as drinking alcohol to excess or misusing drugs. The position of English law is in stark contrast to those of other jurisdictions, notably in some states of the USA, where children, once born, can sue their mothers for taking substances that caused them developmental harm in the womb, for instance, through drug abuse. Some American states will also take pregnant women into custody to protect the foetus from the actions of the mother, and to enforce a caesarean upon the mother when it is deemed necessary for foetal survival (Hull *et al.*, 2004).

Concluding thoughts

Unborn and neonatal children remain under-theorised and under-studied in CYS and there is very limited discussion about whether or not they are in fact children and whether childhood (and indeed life itself) begins at birth, some time before or even some time afterwards. There are also very limited discussions about the embodiment of the unborn, even though technology has made the unborn body increasingly visible. There are many reasons for this reticence – not least questions of personal belief and emotional and individual experience, as this chapter has discussed. However, unborn and neonatal children are both socially constructed and biologically embodied beings and provide an excellent example of the relational nature of children's lives and the way bodies cannot be separated from the objects, spaces, people and other bodies with which they interact.

References

Alderson, P., Hawthorne, J. and Killen, M. (2005) The participation rights of premature babies. *The International Journal of Children's Rights*, 13(1–2), 31–50.

Conklin, B. and Morgan, L. (1996) Babies, bodies, and the production of personhood in North America and a native Amazonian Society. *Ethos*, 24(4), 657–694.

Cornock, M. and Montgomery, H. (2010) Children's rights in and out of the womb. *International Journal of Children's Rights*, 9(1), 1–17.

Dunstan, G. R. (1988) The human embryo in the Western moral tradition. In G. R. Dunstan and M. Seller (eds) *The Status of the Human Embryo: Perspectives from Moral Tradition*. Oxford: Oxford University Press, pp. 39–57.

Einarsdóttir, J. (2008) The classification of newborn children: consequences for survival. In L. Clements and J. Read (eds) *Disabled People and the Right to Life. The Protection and Violation of Disabled People's Most Basic Human Rights*. London: Routledge, pp. 248–264.

Freeman, K. (1994) The unborn child and the European Convention on Human Rights: To whom does 'Everyone's Right to Life' belong? *Emory International Law Review*, 8(2), 615–665.

Gottlieb, A. (1998) Do infants have religion? The spiritual lives of Beng babies. *American Anthropologist*, 100(1), 122–135.

Gottlieb, A. (2004) *The Afterlife is Where We Come From: The Culture of Infancy in West Africa*. Chicago, IL: Chicago University Press.

Greasley, K. (2017) *Arguments about Abortion: Personhood, Morality, and Law*. Oxford: Oxford University Press.

Hardacre, H. (1997) *Marketing the Menacing Fetus in Japan*. Berkeley: University of California Press.

Hull, N. E. H., Hoffer, W. J. and Hoffer, P. C. (2004) *The Abortion Rights Controversy in America: A Legal Reader*. Chapel Hill, NC: University of North Carolina Press.

Isaacson, N. (2002) Preterm babies in the 'mother-machine': metaphoric reasoning and bureaucratic rituals that finish the 'unfinished infant'. In K. A. Cerulo (ed.) *Culture in Mind: Toward a Sociology of Culture and Cognition*. New York and London: Routledge, pp. 89–100.

Jeffry, P. and Jeffry, R. (1996) Delayed periods and falling babies: the ethnophysiology and politics of pregnancy loss in rural north India. In R. Cecil (ed.) *The Anthropology of Pregnancy Loss: Comparative Studies in Miscarriage, Stillbirth and Neonatal Death*. Oxford: Berg, pp. 17–38.

Kehily, M. J. (2010) Childhood in crisis? Tracing the contours of 'crisis' and its impact upon contemporary parenting practices. *Media, Culture & Society*, 32(2), 171–185.

La Fleur, W. (1992) *Liquid Life: Abortion and Buddhism in Japan*. Princeton, NJ: Princeton University Press.

Lancy, D. (2010) Learning 'from nobody': the limited role of teaching in folk models of children's development. *Childhood in the Past*, 3(1), 79–106.

Landzelius, K. (2001) Charged artifacts and the detonation of liminality: Teddy-Bear diplomacy in the newborn incubator machine. *Journal of Material Culture*, 6(3), 323–344.

Layne, L. (2000) 'He was a real baby with real things': a material culture analysis of personhood, parenthood and pregnancy loss. *Journal of Material Culture*, 5(3), 321–345.

Lupton, D. (2013) Infant embodiment and interembodiment: a review of sociocultural perspectives. *Childhood*, 20(1), 37–50.

Miscarriage Association (2017) A Pregnancy Loss Certificate, available at www.miscarriage association.org.uk/2017/01/pregnancy-loss-certificate/ (accessed 29 April 2019).

Montgomery, H. (2009) *An Introduction to Childhood: Anthropological Perspectives on Children's Lives*. Oxford: Wiley-Blackwell.

Moskowitz, M. (2001) *The Haunting Fetus: Abortion, Sexuality and the Spirit World in Taiwan*. Honolulu: University of Hawaii Press.

Mussallam, B. (1990) The human embryo in Arabic scientific and religious thought. In G. R. Dunstan (ed.) *The Human Embryo: Aristotle and the Arabic and European Traditions.* Exeter: University of Exeter Press.

Politi, D. (2019) An 11-year-old in Argentina was raped. A hospital denied her an abortion. *New York Times*, 1 March 2019.

Prout, A. (2011) Taking a step away from modernity: reconsidering the new sociology of childhood. *Global Studies of Childhood*, 1(1), 4–14.

Saadat, S. (2009) Human embryology and the Holy Quran: an overview. *International Journal of Health Sciences (Qassim)*, 3(1), 103–109.

Scheper-Hughes, N. (1992) *Death Without Weeping: The Violence of Everyday Life in Brazil.* Berkeley: University of California Press.

3 Children and young people negotiating gender in context

Naomi Holford

Introduction

Gender shapes children's and young people's lives; at the same time, children and young people shape their gender. From before birth, gender is one of the fundamental factors that categorises human beings. But the way children and young people experience gender varies by context, by culture and by individual. It also varies across time – although there are enduring patterns of gendered inequalities, and the behaviours and attributes associated with a particular gender can and do change. In many contemporary societies there is currently an expansion and rethinking of what gender means. While gender non-conforming children often have a disproportionately bright spotlight shone on them, gender is relevant to all children's and young people's lives, as they negotiate their own identity and how they are perceived by others – in comfortable or uncomfortable ways, which can bring both pain and pleasure.

This chapter will explore some of these pains and pleasures. The first section will consider what is meant by gender. It will then look at some of the ways gendered norms are experienced and enacted in school, including experiences of violence. Next, the chapter will explore how young people negotiate peer cultures of gender online, and finally, the chapter will explore gender diversity.

The meanings and emergence of gender

In this chapter gender is defined as the social and cultural meanings associated with being a boy or man, or a girl or woman. It is closely connected with, but not fully determined by, biological sex – the combination of chromosomes, hormones, internal/external genitalia and reproductive systems that, taken together, lead to the categorisation of a person as male or female (Fausto-Sterling, 2000). Gender identity – which, as with other identities discussed in Chapter 1, can be fluid and changing – is the way a child or young person understands themself as a boy, girl or otherwise. Gender identity often influences gender expression – the way a person outwardly expresses their gender (for instance, through their appearance or behaviour).

Gendered expectations are not uniform; different parts of the world, different societies, different cultures, and even different schools have different constructions of gender. They are shaped by interactions within the family; by traditional media (like children's TV programmes) and social media; by advertising and marketing of toys and other products; by the physical environments children and young people exist within; by the bodies children and young people inhabit.

Many forms of gendered behaviour and difference are frequently considered to be rooted in biology; and certainly biology does have an impact, particularly during and after puberty. However, it is very difficult to distinguish between the effects of biology and the effects of society, since adults – and other children – treat children differently according to their gender from even before they are born. In addition, children's and young people's environments and social experiences affect their bodies and biology. One example of this relates to hormones. Testosterone is thought of as a 'male hormone' (although it is also present in women): a testosterone surge in the womb is responsible for the development of a male reproductive system, and another surge causes the development of facial and body hair, musculature and other secondary sexual characteristics in puberty. It is often associated with risk-taking, competitiveness, physical strength and other traditionally masculine traits. Testosterone is linked with some of these traits – but while testosterone levels affect social behaviour, they are also affected by social behaviour (Fine, 2017). For instance, a study comparing two different cultural groups in Tanzania found that fathers' testosterone levels

Figure 3.1 An ultrasound scan with gendered toys: different expectations begin before birth.

were lower in the group where fathers were closely involved in caring for their children, compared to the group where fathers rarely cared for their children (Muller *et al.*, 2008). This suggests that gendered norms affect hormone levels which, in turn, affect gendered behaviour as a circular process.

Gender is very much embodied; it is experienced within and through the body, through the body's interaction with objects and spaces. In her research with three- and four-year-olds in Wales, Jennifer Lyttleton-Smith (2015) observed the changes that occurred over the first year of nursery. She found that, early in the year, there was little difference between boys and girls in terms of play choices or preference for toys. Over the year, though, particular spaces in the classroom gradually became more divided by gender, and the physical set-up of the classroom and playground shaped how children became involved in different kinds of play. For instance, the 'small world', which featured Lego, cars and blocks and became dominated by boys, was open to the classroom and encouraged narrative games of construction to spread out and be visible. In contrast, the 'home corner', themed around home-making and dress-up play, became dominated by girls and was more secluded and private; achievements in this space were not so recognised. Children's social interactions were also shaped by wider gendered discourses (ways of thinking that circulate within a society), such as the popularity of Disney princess media and marketing of toys on gendered lines. Lyttleton-Smith's research provides an insight into the ways gender emerges and changes through children's interactions with peers and their physical environment, and how gendered expectations can become sedimented and difficult to change early on in children's lives.

Gendered ways of being most associated with men or boys are termed masculinities, while those most associated with women or girls are termed femininities (the plural is used to indicate that there is no single form of masculinity or femininity). Often, masculinity and femininity are seen as oppositional – as reflected in the phrase 'opposite sex' – a trait that is considered masculine is not likely to also be considered feminine. This idea that masculinity and femininity are opposite and separate means that borders and boundaries are set up between them which are enforced and maintained by children and young people, as the following sections explore in more depth.

Gendered boundaries in school and beyond

As will be considered further in Chapter 6, the school is a key site for children's and young people's everyday experiences. Gendered relationships and power relations (both between boys and girls, and between groups of boys or groups of girls) are negotiated throughout different spaces in school. The playground, and other sites where children and young people interact in a less structured way, are particularly key.

Influential research by Debbie Epstein and colleagues (2001) explored children's playground cultures in different schools. In one multi-ethnic London primary school, the small playground was dominated by older boys playing football. This meant that younger boys, boys who did not play football and girls were pushed to the edge of the playground; although some girls wanted to play football they were excluded. Success at football became the key marker of successful masculinity in general, making boys popular with both boys and girls; a local gender culture echoing the wider association of football with masculinity in UK culture. The design of the playground, and unclear rules about how playground football should be played, meant that fights often broke out. Although boys from different ethnic and national groups played on the same teams, these fights often led to polarisation along ethnic and national lines. In another London school with similar demographic intake but a slightly larger playground, space for football was specifically demarcated, and the school organised the space so only particular year groups could play on certain weekdays, and on Fridays only girls could play. This meant that the playground was not so dominated by football; boys as well as girls played a variety of different games. Although there was still gendered conflict and attempts by the boys to exclude girls from football, there was a more mixed culture – boys and girls played together – and different ways to express successful or popular masculinity. Children's gendered use of space and place will be explored further in Chapter 8 in the very different context of a refugee camp in Bangladesh.

Epstein *et al.*'s research gives insight into the ways gendered interactions and identities in school are shaped by a range of factors, including the design and physical environment of the playground and school rules. While children responded in different ways and sometimes reacted against the rules (for instance, in the second school, playing 'wrestling' matches in secret), it indicates how institutions, especially schools, produce certain possibilities for expression of gendered identities, and can shut down other possibilities. The research also highlighted the intersectionality of gender in school, where gender identities were also intertwined with racial identities. Intersectionality is a key theoretical concept developed by Kimberlé Crenshaw that can be used to understand the ways these aspects of identity come together – how they intersect – and what that means. She describes intersectionality as 'a lens through which you can see where power comes and collides, where it interlocks and intersects' (Columbia Law School, 2017). Stephen Frosh and colleagues' research on young masculinities also emphasised intersectionalities, and highlighted boys'

Figures 3.2a and 3.2b Different playground spaces can encourage different kinds of gendered interactions.

different expressions of masculinity in different contexts – for instance, at home or at school. Boys often expressed a 'harder' form of masculinity when in groups with other boys than they did individually.

Similarly, Carrie Paechter and Sheryl Clark (2007) explored girls' construction of different femininities on the primary school playground, and how these related to hierarchies where girls were more dominant or popular. They found that as girls grew older (ten and 11), active play became less socially acceptable, as one participant expressed with regret:

> LUCY:　… apparently you're not allowed to run in Year Six or Year Seven.
> SHERYL: You're not? How come?
> LUCY: Or not that much. Or maybe you are but people just don't want to and you'll feel silly when you do and everybody else is talking.

Instead, 'cool' forms of femininity were associated with walking and talking, and an interest in romance and dating. Lucy played with girls in the year below, lowering her social status, as this was the only way to continue physical activity. These constructions of gender (combined with the dominance of football) meant that the playground space was again dominated by boys, and girls' activities moved to the margins – although the 'cool' girls, resenting this, did sometimes deliberately disrupt games by walking into the middle of the football pitch. Looking ahead to their teenage years, many girls had mixed feelings, anticipating that the range of acceptable femininities would become smaller, and more constrained physically.

Deevia Bhana's research with children and young people (and their teachers) in South African schools focused on gendered relationships, interactions and conflicts (Bhana, 2018). Girls aged 12 to 13, in their final year of primary school in a black low-income township, described an environment where boys were constructed as 'rough', physical and often violent, dominating the playground. Girls made their own spaces, avoiding the violence of the boys and performing a 'gentler' femininity. An important feature of this environment was the boys' frequent attempts to grab girls' lunches. Lunch was the only meal children received at school, in a context where many families suffered food insecurity at home. Bhana emphasises how these constructions of femininity are related to the wider economic and social realities of food insecurity – that 'the protection of the prized commodity of food is directly connected to femininities that accommodate boys' power in the playground' (2018, p. 85). Girls also talked about playing heterosexual playground games involving 'spin the bottle', hide-and-seek and kiss chase – similar to the heterosexual cultures of romance observed in English primary schools (Renold, 2005) – and experienced these as 'both desirable and dangerous' (Bhana, 2018, p. 86).

In this South African school, girls constructed and encountered different forms of femininity, with discussion focused especially around 'dress-up Friday', where children could pay a small amount of money to wear non-uniform clothes. Many girls wore make-up and glamorous hairstyles and outfits, but others were judgemental about these choices:

> MARY: On Fridays … you find girls going extra miles to show off themselves. … They wear very short dresses, exposing their bodies … girls come to school like half naked, wearing short things, showing their bums … the boys, they can't control themselves when they see all that and now they end up forcing themselves onto girls….
>
> HANNA: … and for some girls, it's cool because they're wearing short things. Now the boys think all of us are like that. They take us all like the other girls. But we are not like that and now they take advantage of us.

This conversation highlights a problematic tendency to blame girls for sexual harassment and even sexual assault, removing responsibility from boys who 'force themselves' on girls – a discourse that is still (explicitly or implicitly) prevalent across the Global North and Global South (Gavey, 2018). In this school, 'dress-up Friday' was a way for socially and economically marginalised girls to express themselves. As Bhana says, 'girls gain power through dress amidst economic distress but, contradictorily, they also stand to lose "reputational" value in doing so, as they transgress the normative constructions of femininity' (2018, p. 88) These South African girls' experiences are one illustration of the complexity and contradictions of everyday intersectional gendered identities.

In the next section, I will consider how young people negotiate gendered identities and relationships in online contexts while emphasising that these interact closely with offline experiences and the two cannot be separated.

Figure 3.3 Girls playing football.

Performing gender and heterosexuality in digital spaces

In previous sections, we have explored children's and young people's gendered identities and how they negotiate different spaces. These negotiations can also be linked to the concept of 'gender performance', which has become prominent throughout the social sciences and is most closely associated with the work of Judith Butler (1990). The theory of gender performance argues that gender is not (just) something that we are – an identity – but something that we do, and that we are all constantly engaged in producing our gender through a series of performances (Butler, 1990). A boy is always making himself into a boy through the way he dresses, walks, talks and so on. Through this constant repetition, the category of 'boy' comes to seem natural and unchangeable. But in fact, children and young people (as we have already seen in previous sections) must do a great deal of work to fit into gendered expectations and norms, precisely because gender is unstable and precarious.

Failure to perform gender in these expected ways comes with risk of exclusion, suspicion or harassment by peers as well as adults. This section will explore young people's performances of gender in online spaces. For adults and young people alike, especially in the Global North, many social relations are now mediated through online connections/spaces. One in three internet users across the world are children (Livingstone *et al.*, 2016), 100 per cent of households with children in the UK now have access to the internet (ONS 2019) (although the quality of this connection may vary), and many young people own a smartphone, allowing them to engage with a range of different social networks and communities. Chapter 14 will explore children's relationships with technology in more depth. danah boyd, who has studied young people's online engagement in depth over the past 20 years, emphasises that engagement with social media is 'simply an everyday part of life' (2014, p. 8). She describes online spaces and connections as 'networked publics' that appeal to young people because they allow them to participate in the broader world through connecting with people and having the freedom of mobility – much as physical spaces, like a shopping centre or park, might do. However, networked publics also create new affordances – that is, they make possible particular types of behaviour or interaction. Different technologies have different affordances (for instance, Instagram and WhatsApp allow and encourage different kinds of behaviour), although certain affordances are common across many networked publics.

Just as gendered identities are negotiated in school playgrounds, they are negotiated through social networks. This chapter cannot cover the wide and varied range of gendered digital practices, but one that is common and everyday, yet provokes substantial anxiety, is young people taking and sharing pictures of themselves (sometimes called selfies). This practice is often associated with young women and femininity, and perhaps because of this association is often judged negatively, as Amy Shields Dobson (2015) argues in her study of young women's self-representations online across a range of platforms. Sometimes this judgement is straightforwardly directed against girls, denigrating their expressions of sexuality as frivolous, 'slutty' or 'attention-seeking'. Other times it is expressed as concern for their vulnerability, with concerns that 'self-objectification' and an over-focus on body image are harmful to young women's mental health (e.g. Orenstein, 2016). However, these concerns, while well-meant, often shade into the same kinds of judgement – with black and ethnic minority young women, as well as working-class young women, bearing the brunt of negative attitudes – and can deny young women agency over their own bodies and sexual self-expression (Egan, 2013).

Of course, young men take and share selfies too. Laura Harvey and colleagues studied young people's (aged 13–15) gendered and racialised digital practices in multicultural London schools, exploring the ways in which young masculinities (and femininities) were negotiated and represented through group interviews and observation of young people's social media profiles (Ringrose and Harvey, 2015). Young men discussed the various different ways of gaining 'ratings' within the different local peer groups inside and beyond school – a form of social status that can be seen as a kind of local cultural capital (a concept explored further in later chapters). Ratings were particularly important in navigating the local streets safely, avoiding harassment, theft or violence from other boys, particularly in certain local territories related to school and gang rivalries. Boys without ratings, who weren't 'known', were more likely to experience harassment and violence. Ratings could be gained in many ways, including being good at football, wearing designer clothes, or being linked through family or friendship with well-known older men in the area. One way of expressing this idealised form of masculinity online was through posting topless mirror selfies focused on 'six-pack' or back muscles, often including designer watches or belts. These pictures might also appear among photos taken with friends, and photos of high-end consumer goods (although posting such pictures was not by itself sufficient – peers had to consider the young man as 'authentically' capable of possessing such goods). What this study highlights is how online and offline practices are inextricably intertwined: young men's performance of masculinity online was embedded in their peer groups and navigation of local contexts offline. Again, identity is intersectional, with successful masculinity being linked to wealth.

Young men in this context also talked about gaining social status through performing a successful heterosexual masculinity; being seen as popular with girls and having (or appearing to have) sexual experience. Here the concept of technological affordances can help when considering the changes, and the continuities, of gendered relations. It is certainly nothing new for young men to gain status through sexual experience with women (Holland *et al.*, 2004; Lees, 1986). What is offered by technologies is the *visibility* (see boyd, 2014) where a young man could 'prove' his sexual success through showing, for instance, a screenshot of a young woman flirting with him or asking him to meet up. The *spreadability* is also increased – pictures can be easily circulated. Young men could gain ratings through collecting pictures of girls' bodies, particularly their (clothed or topless) breasts, as indicated in this discussion with a 15-year-old boy:

> INTERVIEWER: And what are they – like, what is like the purpose of keeping them all?

KAJA: Don't know, they are just on my phone. But I don't watch them unless I am showing someone.

INTERVIEWER: So, like, you have got them on your phone and so that is just so that you can say, 'I've got thirty pictures on my phone'?

KAJA: Kind of, like say other people they are like 'Oh I got this girl to do this', I will be like, 'Look at my phone'.... Say if I got a popular girl to do it that looks like one of those girls who wouldn't do it then it would make me look even better.

Here, photos of girls' bodies become commodities – and the more difficult it was to attain a photo, the more status the boy received. Overcoming a girl's resistance was considered a bonus for his performance of masculinity. This can be read as a troubling reflection of an enduring discourse whereby men are seen as active and valorised for persisting with sex, and women's sexual role is to resist that pressure in order to retain respectability (Powell, 2010). This reflects a set of beliefs and practices that has recently become more widely discussed under the term 'rape culture' (see Mendes *et al.*, 2019).

Girls could gain social value (and enjoyment) from being seen as heterosexually desirable through receiving compliments from boys and being asked for photos online. Along with other participants, Jodie often found ways to reject these requests (some did this through humour, such as sending a photo of a cat in response to a request for a 'pussy' photo). But, as Jodie made clear, 'whether she did or did not send a photo she ran the risk of being called a "sket"' (Ringrose *et al.*, 2013, p. 311) – a common slang term used to denigrate women as 'slutty'. It is important to emphasise that it is not the sending of a photo in and of itself that is problematic, despite media anxiety and campaigns against 'sexting' which often focus on discouraging girls from sending photos (Dobson and Ringrose, 2016). Rather, it is the peer culture that judges girls' bodies and behaviour, and requires them to perform femininity through being sexually desirable but at the same time denigrates their sexual agency. These judgements and comments were also often racialised – for young black girls their buttocks were under particular scrutiny from boys, and again this was embedded in a wider context, with harassment being directed at them at school and in the street (Ringrose and Harvey, 2015).

This gendered double standard around sending/sharing photos (sometimes termed 'sexting', although young people do not often use this term) has been echoed across research with young people (Setty, 2019; Salter, 2016; Lippman and Campbell, 2014). Young men's sexting can be considered neutrally or positively, a way for them to seek pleasure and show pride in their bodies, and can work to enhance their masculinity and status. Conversely, for young women, sexting is seen as problematic; young people are reluctant to accept that girls might engage in it for reasons of pleasure or desire, instead considering it as a sign of low self-esteem, and girls who do send pictures are judged negatively. As one 16-year-old boy put it:

[H]e ... requests and she's the one who is accepting them, the guy has to go out and make these requests, it's the same thing as sending a picture of himself. At some point, he doesn't care, he just feels like a macho character and he can send all these photos around and he doesn't care, but the girl … she is like a gem and everyone is chasing after that and once she gives that away, it's like she's … lost her value.

(Setty, 2019, p. 591)

It is important to note that consensual sharing of photos can be pleasurable and enjoyable for young men and women in a context of trust and desire (Hasinoff, 2015). However, it is difficult for young people to find space for these interpretations in the peer culture. For instance, in Setty's study, several girls described (especially in one-to-one interviews as opposed to group interviews) enjoying sending pictures – as 'fun', 'playful' and bolstering self-worth ('I feel good about myself'). Nevertheless, one of these young women whose images had been shared against her will later blamed herself, feeling intense self-loathing; another, who continued to find pleasure in sexting, still received social shaming for it. In addition, young people under the age of 18, even those over the age of sexual consent, theoretically run the risk of criminalisation for creating child pornography by producing sexual pictures of themselves (Karaian, 2014).

Trans, queer and non-binary young lives

The majority of this chapter has focused on children and young people whose gender identity (their sense of self as a boy or a girl) is aligned with the gender they were assigned at birth, although it has explored ways in which gendered expectations can be stifling and challenging. In recent years, an increasing number of people, including children and young people, have begun to express different gender identities; as transgender (or trans), meaning that their gender does not match the one they were assigned at birth, and/or non-binary, meaning they do not consider themselves male or female. Language around gender is changing and contested as people seek compelling and comfortable ways to describe themselves. Thus, while I will seek here to use terms that respect individuals' and communities' self-descriptions as far as possible, different terminologies may be current by the time you read this chapter.

There have always been people who do not conform to the gender binary. Although all societies have a concept of gender, and it is usually broadly associated with different reproductive capabilities, the meanings of gender and sexuality differ across time and space. For instance, among the Native American Navajo, nádleehí were considered simultaneously both male and female, or as a third gender (Epple, 1998). Many Native American peoples today recognise some form of alternate gender, with 'two-spirit' being used as a general term; some two-spirit people consider themselves trans, gay, bisexual or lesbian, but others do not (Adams and Phillips, 2006). In British history, there are examples of people assigned female at birth living the majority of their lives as men, and vice versa. In current Global North societies, sexual orientation (whether you are straight, gay, pan-sexual or bisexual) and gender identity are generally considered to be separate, but this has not always been the case. Many of our ideas about gender are still connected to ideas about sexuality – gendered expectations are often connected to an assumption of heterosexuality.

This historical perspective is included here to argue that the current expansion of gender diversity is not an anomaly, but another shift in a social and historical context. It is undeniable, though, that gender diversity has become rapidly more visible in public life over the past decade. At the same time there has been a backlash, with right-wing governments in countries like Russia, Brazil and the USA seeking to limit trans (and gay) people's civil rights. In addition, certain trans-exclusionary sections of feminism, particularly within the UK, consider that trans people's rights endanger those of cis (non-trans) women (Ditum, 2018; Jeffreys, 2014); a claim countered by trans-inclusive feminists, who argue that there is little evidence for such risk, and that an intersectional approach to feminism should include trans women (Hines, 2019; Finlayson *et al.*, 2018). These political and cultural contexts have an impact on young people, both directly as young people engage with media and news, and indirectly through their parents, teachers and other adults.

Trans young people have a much higher rate of suicide, attempted suicide, self-injury and mental health problems than other young people (Mcneil *et al.*, 2017); but this is not inherent in the experience of being trans. Instead, discrimination and harassment of trans people increase their likelihood of suicide and mental health struggles (Arcelus *et al.*, 2016). Conversely, supportive family and peers, and affirmation of a young person's gender, such as using a child's chosen name and pronoun, have a positive effect on trans young people's well-being (Olson *et al.*, 2016). Many trans and gender-diverse young people find supportive communities online (Cavalcante, 2016). In exploratory research, Paul Byron and Jessie Hunt (2017) highlighted the ways young people of colour in Australia supported each other through sharing and discussing experiences in, and around, youth groups.

In some cases, gender affirmation may include medical intervention, such as using puberty blockers to delay the permanent development of biological characteristics which conflict with a child's internal understanding of their own gender – an embodied experience which can be highly distressing. Medical intervention of this kind can be controversial; some feel that it is problematic to medicalise experience of gender dysphoria (feeling unhappy with one's sex/gender), or that it may push children to conform to rigid gender binaries. However, medical treatment is only offered to children who express a persistent, distressing and long-lasting disconnect between their assigned sex and gender identity. Moreover, puberty blockers – which are reversible – have been used for several decades to delay early onset of puberty, without adverse effects (Roberts, 2015). Following a children's rights approach, this allows children autonomy over their own bodies, and recognises the child's right to express their views in matters affecting them and to have them taken seriously (UNCRC, article 12); though as with other medical treatment in the UK, those under the age of 16 can consent only if they are deemed competent enough.

Sara Bragg and colleagues conducted research across England in a range of different schools and LGBTQ+ youth groups, exploring young people's (13–19 years old) feelings about gender in the context of their everyday lives (Bragg *et al.*, 2018; Renold *et al.*, 2017). They found that experiences and understandings of gender could vary widely. In the same school, one friendship group were confident and supportive of each other in exploring different gender and sexual identities, while another boy was bullied for liking 'girl' things, but also for being in foster care; another example of the need to consider gender in a wider, intersectional context. Generally, young people felt that their generation was more accepting of gender diversity and equality, and they expressed support for the idea of gender fluidity, rejecting a rigid gender binary. However, despite these attitudes, they also talked of enduring everyday gendered norms, including harassment and violence as discussed earlier. They described the role of consumer culture in creating gendered categories and emphasised the role of school as reinforcing the gender binary, particularly school uniforms, but also sports and facilities. Research with teachers also suggests a tendency towards anxiety and discomfort around trans students (Payne and Smith, 2014); US teachers tended to focus on the logistics of fitting trans students into existing binary structures rather than questioning those structures. However, encountering gender-diverse, especially non-binary, children can also lead to reflection and change in teachers' practice (Neary, 2018).

Concluding thoughts

This chapter has explored children's and young people's negotiations of gender in different contexts across the UK and internationally. It has emphasised the importance of intersectionality – seeing gender as one of a range of different aspects of identity. Children's and young people's experience of gender is one of both continuity and change. Gendered inequalities continue to endure, even as they are played out through new technologies; but at the same time, young people are challenging gendered conventions. Some children and young people can embody successful masculinities or femininities in the gender they were born into; for others it is more of a struggle, whether they are trans or not. Expanding visibility of gender diversity has allowed many children and young people to express a more comfortable identity, but at the same time trans and gender-diverse children and young people still experience harassment and face difficulty navigating gendered structures. Although many experiences of gender are positive and pleasurable, rigid gender binaries and boundaries can cause distress and discomfort, closing down opportunities and options.

References

Adams, H. and Phillips, L. (2006) Experiences of two-spirit lesbian and gay Native Americans: an argument for standpoint theory in identity research. *Identity*, 6(3), 273–291 [Online]. DOI: 10.1207/s1532706xid0603_4.

Arcelus, J., Claes, L., Witcomb, G. L., Marshall, E. and Bouman, W. P. (2016) Risk factors for non-suicidal self-injury among trans youth. *The Journal of Sexual Medicine*, 13(3), 402–412 [Online]. DOI: 10.1016/j.jsxm.2016.01.003.

Bhana, D. (2018) Girls negotiating sexuality and violence in the primary school. *British Educational Research Journal*, 44(1), 80–93 [Online]. DOI: 10.1002/berj.3319.

boyd, danah (2014) *It's Complicated: The Social Lives of Networked Teens*. New Haven, CT: Yale University Press.

Bragg, S., Renold, E., Ringrose, J. and Jackson, C. (2018) 'More than boy, girl, male, female': exploring young people's views on gender diversity within and beyond school contexts. *Sex Education*, 18(4), 420–434 [Online]. DOI: 10.1080/14681811.2018.1439373.

Butler, J. (1990) *Gender Trouble: Feminism and the Subversion of Identity*. New York: Routledge.

Byron, P. and Hunt, J. (2017) 'That happened to me too': young people's informal knowledge of diverse genders and sexualities. *Sex Education*, 17 (3), 319–332 [Online]. DOI: 10.1080/14681811.2017.1292899.

Cavalcante, A. (2016) 'I Did It All Online:' Transgender identity and the management of everyday life. *Critical Studies in Media Communication*, 33 (1), 109–122 [Online]. DOI: 10.1080/15295036.2015.1129065.

Columbia Law School (2017) *Kimberlé Crenshaw on Intersectionality, More than Two Decades Later* [Online]. Available at www.law.columbia.edu/pt-br/news/2017/06/kimberle-crenshaw-intersectionality (accessed 5 August 2019).

Ditum, S. (2018) Trans rights should not come at the cost of women's fragile gains. *The Economist* [Online]. Available at www.economist.com/open-future/2018/07/05/trans-rights-should-not-come-at-the-cost-of-womens-fragile-gains (accessed 2 September 2019).

Dobson, A. S. (2015) *Postfeminist Digital Cultures: Femininity, Social Media, and Self-Representation*. New York: Palgrave Macmillan.

Dobson, A. S. and Ringrose, J. (2016) Sext education: pedagogies of sex, gender and shame in the schoolyards of Tagged and Exposed. *Sex Education*, 16(1), 8–21.

Egan, R. D. (2013) *Becoming Sexual: A Critical Appraisal of the Sexualization of Girls*. Cambridge: PolityPress.

Epple, C. (1998) Coming to terms with Navajo 'nádleehí': a critique of'‘berdache,' 'gay,' 'alternate gender,' and 'two-spirit'. *American Ethnologist*, 25(2), 267–290.

Epstein, D., Kehily, M., Mac an Ghaill, M. and Redman, P. (2001) Boys and girls come out to play: making masculinities and femininities in school playgrounds. *Men and Masculinities*, 4(2), 158–172. DOI: 10.1177/1097184x01004002004.

Fausto-Sterling, A. (2000) *Sexing the Body: Gender Politics and the Construction of Sexuality*. New York: Basic Books.

Fine, C. (2017) *Testosterone Rex: Unmaking the Myths of Our Gendered Minds*. London: Icon Books.

Finlayson, L., Jenkins, K. and Worsdale, R. (2018) 'I'm not transphobic, but …': a feminist case against the feminist case against trans inclusivity. *Versobooks.com* [Online]. Available at www.versobooks.com/blogs/4090-i-m-not-transphobic-but-a-feminist-case-against-the-feminist-case-against-trans-inclusivity (accessed 2 September 2019).

Gavey, N. (2018) *Just Sex? The Cultural Scaffolding of Rape*, 2nd edn. Bristol: Psychology Press.

Hasinoff, A. A. (2015) *Sexting Panic: Rethinking Criminalization, Privacy, and Consent*. Champaign: University of Illinois Press.

Hines, S. (2019) The feminist frontier: on trans and feminism. *Journal of Gender Studies*, 28(2), 145–157 [Online]. DOI: 10.1080/09589236.2017.1411791.

Holland, J., Ramazanoğlu, C., Sharpe, S. and Thomson, R. (2004) *The Male in the Head: Young People, Heterosexuality and Power*, 2nd edn. London: Tufnell Press.

Jeffreys, S. (2014) *Gender Hurts: A Feminist Analysis of the Politics of Transgenderism*. Abingdon, Oxon; New York: Routledge.

Karaian, L. (2014) Policing 'sexting': responsibilization, respectability and sexual subjectivity in child protection/crime prevention responses to teenagers' digital sexual expression. *Theoretical Criminology*, 18(3), 282–299 [Online]. DOI: 10.1177/1362480613504331.

Lees, S. (1986) *Losing Out: Sexuality and Adolescent Girls*. London: Hutchinson.

Lippman, J. R. and Campbell, S. W. (2014) Damned if you do, damned if you don't … if you're a girl: relational and normative contexts of adolescent sexting in the United States. *Journal of Children and Media*, 8(4), 371–386 [Online]. DOI: 10.1080/17482798.2014.923009.

Livingstone, S., Carr, J. and Byrne, J. (2016) *One in Three: Internet Governance and Children's Rights*. Innocenti Discussion Papers, UNICEF Office of Research.

Lyttleton-Smith, J. (2015) Becoming gendered bodies: a posthuman analysis of how gender is produced in an early childhood classroom. PhD Thesis, Cardiff University. Available at http://orca.cf.ac.uk/86260/.

Mcneil, J., Ellis, S. and Eccles, F. (2017) Suicide in trans populations: a systematic review of prevalence and correlates. *Psychology and Sexual Orientation and Gender Identity*, 4 [Online]. DOI: 10.1037/sgd0000235.

Mendes, K., Ringrose, J. and Keller, J. (2019) *Digital Feminist Activism: Girls and Women Fight Back Against Rape Culture*. Oxford: Oxford University Press.

Muller, M. N., Marlowe, F. W., Bugumba, R. and Ellison, P. T. (2008) Testosterone and paternal care in East African foragers and pastoralists. *Proceedings of the Royal Society B: Biological Sciences*, 276(1655), 347–354.

Neary, A. (2018) New trans* visibilities: working the limits and possibilities of gender at school. *Sex Education*, 18(4), 435–448 [Online]. DOI: 10.1080/14681811.2017.1419950.

Office for National Statistics (2019) Internet access – households and individuals [Dataset]. Available at www.ons.gov.uk/peoplepopulationandcommunity/householdcharacteristics/homeinternetandsocialmediausage/datasets/internetaccesshouseholdsandindividualsreferencetables (accessed 23 August 2019).

Olson, K., Durwood, L. and DeMeules, M. (2016) Mental health of transgender children who are supported in their identities. *Pediatrics* [Online]. Available at http://pediatrics.aappublications.org/content/early/2016/02/24/peds.2015-3223.abstract (accessed 1 August 2017).

Orenstein, P. (2016) *Girls & Sex: Navigating the Complicated New Landscape*, 1st edn. New York: Harper (an imprint of HarperCollins Publishers).

Paechter, C. and Clark, S. (2007) Learning gender in primary school playgrounds: findings from the Tomboy Identities Study. *Pedagogy, Culture & Society*, 15(3), 317–331.

Payne, E. P. and Smith, M. (2014) The big freak out: educator fear in response to the presence of transgender elementary school students. *Journal of Homosexuality*, 61(3), 399–418 [Online]. DOI: 10.1080/00918369.2013.842430.

Powell, A. (2010) *Sex, Power and Consent: Youth Culture and the Unwritten Rules*. Cambridge: Cambridge University Press.

Renold, E. (2005) *Girls, Boys and Junior Sexualities: Exploring Children's Gender and Sexual Relations in the Primary School*. London: RoutledgeFalmer.

Renold, E., Bragg, S., Jackson, C. and Ringrose, J. (2017) How gender matters to children and young people living in England [Online]. Available at http://orca.cf.ac.uk/107599/ (accessed 2 September 2019).

Ringrose, J. and Harvey, L. (2015) Boobs, back-off, six packs and bits: mediated body parts, gendered reward, and sexual shame in teens' sexting images. *Continuum*, Routledge, 29(2), 205–217 [Online]. DOI: 10.1080/10304312.2015.1022952.

Ringrose, J., Harvey, L., Gill, R. and Livingstone, S. (2013) Teen girls, sexual double standards and 'sexting': gendered value in digital image exchange. *Feminist Theory*, 14(3), 305–323 [Online]. DOI: 10.1177/1464700113499853.

Roberts, C. (2015) *Puberty in Crisis: The Sociology of Early Sexual Development*. Cambridge: Cambridge University Press.

Salter, M. (2016) Privates in the online public: sex(ting) and reputation on social media. *New Media & Society*, 18(11), 2723–2739 [Online]. DOI: 10.1177/1461444815604133.

Setty, E. (2019) Meanings of bodily and sexual expression in youth sexting culture: young women's negotiation of gendered risks and harms. *Sex Roles*, 80, 586–606.

4 Food, eating and identities

Mimi Tatlow-Golden

Introduction

Food has an ordinary, everyday taken-for-granted quality, as a material feature of our daily lives and of everyday childhoods. Yet underneath this very 'everyday' quality lies the fact that food is also socially constructed and is central to our identities. Food is one of the ways that children, young people and families express their belonging to groups in society, such as class or a particular culture: a literal act of embodiment that creates and maintains self- and group identities. This chapter will consider some of the many intersecting identities children and young people experience and express through food. Drawing upon children's and young people's perspectives, as well as those of adults, it examines ways that food in children and young people's lives articulates identities relating to family, culture, and class, moral and ethical views of the world, as well as generation and gender.

Social identity theories, to which you were introduced in Chapter 1, describe how people come to develop a sense of self, or 'who I am', based on features of the social groups to which they belong. Group identities are essential parts of the self-concept and 'form a socially constructed sense of who and what "we" are and also who and what "we" are not' (Oyserman *et al.*, 2007, p. 1012). The social theorist Erving Goffman (1959, 1963) noted that this sense of self is created and enacted through interactions with others, and that attributes experienced as 'ordinary' and 'natural' are established socially as a way of categorising people. One of the ways in which people can be marked out by attributes that appear 'ordinary' or 'natural' is via the food they eat. Although most people, when asked, will typically describe food in terms of taste, hunger, health or affordability, studies by sociologists, anthropologists, psychologists, historians, economists and others have shown that what people eat and how they do so are shaped by many interacting social, economic, historical and cultural factors (Douglas, 2002; Bourdieu, 1984; Caplan *et al.*, 1998; Spagnola and Fiese, 2007; James *et al.*, 2009; Mennell *et al.*, 1994; Wills *et al.*, 2011). Does your family eat pork? Is seaweed something you enjoy? Do you ever engage in fasting? As the sociologist Deborah Lupton (1996) argues, the body and food are important in creating a self-identity. This includes not just physical appearance but also the foods we eat (and those we don't), and how we eat them.

Food identities can develop both at home and beyond, in peer groups, at school and in the wider world. At home, parents and other family members help transmit food and taste expectations, by training taste-buds in early life and shaping the foods and flavours that become considered acceptable or delicious, or indeed those that are disliked or considered disgusting. Through the symbolism of everyday eating and special occasions, particular foods and food practices become infused with meaning (Spagnola and Fiese, 2007). Beyond family, children and young people themselves often actively use food to explore and construct identities: in classrooms, lunchrooms, playgrounds, in fast food restaurants and on the streets, they choose and share food, building relationships and shaping gender and ethnic identities, marking out boundaries with food just as they do with other commercial-cultural objects such as toys, clothes and consumer devices (Nukaga, 2008; Best, 2017). Furthermore, the commercial world plays an active role in creating food preferences and identities (introduced in Chapter 1), using extensive advertising to develop emotions and symbolism associated with manufactured foods. This chapter will explore aspects of these multiple, intersecting food identities, starting with children's use of food in marking ethnic and classed identities.

Food at school: experiences of ethnicity and class

In the Los Angeles area of the United States, in public elementary schools that were majority Korean but ethnically diverse and mixed-income, Misako Nukaga (2008) carried out an ethnographic study of children's lunchtimes. She carried out observations when the fourth-graders (about ten years old) 'associate freely with their peers under minimal adult surveillance and form a strong sense of solidarity through sitting and eating together' (p. 350). Both boys and girls gave different kinds of foods as gifts, shared and traded them. Observing these exchanges, Nukaga identified how various foods, as material, cultural items, were used to create closeness with peers, exert power over others and establish identities.

Children across ethnicities shared and bartered mass-produced processed foods at the school. Widely exchanged items included biscuits (e.g. Chips-Ahoy), chocolate (e.g. M&Ms, Twix, Milky Way), sweets, crisps (e.g. Doritos, Cheetos, Fritos) and prepackaged Lunchables crackers with meat or cheese. The children called these packaged foods 'dry food'. In addition, trade in home-made 'wet food' took place – but usually only between the Korean children who often showed pride in their homemade Korean food:

> Cindy opened the lid of her thermal lunchbox. Inside, she found pieces of meat that looked like Bulgogi (Korean BBQ meat) and cooked bean sprouts on top of steamed rice. She exclaimed with joy, 'Oh, I love this!' When I asked what they were, Cindy replied, 'I don't know what it's called, but it's Korean.'
>
> (Nukaga, 2008, p. 361)

Figure 4.1 Peer food identities at school: children may trade foods they bring from home while others eat free school meals.

Indeed, even Korean seaweed, a salty packaged snack, had become a sought-after commodity at the schools in Nukaga's study: a 'dry' food, yet Korean, it became a widely circulated item in the children's school food economy that only the Korean children had access to.

The multiple forms of 'wet' and 'dry' food capital that the Korean children could distribute contrasted with many of the Latino and African American children who qualified for free/reduced cafeteria lunches and had less or no food to exchange – thus lacking edible resources with which to build relationships. Nukaga thus found that the middle-class Korean children at these schools, who had access not only to 'dry' commercial packaged foods but also to hot cooked food from home, had more opportunities than those of other ethnicities and social classes to use food exchange to develop ethnic identities and mark boundaries. In their food gifting and sharing of both dry and wet foods at school, Korean children established cross-ethnic egalitarian friendships and also built ethnic and class boundaries. They collaboratively created an intricate food economy with which they negotiated ties to others and marked, maintained and muted social differences.

Nukaga describes the children in her study as 'active economic agents' (Zelizer, 2002, p. 377). Certainly, parents or other adults played a role in these exchanges, in that they provided the 'wet' and 'dry' foods. Yet Nukaga found that children actively engaged in creating this school-based economy of food sharing. In doing so she contrasts her findings with adult-centred socialisation frameworks in which children are described as passive recipients who internalise adult culture and practices, including those around food. This ethnography of a school lunchtime food economy showed how young children actively 'do' race and ethnicity through food exchange and eating: building and negotiating relationships with their peers and at the same time developing their ethnic identities.

For the children in these majority-Korean, mixed-ethnicity Los Angeles elementary schools, Korean foods, whether 'wet' or 'dry', were sought-after economic and cultural resources. Yet food as a definer of ethnic identity may not always be experienced as a positive resource in school. In the UK, Anna Ludvigsen and Sara Scott (2009) examined school-based lunch cultures in England, interviewing nearly 200 children and young people about what they selected at the school dining-hall and vending machines. A quarter of their interviewees came from Black, Asian or Minority Ethnic (BAME) backgrounds, and many lived in areas experiencing socioeconomic deprivation. Ludvigsen and Scott found that sandwiches, crisps and a chocolate bar were considered normative for school lunches brought from home. When classmates brought foods other than these, it marked them out as different and objects of ridicule, particularly in schools with large BAME populations. Young people who brought cooked foods such as Indian or Chinese food, or salads, were laughed at, as a 15-year-old girl described, giving the example of a boy of Asian ethnicity:

> everyone used to take the piss and he used to sit there and cry.... He used to have chicken legs that his mum would have cooked and he would eat like three of them and everyone used to call him 'chicken boy' because he would have chicken every day for lunch.
>
> (Ludvigsen and Scott, 2009, p. 428)

At this school in England, having home-cooked food at lunchtime also acted as a powerful marker of ethnicity. Yet in contrast to the Korean elementary schoolchildren in Los Angeles, home-cooked food in these UK settings did not allow young people to enact a positive ethnic identity. Instead, strict norms about acceptable foods – majority-ethnicity and commercial-culture foods (sandwiches, crisps and chocolate bars) – were enforced by peers. Any 'different' food that diverged from these norms was interpreted negatively, and as a consequence a food-related ethnic identity was identified by peers but experienced negatively by young people.

There are several possible reasons why having ethnic-identified home-cooked food at school lunchtime played out so differently in these two mixed-ethnicity settings. One may be that cultural acceptability of ethnic diversity in food and eating practices is different in England compared to the west coast of the United States of America. Whether this or other explanations, such as social class, or indeed both, underlie these differences would require research into food identities spanning multiple sites. However, it alerts us to the fact that children's and young people's ethnic identities enacted through food takes multiple forms, may be experienced both positively and negatively, and is sensitive to the social settings in which it is experienced.

Figure 4.2 In England, young people make fun of classmates who have brought cooked food from home.

Food, rituals and family identity

The studies considered above found that ethnic and classed identities are partially trans-mitted through the home-cooked and bought foods provided for children by their fam-ilies. Family food and eating practices – the particular foods eaten and the rituals associated with them – are a key way in which families create a sense of 'who we are'. Family rituals are specific, repeated practices involving two or more family members that have symbolic significance, many involving food, such as celebrations (e.g. birth-days), traditions (e.g. Christmas, Diwali or Eid), but also patterned practices such as family meals (Wolin and Bennett, 1984), whether a Shabbat dinner, Sunday lunch or Friday night takeaway. Mary Spagnola and Barbara Fiese (2007) explain how not just 'special' events but regular family meals function as rituals, since they often include embedded symbolic practices such as stories, prayers or particular foods on specified days of the week: 'rituals are distinct and unique to particular families, reflecting family identity, culture, and shared values … [and] provide a context for the development of children' (p. 285). Amidst these practices, children develop language and social skills, emotional well-being and family and cultural identities through the culturally embedded, patterned interactions they experience in these family rituals, Spagnola and Fiese con-clude. Family rituals also foster autonomy and allow young people to retain their family identity connection as they engage in life transitions throughout childhood to adulthood.

The importance of food-related routines and rituals to identities and well-being is brought into particular sharp relief when families are unable to enact them as a result of external stressors such as separation, migration or poverty. This is often experienced in the context of migrant experiences (Murphy, 2019). As an example, in Ireland, people seeking asylum are required to live in state-funded 'Direct Provision' centres, with no rights to work and minimal financial support, until their applications are heard. Applicants may be waiting many years for a decision, and so the process may encompass a substantial proportion of childhoods for many families. These centres offer basic accommodation where families are housed in very limited quarters, often without access to cooking or food storage facilities, requiring them to eat the rudimentary food prepared by the centres. Keelin Barry (2014) found that parents felt disempowered in these settings and one of the reasons they gave was that they had no control over the food their children ate, and that their children had never seen them cooking meals. They were thus not able to provide food congruent with their cultural, ethnic or religious identities, and were unable to impart their culture and create a family identity through food (Barry, 2014; Murphy, 2019), disturbing their opportunities to shape their children's identities through food and eating rituals.

Intersections of family, migration and class

The importance of food from their country of origin in migrant children's identity construction is further illuminated in a study of Mexican migrants to the United States. Joanna Dreby and colleagues (2019) spoke with over 100 Mexican migrant families, including children and young people aged five to 17 years, in New Jersey, Ohio and New York State. These children and young people nearly always named Mexican foods as their favourites. Sometimes children named North American classics too, such as a ten-year-old girl whose favourites were macaroni and cheese and enchiladas, but they generally chose Mexican food only, such as rice with beans, tacos, tamales and tostados. Young people described these Mexican foods as being important to their sense of extended family, family history, emotional well-being and identity:

> A 15-year-old in a working-class family explained that she liked Mexican food because, 'that's what I grew up 'cause I lived with my grandma, so it feels more, I guess, comfortable.' A 15-year-old in a middle-class family said what he most likes about Mexico is the food. And when asked 'What makes you feel happy about being Mexican?' A 10-year old in a working-class family explained, 'I get to eat Mexican food.'
>
> (Dreby *et al.*, 2019, p. 6)

Many of the mothers invoked taste and health in explaining their belief that Mexican food was superior to 'American' food and often travelled far or worked hard to incorporate these foods into their children's diets. At the same time, migrant families wanted to signal 'integration' into American society and express their new Mexican-American identity through food. Strategies for doing so varied by social class. Working-class

Figure 4.3 Mexican migrant children saw Mexican foods as important to their identity.

migrant families employed American fast foods to signal their American belonging, and to symbolise identification with their new surroundings were more likely than middle-class parents to acquiesce to children's requests for American fast food items such as burgers, hot dogs and pizza. Middle-class families also signalled their absorption into this stratum of US society through food practices, but did so by eating a globalised diet of international foods, and by drawing upon widespread contemporary discourses of 'healthy', incorporating 'American' healthy eating practices such as restricting fats and sugars in their children's diets.

These migrant children's food practices and identities were therefore informed by intersections of migration and social class. Parents in working-class Mexican US migrant families exerted less control over their children's diets, whereas middle-class migrant parents engaged in management of children's eating by restricting items considered to be 'unhealthy'. Dreby and colleagues (2019) draw a parallel between these findings and sociologist Annette Lareau's (2003) characterisation of middle-class and working- and lower-class approaches to parenting, in which she articulates class-based trends in approaches adopted by parents to their child-rearing. Middle-class parents, Lareau concludes, often engage in a 'concerted cultivation' style of child-rearing to shape their children's lives, whereas working-class families are more likely to engage in a more hands-off 'natural growth' approach, giving children freedom and exerting less control within the family. This is one possible explanation for commonly found class disparities in diet.

As in the US, in the UK, the eating of 'healthy' or 'unhealthy' foods is often involved in constructing and enacting children's and young people's classed identities. Young people in England explained to Ludvigsen and Scott (2009) that 'posh' people ate healthy food, as they could afford it, and because eating other foods was associated with a 'down-market' lifestyle (p. 433). Kathryn Backett-Milburn, Wendy Wills and colleagues in a range of studies with working-class and middle-class parents and teenagers in Scotland (Backett-Milburn *et al.*, 2010; Wills *et al.*, 2011) found that middle-class children, at home but also with their friends, were critical of eating unhealthy items or fast food and were encouraged to develop a taste for a range of cosmopolitan foods, and concluded that middle-class parents engage in more constraints in order to cultivate their young people's taste, whereas working-class parents focused on developing autonomy in their children at an earlier stage. These findings again echo Lareau's (2003) analysis of class differences in parenting approaches and suggest that social class identities based on differences in foods eaten may be found regularly in multiple global settings. These studies indicate class-based patterning in family food practices, where working-class parents (when they can afford to, and often because food is a relatively low-cost item) accord children more autonomy over food choices. In contrast, middle-class parents typically constrain their children's access to foods that meet definitions of 'unhealthy', cultivating their taste in a different direction.

Moral and ethical identities of food and eating: health, vegetarianism and more

Similar patterns of class-based 'healthy' eating have also been identified in California and suggest a different analysis of class-based family eating patterns. Priya Fielding-Singh and colleagues explored how young people and mothers discuss food through in-depth interviews with 160 young people and parents. They found that wealthier families frequently discussed healthy eating and food quality, rarely mentioning cost. In contrast, in poorer families, price and affordability were frequent topics of conversation about food, traded off against other attributes such as quality and healthiness (Fielding-Singh and Wang, 2017). Notably, Fielding-Singh (2019) found that in addition to material characteristics of food such as availability and affordability, the young people also drew upon symbolic interpretations of food that characterised some foods as *more moral* than others and transferred these to those who eat such food. Mirroring 'healthy eating' discourses from nutrition and public health campaigns, young people described healthier foods as 'good', 'right' or 'better' (p. 42); eating them was considered effortful and contrasted with being a 'couch potato' (p. 45). Eating healthier foods was thus associated with personal moral superiority. Wealthier young people saw themselves as deriving moral worth from this, even while they acknowledged that financial privilege allowed their families to eat this way. Interestingly, many young people from less well-off families – who could not afford to eat this way – also subscribed to this discourse of morality and healthy food. As a result, their classed identities were shaped as more or less moral depending on the foods they and their families ate:

overall, more privileged adolescents' beliefs about healthy eating enable them to assert themselves as good, moral people, while those shared beliefs challenge less privileged adolescents' abilities to do the same ... beliefs about healthy eating serve as a powerful medium for adolescents to mark and moralize socioeconomic groups, and each other.

(Fielding-Singh, 2019, p. 41)

Beyond the un/healthy distinction, a further food-related ethical-moral identity is on the rise in the Global North. Ethical eaters are adopting diets that meet social, political or moral goals such as animal welfare or environmental protection, adopting an ethical food identity associated with an actively chosen, political-moral stance that is often not congruent with the dominant food culture. This contrasts with cultures that eschew certain foods such as meat for religious or cultural reasons. Chelsea Chuck and colleagues (2016) spoke with 36 young people who had adopted an ethical eating stance in the United States, mostly white, with a median age of 22 years, most of whom were vegetarian. Almost all had adopted their current diet as a response to political encounters and this led to the conscious adoption of a new identity. After encountering a different worldview 'through various routes such as role models, informational materials or visceral emotional experience' (p. 432), they

overtly or implicitly affirmed their diets as part of identity, saying that it enhanced their personal psychological and/or physical self-view, and remained steadfast to their political diet, even in the face of friction or hardships in social interactions.

(Chuck *et al.*, 2016, p. 432)

Drawing upon a model of group identity development that describes a political identity arising from an 'encounter' experience, Chuck and colleagues draw a parallel between these ethical identities and the awakenings experienced by individuals who encounter politicisation regarding race or gender. Thus, this ethical food identity, as an explicitly chosen, overtly political food identity, contrasts with the moralised 'healthy' identity described by Fielding-Singh and colleagues that reflects dominant cultural narratives about 'being good'.

Generationed food: 'children's food' and beyond

Although many young people adopt ethical eating identities in contrast to family practices, parents and their children express many shared meanings about food and eating, and for young people family remains a major influence even in the teenage years, as about two-thirds of what young people eat is consumed at home (Story *et al.*, 2002). Yet some food identities are generationed: they are associated particularly with children and young people. A widespread practice reported in studies in the UK, the US and Canada and elsewhere is of identifying certain foods as 'children's food' (Roos, 2002; Ludvigsen and Scott, 2009; Elliott, 2011). Children consider that their identity as children determines many foods they eat, contrasting these with the foods that adults eat. 'Children's' foods, in these studies across time and continents, include 'junk food', pizza and sweets, and thus highly processed, commercially produced and widely advertised foods carry a symbolic value, defining a 'child' as one who prefers (and deserves) these items.

Interestingly, although young people often seek to mark themselves out from their younger selves, this differentiation is not seen in the case of food, as processed and 'junk' foods feature in many accounts of foods young people choose when they start purchasing food themselves. Teens use 'fast' food and processed food to mark their teen identity and group belonging (Wills *et al*., 2009; Fitzgerald *et al*., 2010), a phenomenon widely reported in the Global North where such foods form a large proportion of many diets. Furthermore, the symbolism of 'junk' or 'fast' food in some settings indicates a shift to modernity. Soula Ioannou (2009) spoke with 25 young people in urban Nicosia, Cyprus aged between 15 and 17 years from diverse socioeconomic backgrounds. She found that foods carried symbolic meanings for them: whereas eating traditional foods such as Cypriot beans was 'a no-no for our times', associated with family and older generations, the young people associated fast food, such as burgers, fried chicken and pizza, with youth attributes such as *'being "cool", "in", "attractive", "independent", "modern" and "casual"'*:

> When you have delivery food you show a different character, more outgoing and attractive than having home-made food prepared by your mum or grandmother. You come over as a person with a degree of independence who does not depend that much on his family; you look cooler.
>
> (Despina, 15 years; Ioannou, 2009, p. 189)

Earlier in the chapter it was noted how peers may police young people's food practices, enforcing norms of eating through ridicule and shaming. In Cyprus, Ioannou (2009) describes a similar phenomenon in the context of young people shaming those whose food choices did not indicate their modern orientation, quoting a young person who said that young people 'make fun of the ones who have home-made food' (2009, p. 190). Failing to align with peer group identities presents similar threats to young people's well-being in other locations, for example, in northwest England where Martine Stead and colleagues (2011) found that teens focused on having to have what were seen as the 'right' commercial food brands, and in Sweden where Jenny Rendahl and colleagues (2018) found that teens identified social risks of not displaying the 'right', gendered image when eating. In these various settings, therefore, teens carefully expressed and negotiated their identities through the foods they chose to eat – or not.

Gender identities

Food is also strongly associated with gendered identities (gender identities are explored in more detail in Chapter 3) in terms of what, and how much, males and females should eat. In general, males express gendered identities by eating more, and eating meat, whereas female gendered identities are frequently associated with eating less, and 'weaker' foods such as milk-based products, fruits and greens. The details of specific foods vary culturally, but very widespread gendered coding generally reflects social constructions about men's and women's roles, and takes the form of men needing more, 'stronger' food (Counihan and Kaplan, 2004).

As with other features of gender identity, these interpretations and practices are encoded from early childhood. In Australia, Murray Drummond and Claire Drummond (2015) interviewed 33 Australian boys at five years of age and found that they had strongly gendered views on food items and portion sizes, views which persisted, as the Drum-monds returned to speak annually with the boys up to the age of nine years. The boys associated masculinity with meat, alcohol and larger portion sizes, whereas fruit, fish, vegetables and yogurt were associated with femininity, as they said that girls were *'not big on eating animals'* (Drummond and Drummond, 2015, p. 286). Their descriptions of their parents' roles in food preparation reflected their understanding that the male domain was outside the home, whereas women's place was within: *'men are more outside people and they do the barbecues'* – *'My dad's a barbie man and my mum's the cooking girl'* (p. 289).

Similarly, in the UK, when schoolchildren were shown photos of a meal of burger and chips and one of brown bread and fruit, and asked to describe someone their own age who would eat these foods, all agreed that boys would eat the burger meal while girls would choose brown bread and fruit (Ludvigsen and Scott, 2009). This was, Lud-vigsen and Scott report, partly due to concerns about body image, particularly weight, as ten-year-old girls said, *'Girls eat nothing – boys eat everything'* and *'When you think of boys you think of sweets, you think of chocolate ... yeah, they think they are already strong so they don't have to go on any diets'* (Ludvigsen and Scott, 2009, p. 432).

Figure 4.4 Children in England thought that burger and chips was more a 'boy' meal than a 'girl' meal.

It should be borne in mind that although the gendered identities associating men with strength and the outdoor domain, and women with caring roles and indoor activities, are consistent, the specific foods linked to these gendered identities can vary from one location to another and across time. For example, young children in Australia described men as needing salad for strength (Drummond and Drummond, 2015), whereas in the UK and the US salad has typically been gendered as female and middle class (Wills *et al.*, 2011; Shapiro, 2008). Another example of contrasting gender encoding of foods is the case of hummus. This chick-pea puree from the Middle East, eaten with bread, is considered the 'food of manly men' in Israel (Hirsch, 2016, p. 337), particularly when eaten in a *hummusiya*, a specialist restaurant where it is made fresh. Yet elsewhere in the Global North, hummus is associated with identities that are more frequently coded as female, such as not eating meat, and hummus is considered a more 'female' food.

Creating and maintaining food identities: social norms and the commercial world

This chapter has considered multiple ways in which families and children themselves may be involved in creating food identities, through family rituals and food provision, by sharing food at school, and by enforcing group identity compliance through ridicule and shaming of peers in the school context. Social norms are implicit perceptions of what others think and do, and they guide people as to what conduct is considered appropriate (Higgs, 2015), and are thus one of the ways in which identities are created and maintained, including food identities. Interestingly, social norms may influence food behaviours even when they are not accurate. Phillippa Lally and colleagues (2011) surveyed 264 16- to 19-year-olds in the UK, and found that young people held distorted social norms about their peers' eating that affected what they themselves chose to eat. The teens believed that people of their age ate more unhealthy snacks and sugar-sweetened drinks, and fewer fruit and vegetables, than they actually did – and these misperceived norms were associated with what the survey respondents ate themselves. This study therefore suggests that people are influenced in food choices by their unconscious assumptions – those of which they are not aware – and that changing young people's perceptions about what their peers eat could shift their own food identities. Considering the kinds of foods that young people thought their peers ate most, which were highly processed, commercially produced, widely advertised foods, this suggests a link to commercial determination of social food norms.

Social norms about food and eating have, since the mid-twentieth century, been powerfully influenced by producers and marketers of branded, highly processed foods. These commercial interests engage in extensive marketing and advertising of their products and brands, building associations of these with positive emotions and cultures and identities of childhood and youth. Children's engagement with these emotions and identities is regularly found in studies of their food knowledge, attitudes and preferences. They are aware of food brand logos by the age of three and have very high recognition levels by age five (Tatlow-Golden *et al.*, 2014), and they consistently

Figure 4.5 Commercially produced fast food is viewed as 'children's food' and 'young people's food' in many cultures.

identify commercial brands as preferable to own-brand or unbranded foods (Ludvigsen and Scott, 2009; Stead *et al.*, 2011). Ludvigsen and Scott found that branded aware-ness started early and that branded goods were a valuable commodity:

> having a popular brand in your lunch box is useful as a bargaining tool to get you into a football game ... peers might try to become your friend if you had a nice brand in your packed lunch. Some nursery children also showed their awareness of brands, by saying that they liked burgers from a well-known fast food chain ... children bringing packed lunches gave very detailed information in the lunch ques-tionnaire about the branding of crisps, chocolate bars and drinks in their lunch box.
>
> (2009, p. 430)

The powerful role that branded processed packaged foods play in children's identities and relationships is still further amplified in twenty-first-century digital media, where young people contribute themselves to the creation of social norms. They do this by transmitting branded content about food, sharing advertising through their networks and responding to content shared by internet 'influencers', prompted by advertisers to do so via 'likes', 'shares', 'tagging' and other means. In this way children and young people are co-opted as economic agents on digital platforms (Tatlow-Golden and Garde, forthcoming) and they become agents in the nexus of activity that sets com-mercially produced, branded foods at the centre of their lives and identities.

Concluding thoughts: food as an expression of intersecting identities

This account of many food-related identities experienced and expressed by children and young people is by no means exhaustive. Yet already it can be seen that a food identity is complex and multifaceted – all food identities are intersectional. Food is a symbolic representation of identity that may be influenced by ethnicity, gender, class, age and political-moral positioning, and individuals are likely to have discontinuous, divided, possibly conflicting food identities. Food both *creates* and *expresses* these multiple identities. Food identities and practices are often absorbed from the family, social, cultural and commercial norms practised in the social surround, and generally this is not a conscious process. At the same time, children and young people engage actively, as social, economic and moral agents, with aspects of their food practices. Studies of families', children's and young people's food practices show that food creates and transmits norms, values, morals, relationships, emotions, status, belonging and more, and that food and diet – although viewed as ordinary, daily necessities – are crucial to signalling children's and young people's identity and belonging.

References

Backett-Milburn, K., Wills, W., Roberts, M.-L. and Lawton, J. (2010) Food and family practices: teenagers, eating and domestic life in differing socio-economic circumstances. *Children's Geographies*, 8(3), 303–314. DOI: 10.1080/14733285.2010.494882.

Barry, K. (2014) *What's Food Got to Do With It: Food Experiences of Asylum Seekers in Direct Provision*. Cork: Nasc, The Irish Immigrant Support Centre.

Best, A. (2017) *Fast-Food Kids: French Fries, Lunch Lines and Social Ties*. New York: New York University Press.

Bourdieu, P. (1984) *Distinction: A Social Critique of the Judgement of Taste*. Cambridge, MA: Harvard University Press.

Caplan, P., Keane, A., Willett, A. and Williams, J. (1998) Studying food choices in its social and cultural contexts: approaches from social anthropological perspective. In A. Murcott (ed.) *The Nation's Diet: The Social Science of Food Choices*. London and New York: Longman, pp. 168–182.

Chuck, C., Fernandes, F. A. and Hyers, L. L. (2016) Awakening to the politics of food: politicized diet as social identity. *Appetite*, 107, 425–436.

Counihan, C. M. and Kaplan, S. L. (2004) *Food and Gender: Identity and Power*. London: Routledge.

Douglas, M. (2002) *Purity and Danger: An Analysis of Concepts of Pollution and Taboo*. London: Routledge Classics.

Dreby, J., Tuñón-Pablos, E. and Lacy, G. (2019) Social class and children's food practices in Mexican migrant households. *Childhood*. DOI: 10.1177/0907568219832640.

Drummond, M. and Drummond, C. (2015) My dad's a 'barbie' man and my mum's the cooking girl: boys and the social construction of food and nutrition. *Journal of Child Health Care*, 19(3), 279–292.

Elliott, C. (2011) 'It's junk food and chicken nuggets': children's perspectives on 'kids' food' and the question of food classification. *Journal of Consumer Behaviour*, 10, 133–140.

Fielding-Singh, P. (2017) A taste of inequality: food's symbolic value across the socioeconomic spectrum. *Sociological Science*, 4, 424–448.

Fielding-Singh, P. (2019) You're worth what you eat: adolescent beliefs about healthy eating, morality and socioeconomic status. *Social Science & Medicine*, 220, 41–48.

Fielding-Singh, P. and Wang, J. (2017) Table talk: how mothers and teenagers across socioeconomic status discuss food. *Social Science and Medicine*, 187, 49–57.

Fitzgerald, A., Heary, C., Nixon, E. and Kelly, C. (2010) Factors influencing the food choices of Irish children and adolescents: a qualitative investigation. *Health Promotion International*, 25, 289–298.

Goffman, E. (1959) *The Presentation of Self in Everyday Life*. Garden City, NY: Double Day Anchor Books.

Goffman, E. (1963) *Stigma: Notes on the Management of Spoiled Identity*. New York: A Touchstone Book.

Higgs, S. (2015) Social norms and their influence on eating behaviours. *Appetite*, 86, 38–44.

Hirsch, D. (2016) Hummus masculinity in Israel. *Food, Culture & Society*, 19(2), 337–359.

James, A., Kjørholt, A. T. and Tingstad, V. (2009) Introduction. In A. James, A. Kjorholt and V. Tingstad (eds) *Children, Food and Identity in Everyday Life*. London: Palgrave Macmillan, pp. 1–12.

Ioannou, S. (2009) Eating beans. That is a 'no-no' for our times: young Cypriots' consumer meanings of 'healthy' and 'fast' food. *Health Education Journal*, 68, 186.

Lally, P., Bartle, N. and Wardle, J. (2011) Social norms and diet in adolescents. *Appetite*, 57, 623–627.

Lareau, A. (2003) *Unequal Childhoods*. Berkeley, CA: University of California Press.

Ludvigsen, A. and Scott, S. (2009) Real kids don't eat quiche. *Food, Culture & Society,* 12(4), 417–436.

Lupton, D. (1996) *Food, the Body and the Self*. London: Sage.

Mennell, S., Murcott, A., Otterloo, A. and Van, H. (1994) *The Sociology of Food Eating, Diet and Culture*. London: Sage.

Murphy, F. (2019) Seeking solidarity through food: the growth of asylum seeker and refugee food initiatives in Ireland. *Studies in the Arts and Humanities*, 4(2), 69–82.

Nukaga, M. (2008) The underlife of kids' school lunchtime. Negotiating ethnic boundaries and identity in food exchange. Journal of Contemporary Ethnography, 37(3), 342–380.

Oyserman, D., Fryberg, S. A. and Yoder, N. (2007) Identity-based motivation and health. *Journal of Personality and Social Psychology*, 93(6), 1011–1027.

Rendahl, J., Korp, P., Pipping Ekström, M. and Berg, B. (2018) Eating and risk: adolescents' reasoning regarding body and image. *Health Education*, 118 (3), 262–276.

Roos, G. (2002) Our bodies are made of pizza – food and embodiment among children in Kentucky. *Ecology of Food and Nutrition*, 41(1), 1–19.

Spagnola, M. and Fiese, B. H. (2007) Family routines and rituals: a context for development in the lives of young children. *Infants and Young Children*, 20(4), 284–299.

Stead, M., McDermott, L., MacKintosh, L. and Adamson, A. (2011) Why healthy eating is bad for young people's health: identity, belonging and food. *Social Science and Medicine*, 72, 1131–1139. https://doi.org/10.1016/j.socscimed.2010.12.029.

Story, M., Neumark-Stainer, D. and French, S. (2002) Individual and environmental influences on adolescent eating behaviors. *Journal of the American Dietetic Association*, 102(3), S40–S51.

Tatlow-Golden, M. and Garde, A. (forthcoming) Digital food marketing to children: exploitation, surveillance and rights violations. *Global Food Security*.

Tatlow-Golden, M., Hennessy, E., Hollywood, L. and Dean, M. (2014) Young children's food brand knowledge. Early development and associations with television viewing and parent's diet. *Appetite*, 80, 197–203.

Wills, W., Backett-Milburn, K., Roberts, M. L. and Lawton, J. (2011) The framing of social class distinctions through family food and eating practices. *The Sociological Review*, 59(4), 726–740.

Wolin, S. J. and Bennett, L. A. (1984) Family rituals. *Family Process*, 23(3), 401–420.

Zelizer, V. A. (2002) Kids and commerce. *Childhood*, 9, 375–396.

5 Everyday violence and everyday places

Jiniya Afroze

Introduction

Globally, one billion children are thought to experience physical, emotional or sexual violence every year (United Nations, 2016, p. xv) taking many forms, including armed conflict, trafficking and prostitution, harmful work, and child genital mutilation among many others. While some forms of violence, such as beatings or physical attacks, can be obvious and visible, other forms of violence, such as insults and bullying in the form of emotional violence, or violence in the forms of structural inequalities and power relationships/dynamics, are entrenched in everyday lives in ways that are often camouflaged as established social practices. The banality of children's experiences of violence is habitually normalised and naturalised to such an extent that such experiences are often not recognised as violence. The UN Convention on the Rights of the Child (UNCRC) – the most ratified human rights treaty that all UN members of state other than the US have endorsed – recognises that all children have the right to be protected from all forms of violence, abuse, neglect and exploitation. It is reassuring to have policies and systems in place, both internationally and nationally; however, the reality is that children and young people across the world continue to experience violence every day – in their homes, communities, streets, schools and workplaces. This chapter will shed light on the notion of everyday violence in order to discuss some of the mundanity and routineness of children's experiences of violence at the intersection of physical, emotional, structural and symbolic violence (Scheper-Hughes and Bourgois, 2004; Wells *et al.*, 2014). It will then draw references to a study I carried out in Bangladesh to bring out discussions of children's and adults' understandings of everyday violence and to learn from children's narratives about how, in a context of precariousness, children negotiate their agency in response to their everyday experiences (Afroze, 2019).

Conceptualising everyday violence

Violence has often been understood as a visible physical force – either as an actual action or threat – with the intention to hurt others which may affect victims' health and well-being. The concept of direct and physical violence in the form of killing and attack however has been criticised as somewhat limited and lacking in nuance because it undermines emotional violence (e.g. humiliation, insults or bullying), and downplays notions of power and inequality (see Krug *et al.*, 2002). Galtung (1969), in his essay 'Violence, peace, and peace research', conceptualised violence in relation to structural inequalities and unequal relationships of power engrained in a social context, explaining that the unequal distribution of resources affects hierarchies and relationships of power so that someone with fewer economic resources, combined with a limited education and poor health, will inevitably find themselves with the least amount of power and influence in a community. In his later work, Galtung (1990) added another manifestation of violence to his broader definition – cultural violence. By cultural violence he meant the cultural practices in the form of prevailing social norms and practices (e.g. child marriage and physical punishments) which make physical and structural violence so normalised that people are unable to perceive, question or challenge those acts of violence as something wrong.

Bourdieu (1991) used the term 'symbolic power' to imply the ways unequal power relationships and domination are routinely exercised in everyday life. The relationships between those who exercise power and those who accept it, according to Bourdieu, are triggered by 'symbolic power' – whereby the 'dominants' do not recognise their exercise of power as violence, while the 'dominated' legitimise their own vulnerability by adhering to the values and beliefs of the dominants, as well as internalising the belief that such domination is simply the way of the world (Bourdieu, 1991). One classic example of symbolic violence is men's violence against women: in the context of patriarchy, masculine ideas and values are considered as dominant cultural practices where, knowingly or unknowingly, power is channelled and imposed upon women in such an 'invisible' way that often it is 'misrecognized' as violence and thus 'recognized' as legitimate (Bourdieu, 1991, p. 24). Social hierarchies and inequalities therefore, according to Bourdieu, are not reinforced by external power – rather they are legitimised by normalising domination in everyday routine practices.

Drawing upon the work of Galtung and Bourdieu, Scheper-Hughes and Bourgois (2004) go on to illustrate how individual, structural and/or symbolic violence are closely intertwined. In their seminal work *Violence in War and Peace: An Anthology*, Scheper-Hughes and Bourgois (2004, p. 20) wrote:

> By including the normative everyday forms of violence hidden in the minutiae of 'normal' social practices – in the architecture of homes, in gender relations, in communal work, in the exchange of gifts, and so forth – Bourdieu forces us to reconsider the broader meanings and status of violence, especially the links between the violence of everyday life and explicit political terror and state repression.

In contrast to communal and political violence, everyday violence is not something extraordinary or 'painfully graphic and transparent' (Scheper-Hughes and Bourgois, 2004, p. 2). Instead it is something that is 'taken for granted', 'routinized' (Scheper-Hughes, 2004, p. 177) and 'utterly banal' (Scheper-Hughes and Bourgois, 2004, p. 19). Thus, Scheper-Hughes and Bourgois have concerns that often this violence is 'invisible or misrecognized' yet may have significant impacts on people's lives. Scheper-Hughes (1996, p. 889) therefore sees everyday violence as invisible – not so much because it is 'secreted away or hidden from the view', rather because it is so taken for granted that it is often not counted as violence.

Scheper-Hughes and Bourgois (2004) develop Bourdieu's work further, arguing that it is important to recognise different forms of violence; placing violence in narrow boxes does not allow a full understanding of how structural inequalities and relationships of power are embedded in our everyday lives. They describe everyday violence as a 'slippery concept' and a 'continuum' as it moves from more physical and direct violence to subtler forms of everyday violence that contribute to daily sufferings in mundane lives. Furthermore, violence also gives birth to violence, so that victim and perpetrator cannot be seen as binary opposites: often those who experienced violence can become violent towards others in a different time and context. It is therefore not surprising that Bourgois and Scheper-Hughes (2004, p. 318) call for ethnographically based empirical studies where researchers can engage with their research participants for an extended period of time while exploring the social and structural processes and practices that shape experiences of everyday violence.

Research studies that focus on everyday violence in relation to children's experiences are relatively rare. Pells and Morrow's (2018) research with the *Young Lives* project in India, Ethiopia, Peru and Vietnam emphasises the importance of understanding children's experiences of violence in connection to children's social context, poverty, ethnicity, caste and cultural norms. Their research shows, for example, how, physical punishment at school can legitimise violence in other contexts so that children bully their peers, and, again, children's experiences of violence in school can also accelerate the risks of violence at home, both being victims of violence and undertaking violence themselves. Another multi-country study in Italy, Peru, Vietnam and Zimbabwe, commissioned by UNICEF, finds violence to be relatively fluid which moves alongside children across a range of time and spaces and recognises that children's experiences of violence are closely linked to the relationships, structures and power dynamics within families, peer groups and communities (Maternowska and Fry, 2018). Bringing together discussions on children's experiences of violence in everyday lives, Wells and Montgomery (2014) argue for a 'social recognition' of children as vulnerable persons – both due to the materiality of their bodies and their social exclusion from full participation – while at the same time recognising the underlying forms of violence to which children are exposed in their everyday lives. They claim that until and unless the 'role of violence in making the world' is acknowledged, it will not be possible to implement children's rights to protection (Wells and Montgomery, 2014, p. 9). While violence, to a certain extent, is very common to children's everyday experiences globally, how children understand and respond to violence is often shaped by their historical, political, structural and socio-spatial contexts.

Children's experiences of everyday violence in Bangladesh

The research context: an Urdu-speaking Bihari camp in Bangladesh

The site where I conducted the study is commonly known as 'camp' and the residents are known as Urdu-speaking Bihari people. The camp residents have their origin in the Indian state of Bihar and a few other Muslim majority regions in India who moved to what was then East Pakistan during the partition of India and Pakistan in 1947. At the end of the British colonial rule in India, many Muslims moved to the Muslim-majority East Pakistan (in part because of its geographical proximity) in the hope of making their homeland among others who shared their religion. However, the Biharis were never able to make East Pakistan their 'home' despite sharing the majority religion, as there were linguistic, cultural, political, social and ideological differences between the Urdu-speaking Biharis and Bangla-speaking Bangalis in East Pakistan. Eventually, political tensions between East Pakistan and West Pakistan turned into a war of independence. After a nine-month-long war, Bangladesh became an independent country in 1971. Many Biharis left their homes and took shelter in 'temporary camps', supported by the International Committee of the Red Cross (ICRC). To this day, these camps continue to be 'home' for many Urdu-speaking Biharis and their children.

I undertook my research in a camp in a suburb in Dhaka where a large number of Biharis settled during the post-partition period in 1947. Historically, this area was a

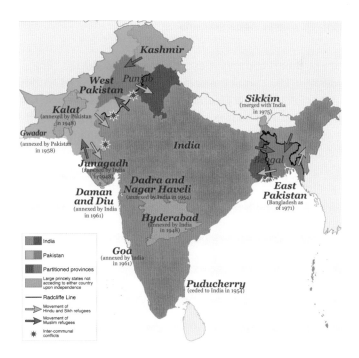

Figure 5.1 Map of India, West Pakistan (present-day Pakistan) and East Pakistan (present-day Bangladesh) following the partition of India and Pakistan in 1947.

Figure 5.2a and 5.2b A few lanes inside the camp.

concentrated hub of Bihari communities; therefore, around the time of the independence of Bangladesh in 1971, many displaced Biharis relocated to this area and took shelter in a number of temporary camps. The camp has around 4500 residents of which 1500 are children. The houses in the camp are mostly made of bricks and concrete with roofs made of corrugated iron sheets. Most of the houses have one room of ten-square-feet space, which is shared by families comprising three generations. The two public toilet spaces in the camp are shared among all the residents. The houses do not have any official access to gas, water and electricity. In the absence of formal structured services, there is informal (and illegal) access to utilities run by local gangs who, in collusion with the local authority, supply water and electricity to the residents for a high price. While most of the houses have some access to electricity, only a few people can afford to connect to clean tap water in their homes; thus they mostly rely on the three communal water collection points which run water twice a day. The economy in the camp broadly revolves around small trades and workshops, among which the most common is work related to hand embroidery (*karchupi*).

Considering the fact that education in Bangladesh is compulsory and free only up until primary level which incorporates students aged between six and ten, many children either do not register in secondary school or they drop out earlier before completing their national-level school final exams at the end of year ten. For a student in

Figure 5.3a, 5.3b and 5.3c Images of a few houses inside the camp.

secondary-level education, it takes around BDT10,000, the equivalent of at least £100, every month to manage the minimum education expenses per child. In the context of extreme poverty where most of the families do not even have a monthly income of £100, it is not surprising that parents in many cases cannot prioritise expenses for their children's education over other basic needs like food and health.

As members of the Bihari community, children and adults living in the camp are historically, ethnically, linguistically and structurally marginalised. For many years, Bihari people experienced discrimination in accessing basic services and securing employment in formal sectors, as they did not have a right to citizenship in Bangladesh until 2008. This social stigma was accentuated by their linguistic and ethnic identity, and to this day they continue to experience discrimination and even hostility. Through embracing ethnographic fieldwork over nine months – using participant observations, semi-structured qualitative interviews, group interviews and group discussions – this study explores the everyday lives of children (aged five to 18) and adults in the camp to illustrate how the concept of everyday violence plays out in children's lives, and how children negotiate their agency in responding to everyday violence.

Everyday violence in everyday spaces

The excerpt below presents a note from the observation of a drama piece that a few children of the camp performed in celebration of Children's Rights Week organised by a local charity that works for children's rights in the camp (Afroze, 2019, p. 158).

> Shuhash, a 14-year-old boy, is in a classroom with his friends. The teacher comes and asks for the homework. She beats Shuhash as he has not prepared his lessons. The teacher even tells him that if he does not do his lessons tomorrow then she would ask him to stand outside the classroom, under the sun. After school, Shuhash cannot join his friends on the football ground, as he must finish his lessons before he goes to work in the afternoon. He is late for work as he struggled to finish his lessons. At work, the *mohajon* (supervisor) scolds Shuhash for being late to work. At the end of the day, he cut his pay for being late. When Shuhash hands over the money to his mother, she yells at him for bringing less money at home. At night, Shuhash has very disturbed sleep. He wakes up a few times screaming, 'Madam, don't beat me, I will do my lesson', '*Ustad* (Sir – to address the supervisor), I will not be late at work again', 'Ma, forgive me, I will not do this again'.
>
> (Extracts from field notes taken on 2 October 2016)

The storyline, collectively written by children with the support of some adults in the community, does not relate the experiences of any individual child, but was a composite of experiences which reflected the everyday life experiences of several participants. The issues featured in the drama were nothing extraordinary or unusual in their lives; they were part of children's 'routine, inescapable, and mundane' experiences of everyday lives (Wells and Montgomery, 2014, p. 1). This provides a glimpse of the ways personal, structural and symbolic violence intertwine with children's everyday experiences in the camp and which the chapter will go on to further elaborate.

Considering its physical, spatial, material and economic conditions, the social space of the camp can easily be compared to other slums in urban Bangladesh. The violence that the camp residents referred to was not necessarily physical violence or attack but illustrated the everyday marginalisation and discrimination in the forms of social exclusion and disadvantages that members of the camp community have experienced for generations because of their ethnic-linguistic identity and their historical roots. On many occasions, children and adults in the camp expressed a shared sense of anguish and anxiety about the social spaces, saying, 'the environment of the camp is very bad', 'the camp is not a good place' 'and this camp is not a liveable place'. They often associated the present situation of the camp with the legacy of deprivation that Bihari people have carried with them since the partition of India and Pakistan in 1947. Children's narratives also showed that they often experience symbolic violence (Bourdieu, 1991) because of the negative connotations associated with the camp. Rodela, aged 17, thinks the term 'camp' has very negative undertones for many people living outside the camp and, indeed, also within the camp. She says:

> It hurts me. Why do they say so? Not everyone in a place can ever be the same. There is no such rule that everyone in the camp will be bad only because the camp is bad.... But wherever you go, you would only hear about the camp – that camp is a filthy place. The camp is [considered to be] a bad place only because of a few children. If I go somewhere [outside the camp] then people would say [in surprise], 'oh, how could you be a good girl since you are living in a camp? That place is bad. Camp is the worst place'.
>
> (Rodela, 17, individual interview)

While attaining citizenship rights in 2008 enhanced opportunities for the Biharis to access basic services, many camp-based Biharis continue to experience discrimination and deprivation because of the social stigma associated with the social spaces of the camp. This legacy of social and spatial deprivation entraps the Biharis in a 'continuum of violence' (Scheper-Hughes and Bourgois, 2004, p. 1) which triggers individuals and groups to produce and reproduce violence within their contexts. Some adults claimed that their experiences of discrimination in accessing education, securing a job and having the right to vote over the past few decades have given rise to a new generation of Urdu-speaking Biharis who are 'burdens' instead of 'blessings', 'criminal' instead of 'capital' to the country. Within the broader landscape of cultural, social and political structures, children and adults in the camp are often positioned in contrast to 'others', be it the Bihari political elites, the government or other Bangladeshis in general. The 'others' have education, wealth, culture, demonstrating all the symbolic capital that Bourdieu (1986) has referred to, which the camp-based Biharis consider they do not have.

Central to the ideas about childhood within the camp are the concepts of *'bhalo'* (good) children, as opposed to *'noshto'* (rotten) or *'kharap'* (bad) children, which reflect the concept of 'rottenness' associated with the camp itself (see also Afroze, 2019). To isolate themselves from the rottenness of the camp, the participants expressed their desire to become 'good' and feared that the 'rotten' environment of the camp might turn them 'rotten' too. The account of Johny, aged 14, shows how his exposure to the 'outer' world enabled him to learn the differences between the 'good' and the 'bad':

> When I started school, made a few friends with boys who live outside the camp, I started to realise that the boys in the camp are really very bad. The boys from outside the camp are very good – they do their prayers ... I haven't made any friend in this camp. The boys here are not good. They don't study, and only do chitter-chatter on the streets. Even young children have mobile phones on their hands; they take cigarettes. That's the reason that I can't get along with them. You can tell looking at them who is good and who is bad, you know, they do swearing and bad words, they do hitting and fights. I don't get out on the street; I mostly stay at home and study.
>
> (Johny, 14, male, individual interview)

Masum, aged 13, gave a glimpse of his journey from becoming a 'good' to a 'bad' boy.

> I learned swearing from this camp. I have not always been as I am today. I was good when I was young. I used to say my prayers. I don't like swearing. But most of the people [in the camp] use bad words ... I grew up hearing bad words, and I learned those too. My mum used to say that she would hit me if I swear. But if anyone swears by my mother then I evidently swear back or strike back.
>
> (Masum, 13, male, individual interview)

To avoid their children being labelled 'rotten' or 'bad', parents often limit their children's mobility within the camp so that they have fewer interactions with people and lesser scope to be seen through the lens of a 'rotten child'. An 11-year-old girl, Shajeda, reflects on such tensions where, by conforming to her mother's instruction, she does not make friends with anyone in the camp. She legitimises the cultural belief that as a girl if she wanders around the camp then it might bring disgrace and disrespect to her family. The generational power practices also support this assumption as she said, 'what my mother says she surely says for my well-being, she surely wouldn't say anything that would be bad for me'.

The gendered experiences of violence are often mediated by the age of the child. Many parents expressed their concerns around their younger children's mobility and safety, and they also believed that younger children were at lesser risk. As girls reach puberty, however, their risks in relation to where they go, with whom they get along become a matter of much greater communal concern. The community therefore starts to keep an eye on the girls which puts pressure on girls to be constantly conscious about the issues of social shame, prestige and issues related to *maan-shomman* (respectability). One girl, ten-year-old Pia, explains:

There is no bar on going outside when we are young. But as we are growing older, they [the adults] won't let us go outside to play. It is correct too – if we, as older children, play in the streets then people would talk badly about us. Whatever we play or do – if we are in the streets [as older children] – then people definitely would talk badly about us.

(Pia, 10, female, group discussion)

Many children explained that they prefer to be silent, as opposed to raising their voices, in order not to jeopardise their reputation of being a 'good child' that they have cultivated over the years. The following extract explains the reasons behind the choices of silence:

I don't do anything even when I get angry. Why don't I do so? Because one word will beget many words. This is the reason that I don't say anything. I tell them [who start bad words] that, 'you have the mouth to throw bad words – so better you continue to do so'. I rather would let those bad words enter through my one ear and leave through the other. I don't have any need to hear those! I don't have any need to fall into the trap of problems.

(Tonima, 13, female, individual interview)

A few participants like 14-year-old Adi said that they prefer to distance themselves from the 'rottenness' of the camp as well as its 'rotten' residents. The strategy to isolate themselves from their Bihari peers is a way of identifying ways to connect and integrate with mainstream Bangla society, to establish relations and build connections and, consequently, to accumulate 'symbolic capital' through this process (Bourdieu, 1991).

Everyday violence and gendered power dynamics

Gender norms and unequal power dynamics constrain everyday experiences of girls and boys in many different ways and through both visible and invisible forms of violence. Gender inequality and discrimination perpetuate violence in many ways, and it becomes particularly visible when girls are married before 18, which is the legal age of marriage in Bangladesh. Parents often view marriage as a safer alternative to the physical risks girls experience in their everyday lives. If any girl is sexually harassed before her marriage then parents fear this may bring shame to the girl as well as to the family, which would lower the chances of the girl receiving a respectable marriage proposal.

Several participants however indicated that child marriage is no longer the norm in the community, and also said that the trend of marrying children off early has reduced significantly over the past few years. Some girls emphasised the importance of 'standing on their own feet' as opposed to getting married too early and being dependent on their husband's income. Urmi, aged 18, was firm in her aspiration that she wants to have 'an identity' of her own instead of relying on her husband. Urmi said, 'I would be able to do everything if I have my own capabilities. I won't have to be a burden to anyone.' Urmi wanted to get a job so that she can support her parents as well as get 'established' before getting married. Rodela, 17, firmly expressed the view that young women must have some academic accomplishments prior to their marriages which might work as 'backup capital' in case their marriages run into difficulties. While most of the families I interviewed were not able to continue with their children's education beyond secondary level, education serves as a protection strategy for many young women who, unlike their parents, do not have an uncritical reliance on and confidence in marriage. The observations and narrations of some of the young women suggest that having an academic certificate gives symbolic power to a married woman which can help her negotiate authority in marital relationships. Changing attitudes and knowledge of the drawbacks of early marriage do not necessarily protect children however, and even though some parents also expressed their aspirations for their daughters to have an education, many children have to drop out of school due to poverty and to fulfil their caring responsibilities. While it may be the case that there is a changing realisation about the importance of education and the negative consequences of child marriage, the constraints of everyday life continue to challenge many parents.

Generational power and inequalities

The everyday life experiences of children throughout the world are embedded in the unequal relationships of power between children and adults. Children's experiences are often mediated by their negotiations of agency in relation to power imbued in spaces, social structures and social relationships. As this chapter has argued, violence takes many forms, but one of the most visible and overt is through discipline and socialisation. The term 'physical violence' is a broad term used by academics and practitioners to include physical and corporal punishments as well as humiliation and violent forms of discipline. However, it is important to note that while the use of bad language and shouting creates a culture of everyday violence in the camp, the people in the camp often do not recognise it as violence or humiliation. The use of bad language and swearing was rarely discussed as punishment by the participants in this research; however, its absence or presence was clearly a critical issue for them and a marker of good/rotten spaces of the camp. Milon, aged 16, however, described swearing as the key negative factor that affects children in relation to their everyday use of space in the camp.

> Young children start swearing even before they start uttering the word mum. I feel so bad – but what to do! There are few people who get fun seeing that a baby has said a bad word! But that's not something good at all! If they had taught the baby alphabets and letters, then that would have been something worthwhile! The baby is using bad words and they are getting fun out of it! I probably can teach the baby – but what to do with the grown-ups? It does not look good if I explain the grown-ups being a child myself! Yet I try to explain to them whenever I can. I just pray that nothing like this happens again. The bad words and swearing can only bring loss – not to our camp only, to our country, to the world.

While some children talked about some apparently less visible but predominant violence like swearing and discrimination, others discussed more apparent forms of violence, including physical violence. The role of everyday violence in the shape of discipline in the camp was discussed explicitly by Bablu, ten, and Shurjo, seven, who shed light on the cultural norms about social relationships between older and younger people:

> BABLU: Yes, they [my parents] hit me. Why won't they [he says with stress in his tone]? They have the *odhikar* (right) to hit our bodies. As grown-ups, they surely can hit us.
>
> SHURJO: They are our parents. Why won't they hit us?
>
> BABLU: [Suppose] we are taking a wrong path. Ma beats me to discipline me. She says, 'you should take the right path. If you take this [right] path, then it will be for your good. If you take that [wrong] path, then it will be bad for you.' This is what we have learned. Nothing works without a beating up. If I try to explain [to the other person], then it won't work. Now you see, here [among the three other boys in that group] I am the oldest. Would it be a problem if I slap him [Bablu refers to Shurjo]? There is no 'fault' [he says that in a self-assuring tone]. Now they [parents] hit me, they as adults can hit me. It doesn't matter at all [said with confidence].
>
> (Extracts from a group discussion, boys' group)

Bablu's exercise of his authority shows how violence becomes legitimised and how older children use violence towards those who are younger as a way of displaying their increased symbolic power, which they have accrued with age.

Adult–child relationships in Bangladesh are embedded in hierarchical relationships of power, through which adults validate their exercise of power over children, while children also largely acquiesce and even support adults' authority. Parental use of violence in the form of physical discipline is widely supported and seen as legitimate by both parents and children.

> SHIMANTO: Parents are *boro* [grown-ups]. We are *chhoto* [young]. We remain *nichu* [low] with them.
>
> JINIYA: What is the reason for doing that?
>
> SHIMANTO: We must be afraid of our parents. They are our parents, aren't they? We must obey them.
>
> MISHUK: Nothing would happen even if they hit us. Children are always *chhoto* [young] in their mothers' eyes.
>
> NAVEED: Doesn't matter how big we grow up, we are always young in parents' eyes.
>
> MUKUL: [Parents] hit for our betterment. So that we don't become *kharap* [bad]. They hit for our *bhalo* [good].
>
> (Extracts from a group discussion, boys' group)

While children may have strong views about what they consider legitimate and illegitimate forms of violence, this does not mean that they passively accept even legitimate forms. While they spoke in some instances about their belief in the need to conform and comply with all forms of adult authority, they also had techniques and strategies to undermine it. Children's narratives also show how they negotiate with adults to stop violent practices, and what role family culture plays in mediating these processes of negotiations. Nishi, a 16-year-old young woman, is aware of the 'rotten' side of the camp but is unwilling to take it for granted that, as a resident of the camp, she must embrace its 'rotten' culture. While her parents do not practise harsh disciplinary practices, Nishi has had conversations about power and authority in the household and the need to break cycles of everyday violence:

> I told my dad, 'If you [tells her father] scold or beat me – for no reason – one day I might throw this back to you. You would then say, how come that a daughter talks so badly with a dad! But it is you who started the *galagali* [yelling].' ... We have friends in school. They are wealthy and rich – even then, they are my friends. If I ever get used to this *galagali* [yelling and bad words] [because of the negative influence of the camp/family practices], then I might start using those with my friends too. They would then think that I have learned all these *galagali* as I grew up in the camp.
>
> (Nishi, 16, female, individual interview)

Children's economic power and contribution to the family are often the stimulus to negotiate and create strategies to resist violence. Rima, 12, said that she stopped going to the *karchupi* workshop, as her supervisor smacked her if she did not do her work well. Hitting, smacking and shouting are so normalised in this context that they were not considered violent by Rima's family members, let alone any justifiable reason to refuse to work. Nevertheless, Rima could stand firm on her position because of the power of her economic influence, and her potential to bring in income in the future. Her mother did not want to upset her, as the family values even the little contribution she makes; in the context of extreme poverty her earnings are the only steady source of income for the family.

Concluding thoughts

The findings discussed in this chapter illustrate children's complex relationships with the everyday spaces of the camp, the impact of cultural norms and structural realities, and how that influences and shapes the way children experience their everyday lives in the camp. Most important in children's everyday experiences is the construction of goodness and rottenness, and the ways rottenness of the camp can influence and turn children themselves rotten. Discussions about the concept of *maan-shomman* (respectability) illustrate how the notion of good and bad child link to the inter-generational and gendered cultural practices, where conforming to adults' authority endorses children's sense of belonging in the communal construct of good children. The discussions also shed light on the symbolic power of social relations and social spaces, while reflecting on the ways that influence children's experiences of violence in everyday lives. The findings also bring out how, within the complex historical, political and structural milieu of the camp, while many children conform to the way of the world, others also find ways to express themselves by negotiating and contesting their agency within the constraints.

References

Afroze, J. (2019) Realising childhood in an Urdu-speaking Bihari community in Bangladesh. In N. von Benzon and C. Wilkinson (eds) *Intersectionality and Difference in Childhood and Youth: Global Perpsectives*. London: Routledge, pp. 158–172.

Bourdieu, P. (1986) The forms of capital. In J. Richardson (ed.) *Handbook of Theory and Research for the Sociology of Education*. Westport: Greenwood Publishing Group, pp. 241–258. doi: 10.1002/9780470755679.ch15.

Bourdieu, P. (1991) *Language and Symbolic Power*, edited by J. B. Thompson, translated by G. Raymond and M. Adamson. Cambridge: Polity Press.

Galtung, J. (1969) Violence, peace, and peace research. *Journal of Peace Research*, 6(3), 167–191.

Galtung, J. (1990) Cultural violence. *Journal of Peace Research*, 27(3), 291–305.

Krug, E. G., Dahlberg, L. L., Mercy, J. A., Zwi, A. B. and Lozano, R. (2002) *World Report on Violence and Health*. Geneva: World Health Organization. doi: 10.1136/ip.9.1.93.

Maternowska, M. C. and Fry, D. (2018) The multi-country study on the drivers of violence affecting children: an overview. *Vulnerable Children and Youth Studies*, 13(sup.1), 12–25. doi: 10.1080/17450128.2018.1476748.

Pells, K. and Morrow, V. (2018) *Children's Experiences of Violence: Evidence from the Young Lives Study in Ethiopia, India, Peru and Vietnam*. Oxford: Young Lives. Available at www.younglives.org.uk/sites/www.younglives.org.uk/files/YL-ViolenceAffectingChildren-A4-Feb18.pdf.

Scheper-Hughes, N. (1996) Small wars and invisible genocides. *Social Science and Medicine*, 43(5), 889–900. doi: 10.1016/0277-9536(96)00152-9.

Scheper-Hughes, N. (2004) Bodies, death, and silence. In N. Scheper-Hughes and P. Bourgois (eds) *Violence in War and Peace: An Anthology*. Malden, MA: Blackwell Publishing, pp. 175–185.

Scheper-Hughes, N. and Bourgois, P. (eds) (2004) *Violence in War and Peace: An Anthology*. Malden, MA: Blackwell Publishing.

United Nations (2016) *Celebrating Childhood: A Journey to End Violence Against Children*. New York: Office of the SRSG on Violence against Children. Available at https://sustainabledevelopment.un.org/content/documents/2467Celebrating_childhood_report.pdf.

Wells, K. and Montgomery, H. (2014) Everyday violence and social recognition. In K. Wells *et al.* (eds) *Childhood, Youth and Violence in Global Contexts: Research and Practice in Dialogue*. Basingtoke: Palgrave Macmillan, pp. 1–15.

Wells, K., Burman, E., Montgomery, H. and Watson, A. (eds) (2014) *Childhood, Youth and Violence in Global Contexts: Research and Practice in Dialogue*. Basingtoke: Palgrave Macmillan. doi: 10.1057/9781137322609.

6 Getting ready for school

Who's playing?

Karen Douthwaite

Introduction

The early period in children's lives prior to formal schooling, commonly referred to as the 'early years', has come under increasing scrutiny as a time when children's development and learning can be supported through the provision of care and education services. Recognising the value of play as a context in which children are driven to explore their wider worlds and their place within them, 'play-based learning' is widely promoted as a suitable approach to underpin children's experiences in these contexts (OECD, 2012). While play is typically considered to be an activity led by children's curiosities and agendas, its potential to lead to the acquisition of knowledge and skills has drawn political attention to the early years period as one in which prescribed outcomes might be derived to prepare children for the challenges of school and later life (NAEYC, 2009; Broström, 2017). Early years settings are increasingly becoming a context in which adult educators are held accountable for the outcomes from children's play and early experiences, shaping the way they engage with children and make provisions. This chapter explores a range of historical, political and theoretical perspectives of the purpose of early years provisions and their relevance to young children's play and learning relationships. The chapter has a particular focus on England as a context in which government intervention through curriculum guidance impacts upon children's provisions for play, but reflects a broader international debate about what it means to get ready for school.

The early years setting: a site for education and care

Early Childhood Education and Care (ECEC) is an umbrella term used at an international level to describe the early provisions for children outside of the home, and typically prior to the start of mandatory schooling (OECD, 2017). The terms 'education' and 'care' reflect two different purposes of provision that have integrated over time, with many contemporary settings, such as preschools, nurseries and kindergartens across Westernised countries, offering some aspects of both. In the nineteenth and early twentieth century, services for young children were typically founded by charitable, religious or private organisations with the aim of caring for disadvantaged children or providing middle-class children with an education. Following World War II, a vast increase in women entering the workforce and an explosion of social welfare policies led to a significant increase in publicly funded or subsidised childcare provisions, for example in the US and parts of Europe (Kamerman, 2006; Kamerman and Gatenio-Gabel, 2007). As well as a focus on quantity of provision and equity of access, public spending drew government interest in quality, and the past few decades have seen an abundance of national and international policies on the experiences and outcomes children should have as a result of their ECEC experiences (OECD, 2017).

Snapshots of the activities taking place in early years settings across Westernised contexts are likely to reveal environments resourced in part, for children's learning-through-play supported with guidance from educators, known as teachers or practitioners (Wall *et al.*, 2015). The provision of supported play-based activities has become embedded in early years settings as an age-appropriate educational practice, or pedagogy, in which children's own ideas and curiosities drive their cognitive, emotional and social development (Bredekamp, 1987; NAEYC, 2009).

> [Play] gives them opportunities to develop physical competence and enjoyment of the outdoors, understand and make sense of their world, interact with others, express and control emotions, develop their symbolic and problem-solving abilities, and practice emerging skills.
>
> (NAEYC, 2009 p. 14)

However, the opportunities children have to play, the resources provided and the guidance from practitioners are changing in some contexts (Broström, 2017). In a comparative study of nationally representative datasets of kindergarten practices for five-year-olds in the US from 1998 and 2010, for example (Bassok *et al.*, 2016), researchers found that modern kindergartens were less likely to include areas for art, domestic role-play and exploratory activities, but made greater use of teacher-led instruction, textbooks and worksheets. Teachers demonstrated a significant increase in the numeracy and literacy content of their provision and were twice as likely to agree that children should leave the kindergarten able to read. The researchers' findings led them to pose the question: 'Is kindergarten the new first grade?' in recognition of the pedagogic approaches more typically observed higher up the educational system (Bassok *et al.*, 2016, p. 1).

Challenges to play-based learning as the dominant pedagogy in early years settings originate with a standards and accountability movement of the latter half of the twenty-first century. The growth of global economic competition and concerns about achievement gaps in increasingly diverse populations, led to a focus on children's outcomes from school, and on making an early start on the educational ladder (Kamerman, 2006; NAEYC, 2009; Miller and Pound, 2011). Some international government perceptions of the early years as a discrete period in its own right began to shift towards its role as a preparatory stage in readiness for school. While the term 'school readiness'

Figure 6.1 Play-based pedagogies have typically dominated ECEC provisions to date.

lacks explicit definition, prescriptive curriculum frameworks increasingly qualify the sentiment with specific cognitive and linguistic skills each child should acquire before entry to school; increasing the prevalence of goal-directed and adult-led instruction (Bingham and Whitebread, 2012; Sylva *et al.*, 2015; Broström, 2017). This chapter considers the implications of these challenges to play-based pedagogies **for** young children's experiences, learning and relationships.

Why play?

A definition of play is difficult to establish; ephemeral in nature, its characteristics are hard to capture, but an understanding of its benefits as a driver for learning becomes clear when children's imaginative, creative and playful activities are observed (Moyles, 2015). Consider the following example of children's play in a *nidi d'infanzia* (nursery) for children aged 3 months to 3 years in the city of Pistoia in the Tuscan region of Italy. There is no formal curriculum in Pistoia; children's learning is represented in wall panels which display their paintings and drawings as well as photographs and written commentaries from their teachers. Documentation acts as a 'window and a mirror', making children's learning visible to the whole community and facilitating reflective practice for teachers (Barr and Drury, 2017, p. 3). This window to children's learning enabled researchers Barr and Drury to describe the learning-through-play that took place over many months:

This work began with one child, Leonardo, constructing a slide out of a hollowed out piece of wood. Leonardo 'silently and repeatedly experimented with sliding twigs, stones and shells' down this natural slide. Many children were attracted to this activity and began to make and play with wooden slides. In November, Leonardo began to construct slides with everything he could find, rolling wooden rings down inclined rods and building slides with wood blocks and other materials. ... The work continued in the classroom and in the following summer holiday, parents were invited to send in objects that could be rolled down slides ...

... Bigger and bigger slides were created and the slide idea even became part of lunchtime too, as Milo slid a meatball down his fork and created a 'fork-slide'. Children went on to look at shapes that slide easily, what helps them to slide (the inclination of the slide, the strength they are pushed with), which objects slide quietly, and which noisily. In the park adjacent to the nido they also found natural slides, such as 'water slides' where leaves slid down a small waterfall, and they slid and rolled their own bodies down steep banks in the park. In school, they invented games with rules, rolling balls to each other and creating tunnels with their bodies to send the balls through. This whole long project was marked by successive discoveries as children grasped the principle of what was needed to make a workable slide, what objects were best for sliding, and explored – in a scientific way – physical forces such as force, friction, and gravity.

(Barr and Drury, 2017, pp. 11–12)

This account shows that children's playful enquiries were central to the construction of new knowledge, supported by engagement with teachers and the environment. Learning was not merely cognitive but embodied, social and emotional, as children tested their physical capabilities, created and experimented with rules and experienced different ways of participating in the action. The philosophy underpinning the pedagogy in Pistoia is one founded on 'listening relationships', a child-centred approach in which children's perspectives are valued and serve as the starting point for teacher guidance that facilitates shared meaning-making across the learning community (Rinaldi, 2005). If teachers in Pistoia have any concern about school readiness it is in introducing children to a culture of learning, and there is no evaluative assessment of children's play (Mantovani, 2001). This child-centred but social perspective of play as a context for children's holistic development has a rich heritage, and a review of this extensive history is beyond the scope of this chapter. However, a brief consideration of the teachings of some significant pioneers explores the enduring conceptualisation of play as an appropriate pedagogy for learning and demonstrates the strength of its relevance in the debate about what it means to prepare children for school.

The rise and enduring appeal of play-based pedagogies

The establishment of the early years setting as a context for education is widely credited to educationalist Friedrich Froebel (1782–1852), founder of the first kindergarten (children's garden) in Germany in 1839. Influenced by the dominant philosophy of

Romanticism, Froebel considered play to be a natural way for children to explore the connected relationship of man, God and nature (Braun and Edwards, 1972). Inspired by the work of Swiss pedagogue Johann Heinrich Pestalozzi (1746–1827) who promoted 'learning through doing', Froebel developed a series of objects such as wooden cubes and spheres (gifts) and activities such as weaving and needlework (occupations) to engage children in constructing knowledge about universal laws of the world (Manning, 2005). Froebel positioned the child as an active learner, and promoted the women who worked with children, as educators, nurturing children's ideas through observation and guidance (Bruce, 2012). Froebel's ideas had international appeal, and child-centred approaches to learning can be seen in the teachings of many early years pioneers (Jarvis *et al.*, 2017).

Play-based pedagogies gained significant traction with the teachings of American philosopher and educator John Dewey (1859–1952). Responding to an increase in immigration to the United States and its expanding industrialised workforce towards the end of the twentieth century, Dewey considered the traditional approaches to learning discrete subjects in schools to be ill-suited to the needs of a culturally diverse population (Weiss *et al.*, 2005; Lindsay, 2016). Dewey praised Froebel's promotion of the active learner but aspired to more democratic practices than those offered by prescriptive learning materials. For young children, Dewey promoted 'free play' and creative activities such as art and drama, resourced and supported by skilled educators to facilitate individual agency and social participation; central tenets of liberal democracy (Dewey, 1916). Dewey's approach had significant influence in the US and overseas (Beatty, 2017), and is acknowledged, for example, as a source of inspiration in the educational philosophy founded by educators and parents in Reggio Emilia, Italy as they sought to develop a democratic educational system following World War II and years of fascist oppression (Lazzari and Balduzzi, 2013). The Reggio Emilia approach promotes children as competent protagonists in their own learning, supported to share their perspectives in close relationships with guiding teachers through multiple modes of communication such as art, music, play and drama, described by the founding teacher Loris Malaguzzi as the 'hundred languages' of children (Lindsay, 2016, p. 4).

Unlike the metaphysical origins of Froebel's philosophy, Dewey's assertions and their international growth were rooted in the emerging field of child psychology, in particular ideas around sequential mental maturity (Hall, 1906). Developmental psychology was heavily influential through the twentieth century in understanding children's learning and development, and consequently identifying appropriate pedagogic strategies for teaching. Swiss psychologist Jean Piaget (1896–1980) was particularly instrumental in promoting play as a developmentally appropriate tool for constructing knowledge. Piaget proposed that abstract and logical thinking was not possible until children had progressed through other sequential stages of development, for example, constructing knowledge through sensory engagement with the environment in infancy, and representational use of objects in early childhood (Piaget, 1929; Smidt, 2006). Piaget's theory of cognitive constructivism, in which children construct knowledge based on their experiences and stage of development, has relevance to the children's experiences, reflected in the wall panels in Pistoia. Children were not taught about abstract concepts such as force, friction and gravity didactically but were supported to experience the concepts in action through sensory and representational activity in a carefully resourced environment.

Perhaps most relevant to the pedagogy of relationships seen in Pistoia is the work of Soviet psychologist Lev Vygotsky (1896–1934). While Piaget promoted the role of the physical environment to children's learning, Vygotsky promoted a more social form of constructivism, with an emphasis on the relevance of children's social and cultural experiences. Vygotsky proposed that in imaginative and dramatic play children begin to explore ideas beyond their current experiences, enabling them to 'operate at their highest possible cognitive level' (Smidt, 2006 p. 46). In this state, adults as more experienced guides might tune into children's play, and recognise a 'zone of proximal development' where children's ideas can be extended through the co-construction of new knowledge using shared cultural tools such as language and gesture (Vygotsky, 1962, 1978). Consider the journey from Leonardo's wooden slide in the Pistoian *nidi* to broader experimentation with ideas about shape, size and force, supported by the provocations of teachers attuned to children's intentions. The sociocultural nature of play-based pedagogies means that learning is not only cognitive but satisfies children's feelings of agency and relatedness, and develops emotional self-regulation as children grow in their ability to act in coordination with others (Smilansky and Shefatya, 1990).

This brief consideration of some key players in the development of early years pedagogies has demonstrated the positioning of the child as an active learner, constructing

Figure 6.2 Adults join children's imaginary play and promote new ideas for shared learning.

knowledge through play in close relationships with educators. Play harnesses children's curiosities, and, through sensory, imaginative and social consideration of those curiosities, new ideas can be introduced, examined and consolidated. This need for sensory, experiential and social learning contexts in which children's agency and intentions have value led to a mantra of 'developmentally appropriate practice' for much international provision through the twentieth century (Bredekamp, 1987). In play-based provision children develop functional skills, knowledge of their worlds, positive learning dispositions and the ability to regulate emotions; arguably foundational skills for starting school. However, the standards and accountabilities movement, which gained significant pace at the beginning of the twenty-first century, increasingly aligns 'school readiness' with achievements in discrete subjects, attracting more adult-led teaching and less child-led play in some Western settings (Sylva *et al.*, 2015; Broström, 2017). The remainder of this chapter explores the complex dynamic in settings in England, where children's opportunities for play and relationships with educators are negotiated amidst policies, prescriptions and perceptions of school readiness.

Early learning in England: a battleground for play?

The 1988 Educational Reform Act in England, driven by the rhetoric of raising standards, introduced a statutory curriculum for schools, with literacy and numeracy hailed as a priority for five- to seven-year-olds. Traditional approaches to learning rooted in play-based pedagogies that had dominated infant schools were set aside, and resources such as sand and water trays, role-play and construction toys moved to the peripheries of classrooms in favour of teacher-directed learning activities (Anning, 2015). The potential implications of restricted opportunities for play are considered in Howe's (2016) research in a Year 1 classroom (for five- to six-year-olds) in England, in which children expressed discontent with the lack of opportunity to make friends, as well as with the limitations on their autonomy within the classroom.

> As James was walking to school one morning about three weeks after he had started in Year 1 he turned to his mother and said 'I don't want to go to school any more'. When she asked him why not he said 'Well, I don't mind doing literacy and I don't mind numbers, but I always have to do what the teacher tells me to do'.
>
> (Howe, 2016, p. 748)

Observations of children's actions in the classroom demonstrated that the rare opportunities for play resulted in higher level thinking, motivation and perseverance. Writing menus in a café role-play area facilitated engagement with writing; playtimes enabled the development of social and language skills, and opportunities for collaborative creativity supported participation within the wider school (Howe, 2016). Such findings are consistent with other research which suggests that children engage in more purposeful problem-solving and independent thought where they perceive an activity as play and have agency in setting the activity goals (McInnes *et al.*, 2009). Howe's research takes place in the formal context of mandatory schooling, where children join the year from their Reception classes, governed by a different, nominally play-based curriculum. However, as the discussion that follows demonstrates, even a statutory declaration about the importance of play cannot secure its place as children's dominant experience in practice.

Rapid expansions in funded childcare in England at the beginning of the twenty-first century, designed to provide universal provision for three-year-olds, led to the definition of a *Foundation Stage* for three- to five year-olds, supported with a statutory curriculum (Anning, 2015). The Foundation Stage curriculum has undergone a number of revisions, extending its reach from birth to age five, and prescribes the outcomes children require in 'readiness for school' as well as recommending the pedagogies to achieve them (Bingham and Whitebread, 2012). Reflecting the enduring social pedagogies for children's early learning, the curriculum guidance makes a strong statement about the place of play in practice.

> Each area of learning and development must be implemented through planned, purposeful play and through a mix of adult-led and child-initiated activity. Play is essential for children's development, building their confidence as they learn to explore, to think about problems, and relate to others. Children learn by leading their own play, and by taking part in play which is guided by adults.... Practitioners must respond to each child's emerging needs and interests, guiding their development through warm, positive interaction.
>
> (DfE, 2017, p. 9)

The learning context implied here is playful, sociable, often led by children's interests and guided by supporting practitioners. However, the curriculum also calls for every child to reach specific learning outcomes in a range of cognitive, social and physical domains by the time they enter the National Curriculum stage in Year 1. For example, the following goals for literacy and numeracy are featured:

- Children use their phonic knowledge to write words in ways which match their spoken sounds
- They write simple sentences which can be read by themselves and others. Some words are spelt correctly and others are phonetically plausible
- Using quantities and objects, they add and subtract 2 single-digit numbers and count on or back to find the answer
- They solve problems, including doubling, halving and sharing

(Standards and Testing Agency, 2018, pp. 30–31)

The English curriculum is underpinned by conflicting perceptions of child development, promoting learning through social interaction in child-led play alongside individualist outcome-driven trajectories (Rix and Parry, 2014). Curriculum guidance simultaneously positions the practitioner as a carer, researcher and technician (Moss, 2006) charged with guiding children's development through 'warm interaction' and knowledge of individual needs, as well as with meeting universal prescribed outcomes. Whether to lead children or nurture their knowledge through their play becomes a complex process of negotiation for the practitioner, not just of policy but of associated discourse, the power of which changes with context (Walkerdine, 1990). In Pistoia, for example, where children's play is not regarded as a focus for assessment, nurturing relationships are held in the highest esteem by the whole community; as a bedrock of professional practice (Barr and Drury, 2017). In England, the dominance of schooling and assessment aligns the discourse of professionalism more readily with didactic teaching and outcomes, denigrating the emotional labour required in ECEC practice (Osgood, 2012). Holding firm to child-led, play-based pedagogies can be difficult where settings are physically situated within school environments driven by an assessment culture, or where perceptions of care align the work of a predominantly female workforce with maternal intuition.

Consider, the complexity of negotiating a professional identity for this practitioner who comments on the aspirations of parents.

> There are those at one end of the spectrum that think it is just play and then at the other end you have parents who want their children reading and writing, you know that think we are in the business of cultivating little Einsteins ready for real school.
>
> (Osgood, 2012, p. 105)

Or the difficulties for this Early Childhood university student in promoting the value of the play-based pedagogies they have been taught in a Reception class attached to a school.

> Mark making in sand, gloop or other materials did not count, it needed to be writing with pencil and paper. Although I put forward my justification for not making the children formally 'write' every day, I was told that it needed to happen because 'before long these children will be in class 2 and they will need to write everyday'.
>
> (Rose and Rogers, 2012, p. 49)

Although the Early Years Foundation Stage curriculum makes a clear case for social, child-centred, play-based pedagogies, conflicting references to individualist academic outcomes for school readiness create complexities for practitioners designing provision. The culture of listening relationships implied in the long-term learning project in Pistoia is difficult to translate into practice in England, as the negotiation of standards and accountabilities questions who should lead and who should listen.

Who leads? Who listens?

Bringing together curriculum goals and pedagogies of play is challenging for practitioners who seek to resolve the dissonance between adult-driven outcomes and developmentally appropriate child-led learning inherent in the English curriculum. Using

Figure 6.3 Practitioners negotiate a range of discourse that impacts upon their practice with children.

prescribed outcomes to direct the nature of children's play can limit children's agency and engagement, and narrow interpretations of their meaning-making. Consider the following example of an activity provided in an Early Years Foundation Stage setting in rural England for three- and four-year-olds. Although the activity is intended to be playful, its purpose is defined by the adult educator, aligned with curriculum goals concerned with social and physical development. Note how children subvert the intentions of the activity and make it their own.

[Observation]: Outdoor play with hollow blocks: Alfie, Max, Joseph, Joel, Leanne, Henry

The large hollow blocks have been laid out in a circle by the adults, in one layer, with a small gap between them, and a foam mat in the centre. The intention is for the children to develop their gross-motor and loco-motor skills (especially balancing), sharing and co-operation, by stepping from one block to another. The activity is well within their capabilities, but for the first four minutes they use the blocks as they have been laid out. Leanne pretends to wobble and 'falls' onto the mat. 'Look, I can't do it. I'll have to fall in the sea'. The children make a game of this. There is some rough and tumble play and they 'swim' back to the blocks and 'rescue' each other.

Max has been experimenting by jumping rather than stepping between blocks. He extends the challenge as he puts one block on top of another. This widens the gap, and Max tries to jump between the blocks. Alfie, Joel, and Joseph watch carefully, as if they are assessing the challenge before they join in. A new rule is invented: They jump from one block to another then 'dive' into the 'sea' where they do forward and backward rolls. The NT [educator] intervenes to stop their activity as it is not safe. She reminds them they are allowed the blocks in one layer only. The children return to the stepping activity, going round in a circle, but with little interaction.

(Wood, 2014, p. 10)

In the children's imaginary narrative of swimming and diving in the sea, children exercise both individual and collective agency to challenge the dynamics of institutional power that dictate the purpose of their play (Wood, 2014). In this scenario, curriculum goals that position adult practitioners as leaders of provision and children as followers meet with resistance, and ultimately disengagement with the learning outcomes, as the activity is restored to its original goal-centred intentions.

Children's disengagement from learning provision has considerable implications for the development of skills in readiness for school and beyond. In England, concerns have been raised about outcomes for boys, who are seen to underachieve in reading, writing and mathematics prior to starting school and across their entire school career (Adock *et al.*, 2016). Prescribing early years curriculum goals in these academic subjects has set a bar for school readiness, but without pedagogic strategies that value children's agency and perspectives, learning opportunities may attract limited engagement (NAEYC, 2009). In one setting in a children's centre in Islington, Head Teacher Anita Mohindra describes how following rather than leading the play of boys was crucial in developing their cognitive, social and emotional skills for learning (Islington Primary Strategy Early Years Team, 2007). Mohindra describes how the boys' frequent choice of weapon play was initially banned for its association with aggression and anti-social behaviour. However, practitioner concerns about the implications of marginalising boys' play led to a relaxation of the ban, and a tuning-in to weapon play narratives. Children and practitioners co-constructed a new culture involving chasing and rescue games, den building and superhero play. New ways of framing aggression and its impact were considered by exploring alternatives such as magic potions and superpowers. By following the narratives and curiosities of boys' play rather than leading with curriculum goals, the whole community engaged in meaningful learning. Once children are operating at their highest cognitive level in play, learning in the curriculum areas, such as literacy and numeracy, can be extended. For children in Mohindra's setting, it is clear that counting sticks for Batman's cave or writing potion ingredients might easily become part of engaged community play.

The approach Mohindra describes can be considered a 'playful pedagogy' in which children's interests in play serve as the starting point for guiding their development. In playful pedagogies, practitioners can set aside curriculum goals, confident in the knowledge that learning will take place for documented evaluation post-play (Gooch, 2008).

Figure 6.4 Guided participation engages children in a collaborative search for new understandings.

This is not 'just play' but a professional strategy in which practitioners seek the 'teach-able moment' (Ephgrave, 2015, p. 2) akin to Vygotsky's 'zone of proximal develop-ment' (Vygotsky, 1962, 1978). Sociocultural thinker Barbara Rogoff (1990) extends Vygotsky's teachings to promote the relationship in playful pedagogies as one of 'guided participation', in which the practitioner engages the child in a dynamic and collaborative search for new understandings that evolve from children's interests. Lis-tening and leading are shared actions in the relationship as ideas are passed back and forth, and previously held meanings are transformed. As active negotiators in the development of the learning culture, children not only co-construct new knowledge but develop the functional and emotional regulation skills required to be active in any learning community, including schools (Rogoff, 1990).

Strong associations between narrative, imaginary play and early literacy develop-ment (Roskos *et al.*, 2010) suggest that playful pedagogies which guide children's stories into the open for collaborative meaning-making form a particularly pertinent approach to marrying play-based and goal-centred directives. Many settings in England are embedding storytelling and story-acting practices in their provision inspired by the writings of American kindergarten teacher Vivian Gussin Paley, and the pedagogies of her 1970s kindergarten classrooms (Cremin *et al.*, 2018). Paley (2004) recognised that children express their motivations in their play, and by guiding their stories into the community domain, first through narration and then dramatisation, ideas can be exchanged and developed building individual and collective identities.

> If readiness for school has meaning, it is to be found first in the children's flow of ideas, their own and those of their peers, families, teachers, books, and television, from play into story and back into more play.
>
> (Paley, 2004, p. 11)

Consider Monesha's story, narrated to an adult in an English nursery. Armed with the knowledge that her story would be dramatised, Monesha creates numerous meaningful roles in her story for her friends, drawing upon common shared cultural themes from books, TV and home to engage their collective interests.

> First there was Goldilocks and the three bears. The mummy bear cooked some porridge for dinner and Hello Kitty was making some cornflakes for dinner. And Barbie had a big, big friend called Teddy. And the second name of Teddy was Ravi. And Power Rangers had a fire in their house and the ambulance came to put it out. The end and then they bowed.
>
> (Faulkner, 2017, p. 98)

The processes involved in documenting children's stories and bringing them to the stage require a shared dynamic of listening and leading between adults and children, as roles are negotiated and understandings checked. Through guided participation, children are encouraged to 'try on' different roles in other people's stories and take these different perspectives back into play for further exploration. The use of shared cultural interests and literary conventions in Monesha's story show that the agency afforded to her through playful pedagogies contributes to an evolving readiness to participate in the social and academic activities that starting school will bring.

Concluding thoughts: school readiness, a case for play and the play professional

In a critical review of perspectives and evidence on 'school readiness' in England, Bingham and Whitebread (2012) assert that pre-primary pedagogies that promote the transmission of discrete knowledge from adult to child limit opportunities for children to develop broader skills relevant to their participation in learning communities. The authors suggest that for children to be confident learners in school they need to develop dispositions such as motivation, cooperation and persistence, attributes known to develop through play where children experience emotional security, agency and cognitive challenge. If policy-makers in England and beyond continue to measure the success of ECEC provision through notions of 'school readiness', they might look to the pedagogies in place in daily practice to develop coherent enabling curriculum frameworks. While the secret to being ready for school might lie in developing phonic knowledge and counting backwards, it is more likely to be found in children's stories, nurtured into the open by skilled play professionals for collaborative and negotiated meaning-making.

References

Adock, A., Bolton, P. and Abreu, L. (2016) *Educational Performance of Boys: Debate Pack* [Online]. House of Commons Library. Available at https://dera.ioe.ac.uk/27199/1/CDP-2016-0151.pdf (accessed 10 October 2019).

Anning, A. (2015) Play and the legislated curriculum. In J. Moyles (ed.) *The Excellence of Play*, 4th edn. Maidenhead: Open University Press, pp. 3–13.

Barr, M. and Drury, R. (2017) 'Documentation' in Pistoia preschools: a window and a mirror. *International Research in Early Childhood Education*, 8(1), 3–20.

Bassok, D., Latham, S. and Rorem, A. (2016) Is kindergarten the new first grade? *Aera Open*, 1(4), 1–31.

Beatty, B. (2017) John Dewey's high hopes for play: democracy and education and Progressive Era controversies over play in kindergarten and preschool education. *The Journal of the Gilded Age and Progressive Era*, 16, 424–437.

Bingham, S. and Whitebread, D. (2012) *School Readiness: A Critical Review of Perspectives and Evidence, A TACTYC Research Publication* [Online]. Available at TACTYC.org.uk (accessed 3 October 2019).

Braun, S. J. and Edwards, E. P. (1972) *History and Theory of Early Childhood Education*. Belmont, CA: Wadsworth Publishing Company.

Bredekamp, S. (Ed.) (1987) *Developmentally Appropriate Practice in Early Childhood Programs Serving Children from Birth through Age 8*. Washington, DC: National Association for the Education of Young Children.

Broström, S. (2017) A dynamic learning concept in early years' education: a possible way to prevent schoolification. *International Journal of Early Years Education*, 25(1), 3–15.

Bruce, T. (2012) The whole child. In T. Bruce (ed.) *Early Childhood Practice: Froebel Today*. London: Sage, pp. 5–16.

Cremin, T., Flewitt, R., Swann, J., Faulkner, D. and Kucirkova, N. (2018) Storytelling and story-acting: co-construction in action. *Journal of Early Childhood Research*, 16(1), 3–17.

Department for Education (DfE) (2017) *Statutory Framework for the Early Years Foundation Stage*. London: DfE.

Dewey, J. (1916) *Democracy and Education*. New York: Macmillan.

Ephgrave, A. (2015) *The Nursery Year in Action: Following Children's Interests Through the Year*. Abingdon: Routledge.

Faulkner, D. (2017) Young children as storytellers; collective meaning making and sociocultural transmission. In T. Cremin, R. Flewitt, B. Mardell and J. Swann (eds) *Storytelling in Early Childhood: Enriching Language, Literacy and Classroom Culture*. Abingdon: Routledge, pp. 85–100.

Gooch, K. (2008) Understanding playful pedagogies, play narratives and play spaces. *Early Years*, 28(1 March), 93–102.

Hall, G. S. (1906) *Youth*. New York: David Appleton & Co.

Howe, S. (2016) What play means to us: exploring children's perspectives on play in an English Year 1 classroom. *European Early Childhood Education Research Journal*, 24(5), 748–759.

Islington Primary Strategy Early Years Team (2007) *Engaging Boys in the Early Years; The Experiences of Three Early Years Settings* [Online]. Available at www.westsussex.gov.uk/media/5567/engboys.pdf (accessed 26 March 2019).

Jarvis, P., Swiniarski, L. and Holland, W. (eds) (2017) *Early Pioneers in Context.* Abingdon: Routledge.

Kamerman, S. B. (2006) 'A Global History of Early Childhood Education and Care'. *EFA Global Monitoring Report 2007, Strong Foundations: Early Childhood Care and Education*. UNESCO.

Kamerman, S. B. and Gatenio-Gabel. S. (2007) Early childhood education and care in the United States: an overview of the current policy picture. *International Journal of Child Care and Education*, 1(1), 23–34.

Lazzari, A. and Balduzzi, L. (2013) Bruno Ciari and 'educational continuity': the relationship from an Italian perspective. In G. Dahlberg and P. Moss (eds) *Early Childhood and Compulsory Education: Reconceptualising the Relationship*. Abingdon: Routledge, pp. 149–173.

Lindsay, G. M. (2016) John Dewey and Reggio Emilia: worlds apart – one vision. *Australian Art Education*, 37(1), 21–37.

Manning, J. P. (2005) Rediscovering Froebel: a call to re-examine his life and gifts. *Early Childhood Education Journal*, 32(6), 371–376.

Mantovani, S. (2001) Infant–toddler centers in Italy today: tradition and innovation. In L. Gandini and C. P. Edwards (eds) *Bambini*. New York: Teachers College Press, pp. 149–173.

McInnes, K., Howard, J., Miles, G. E. and Crowley, K. (2009) Behavioural differences exhibited by children when practising a task under formal and playful conditions. *Educational and Child Psychology*, 26(2), 31–39.

Miller, L. and Pound, L. (2011) Taking a critical perspective. In L. Miller and L. Pound (eds) *Theories and Approaches to Learning in the Early Years*. London: Sage, pp. 1–18.

Moss, P. (2006) Structures, understandings and discourses: possibilities for re-envisioning the early childhood worker. *Contemporary Issues in Early Childhood*, 7(1), 30–41.

Moyles, J. (2015) Starting with play: taking play seriously. In J. Moyles (ed.) *The Excellence of Play*, 4th edn. Maidenhead: Open University Press, pp. 14–24.

National Association for the Education of Young Children (NAEYC) (2009) *Developmentally Appropriate Practice in Early Childhood Programs Serving Children from Birth through Age 8* [Online]. NAEYC. Available at www.naeyc.org/sites/default/files/globally-shared/downloads/PDFs/resources/position-statements/PSDAP.pdf (accessed 10 October 2019).

OECD (2012) *Starting Strong III – A Quality Toolbox for Early Childhood Education and Care*. Paris: OECD Publishing.

OECD (2017) *Starting Strong 2017: Key OECD Indicators on Early Childhood Education and Care*. Paris: OECD Publishing.

Osgood, J. (2012) *Narratives from the Nursery: Negotiating Professional Identities in Early Childhood*. Abingdon: Routledge.

Paley, V. G. (2004) *A Child's Work; The Importance of Fantasy Play*. Chicago, IL: The University of Chicago Press.

Piaget, J. (1929) *The Child's Conception of the World*. London: Routledge and Kegan Paul.

Rinaldi, C. (2005) Document and assessment: what is the relationship? In A. Clark, A. T. Kjorholt and P. Moss (eds) *Beyond Listening: Children's Perspectives on Early Years Services*. Bristol: Policy Press.

Rix, J. and Parry, J. (2014) Without foundation: the EYFS framework and its creation of needs. In J. Moyles, J. Payler and J. Georgeson (eds) *Early Years Foundations: Meeting the Challenge* (2nd edn). Maidenhead: Open University Press, pp. 203–214.

Rogoff, B. (1990) *Apprenticeship in Thinking: Cognitive Development in Social Context*. New York: Oxford University Press.

Rose, J. and Rogers, S. (2012) Principles under pressure: student teachers' perspectives on final teaching practice in early childhood classrooms. *International Journal of Early Years Education*, 20(1), 43–58.

Roskos, K. A., Christie, J. F., Wildman, S. *et al.* (2010) Three decades in: priming for meta-analysis in play-literacy research. *Journal of Early Childhood Literacy*, 10(1), 55–96.

Smidt, S. (2006) *The Developing Child in the 21st Century: A Global Perspective on Child Development*. Abingdon: Routledge.

Smilansky, S. and Shefatya, L (1990) *Facilitating Play: A Medium for Promoting Cognitive, Socio-emotional, and Academic Development in Young Children*. Gaithersburg, MD: Psychosocial & Educational Publications.

Standards and Testing Agency (STA) (2018) *Early Years Foundation Stage Profile: 2019 Handbook*. London: STA.

Sylva, K., Ereky-Stevens, K. and Aricescu, A-M. (2015) *Overview of European ECEC Curricula and Curriculum Template*. Utrecht: Utrecht University – CARE Project.

Vygotsky, L. S. (1962) *Thought and Language*. Cambridge, MA: Harvard University Press.

Vygotsky, L. S. (1978) *Mind in Society. The Development of Higher Psychological Processes*, edited by M. Cole. Cambridge, MA: Harvard University Press.

Walkerdine, V. (1990) *School Fictions*. London: Verso.

Wall, S., Litjens, I. and Taguma, M. (2015) *Pedagogy in Early Childhood Education and Care (ECEC): An International Comparative Study of Approaches and Policies*. Department for Education/OECD.

Weiss, S., DeFalco, A. and Weiss, E. (2005) Progressive = permissive? Not according to John Dewey … subjects matter! *Essays in Education*, 14 [Online]. Available at https://openriver.winona.edu/eie/vol.14/iss1/7/ (accessed 27 September 2019).

Wood, E. A. (2014) Free choice and free play in early childhood education: troubling the discourse. *International Journal of Early Years Education*, 22(1), 4–18.

7 Children and young people's experiences of school

Do we listen hard enough?

Lucinda Kerawalla

Introduction

Although children and young people in the United Kingdom (UK) spend around 190 days a year at school, it is only in recent years that their perspectives on life in the state school (non-fee-paying) classroom have been sought (Sheehy, 2018). This chapter discusses some of this research and prioritises the voices of children and young people over academic theory. There has been relatively little research on what children *like* about school and rather more research on what children *dislike* about school, and areas which could be improved. The intention of this chapter is to provoke thought about the value of listening to children and young people's perspectives on their experiences of life in their classrooms, and the extent to which their right to be heard and listened to is made possible by schools and policy-makers.

In 1991, the UK ratified the United Nations Convention on the Rights of the Child (UNCRC, 1989), although it has not been incorporated into national law (DfE, 2014). It is important to acknowledge that the implementation of children's rights is often constrained by the realities of society (e.g. the authority assumed by some adults) so that implementation varies across different contexts. A balance often needs to be struck between considering different voices that might be loud, quiet, older, younger, more or less authoritative, etc. For example, children and young people in the UK do not have the right to choose whether to attend school. However, while they are in school, children and young people today do have a right to have their voices heard. In recent decades, various attempts have been made at national, regional and institutional levels in the UK to recognise that children are active participants in society who have the right to voice their opinions, including those about their education (Sheehy, 2018). These efforts include the instigation of various 'pupil voice' initiatives (e.g. DfE, 2014; UNICEF), and large national and regional surveys of the opinions of children and young people about their experiences of various aspects of their education (e.g. Ipsos MORI, 2013).

This chapter cannot cover all aspects of all children's and young people's experiences of the classroom; that would need a whole book. What follows is a

Figure 7.1 Children and young people have the right to be heard in school.

discussion of some of the research published since the year 2000, which gives the reader a glimpse of what life in UK state school classrooms is like from the perspectives of some of the children and young people who spend a significant proportion of their lives there.

The chapter begins by considering children's and young people's perspectives on being part of the school system. It then takes a closer look at classroom life by considering children's and young people's experiences of different teaching styles, assessment and ranking, fear in the classroom, and their perspectives on how a low family income can affect their participation in school activities. The chapter ends on a positive note by considering children's and young people's wishes for what their schools could be like, and then discusses the differences which the new 'rights respecting school' award from UNICEF has made to the experiences of thousands of children and young people today.

Schooling for future life

To some extent, schooling has been shaped by decades of psychological theories which presents an image of the child as an initially immature individual who passes through a number of developmental stages until they become a mature adult (see Piaget, 1969). Within this framework the child is conceptualised as a novice learner.

Saevi (2015) argues that the notion of 'education' necessarily creates an asymmetric relationship between the mature, expert teacher and the immature, inexpert child, within which the teacher has control over the freedom of the child. Austin *et al.* (2003) take this argument further and suggest that cultural practices in schools *ensure* that children and young people are positioned as pre-competent. These authors give the example of a certain type of classroom talk, where teachers ask questions they know the answers to, and children are required to show that they have learnt the answers to them, as a way in which the pre-competent status of children and young people, and the expert status of teachers, is normalised and maintained.

Practices such as these, together with psychological theories which describe and differentiate human beings in terms of their stage of developmental maturity, contribute to the widely held notion that children and young people are in a perpetual state of 'becoming' (e.g. Corsaro, 2011). The focus is on their future – on children and young people developing into, or becoming, educated adults. Children are therefore seen as adults-in-the-making. Interestingly, this focus on the future is often reflected in children's and young people's responses to researchers who ask them 'Why do you go to school?':

- 'it's very important to get a good job' (girl aged 10)
- '... so you know things when you have your own kids' (girl aged 11)
- '... so you can have enough money to live' (girl aged 11)
- 'in case you get a good job and wouldn't be able to write or anything' (girl aged 10)

(Horgan, 2007, p. 13)

Figure 7.2 Schooling can open doors to a good future.

It has been argued that viewing children's experiences of childhood through a lens that is focused on their futures has the effect of side-lining the fact that children and young people are competent and autonomous 'beings' in the world *today* (Corsaro, 2011). Conceptualising children and young people as 'inexpert, pre-competent, developing, becomings' means that school can be conceptualised as a 'designated site of childhood, a space organised and controlled by adults to aid an ordered transition from childhood to adulthood' (Burke and Grosvenor, 2003, p. 93).

Over the years, schools have taken on more and more responsibility for the creation of 'good' citizens of the future who are educated, well-rounded and able to become an effective member of the workforce. One young person has described their experience of this process as being 'treated like herds of an identical animal *waiting to be civilised* before being let loose on the world' (Burke and Grosvenor, 2003, p. 94, italics added). In her award-winning entry to the Scottish Schools' Young Writer of the Year competition organised by the Scottish Review, 16-year-old Harriet Sweatman (2019) wrote:

> In here [school], you are manufactured. You move along the conveyor belt of exam seasons, hoping for the grades you need, so you can be packaged up with a pretty label saying you got straight As and are shipped off somewhere else.

The strong educational focus on the future can result in some young people expressing exhaustion and frustration with how things are *now*: 'They nag you and nag you. They say you need to do this job, you need to do that job, oh you need an A in English to do this job. That just really gets on your nerves' (Boy, year 6) (Chamberlain *et al.*, 2011, p. 17). This child seems to be yearning for recognition of his current 'being', instead of his school's focus on his becoming. His autonomy as an individual, and his opportunities to voice his opinions and participate in decision-making today, as the UNCRC suggests, is therefore contested.

Experiences of authoritative and student-centred classrooms

When asked about the kinds of classroom activities they prefer, primary school children mention activities that are 'fun', 'easy' and 'interesting', whereas young people attending secondary school consistently mention interactive, lively teaching which includes group work, trips, external speakers and opportunities for creativity and choice (Lord and Jones, 2006, p. 33). And yet these views are often at odds with children's and young people's experiences. Teachers often employ a range of different teaching approaches and strategies depending on the topic being taught, the aims of the lesson and the learning needs of their students. Sometimes a teacher might stand at the front of the class and *transmit* knowledge to their students (i.e. tell them what they need to know). On other occasions they might ask their students to form small groups and *construct* knowledge by talking to each other (Mercer and Littleton, 2007). Sometimes, however, a teacher might be perceived by their students to be too authoritative, which can render the children and young people in the class relatively powerless and often gives rise to fear (Hargreaves, 2017). Hargreaves (2017) argues that teachers need to focus on developing 'children's own authority rather than relying on the teacher's authoritarianism' (p. 24).

The extent to which children and young people feel empowered and agentic in the classroom is linked to the extent to which they have control over the activities in which they are engaged. Student-centred approaches to teaching and learning attend to the voices of children and young people, who are given choices over what and how they learn. Children and young people are encouraged to take on responsibility for their own learning and to develop skills which they can apply to a range of learning situations. Teachers who adopt a student-centred approach with older children and young people are more likely to create opportunities for children and young people to work together in collaborative groups where they create their own understandings, together, facilitated by the teacher. Research suggests that when children and young people are given choices in the primary classroom they are more likely to be proactively engaged in learning (Hargreaves, 2017). The following studies contrast children's and young people's perspectives on being part of an authoritarian versus student-centred classroom.

Quick (2015 cited in Hargreaves, 2017, pp. 44–48) carried out some research with a year 5 class (nine years old) in London. Quick reports that the children describe being 'bossed around' and said that they had developed 'tricks' to overcome their feelings of being controlled. The tricks were developed by the children in order that they appeared to do what the teacher asked without actually doing so. For example, one child described how, when asked to cross her legs when sitting on the floor, she would bend one leg so that from the teacher's chair it looked like she had her legs crossed. The children talked about how their tricks made them feel 'powerful' because 'it feels like *we* control *them* [her emphasis], all the teachers. It feels free – free!' Quick argues that the tricks give the children a sense of autonomy and competence which their authoritative teacher was unable to facilitate, but it did mean that the children were more focused on appearing to do what the teacher asked of them rather than spending time on their learning. Tricks and strategies such as these are examples of children concealing their 'dissatisfaction behind a veil of compliance' (Fisher, 2011, p. 121).

In comparison, Maitles and Gilcrist (2004) carried out a study in a Scottish secondary school where a class of 30 young people aged 13 to 15 years were involved in decisions about the content and teaching of their religious and moral education lessons. In their responses to a questionnaire about their preferred learning styles, the young people said that they did not learn from authoritative teaching. Instead, they enjoyed learning together in groups of their choosing, listening to visiting speakers and learning from books or the internet. Eighty per cent of the class said they would be interested in communicating with, and learning from, young people in other countries. They also asked for outings and some of the young people said they would enjoy learning by presenting their work to the rest of the class. These requests were implemented by the teacher and later one young person described how:

> I thought it was really good to be part of a democratic class because the teacher was letting us in on the whole learning bit. It was good but quite scary at the same

time because somebody is saying, 'How would you like to be taught?' and we've never been asked that before.

(Maitles and Gilcrist, 2004, p. 93)

This study illustrates the benefits of giving young people age-appropriate control over how they are taught. When young people are given choices, and when their voices are listened to and acted upon in a student-led classroom, they appreciate their involvement (Maitles and Gilcrist, 2004). Yeomans (2013 cited in Hargreaves, 2017, pp. 73–77), a teacher and researcher, interviewed young people in her own secondary school about choice in lessons and they gave three main reasons for why they appreciated it:

1   **Choice involves taking an active part in lessons.** One young person in year 7 said that choice 'makes us more creative … encourages you to think for yourself'. Another young person in year 9 pointed to the importance of being able to choose who they work with because when teachers choose groups it's harder because you don't always feel comfortable sharing ideas'.
2   **Choice makes you feel happy, trusted, mature and responsible.** The young people described feeling 'happier', 'more comfortable' and 'relaxed' when given choices in lessons. Anita, in year 9, said, '[Choice] makes you feel like you have more freedom'. Sophie (year 7) said, 'it makes you feel happier that you are trusted to make your own choice'. Tom (year 9) said, 'It makes you feel like you are in charge and more responsible for what you do … it makes you more enthusiastic about what you do'.
3   **Choice means that learning is personalised.** Debbie (year 7) described how 'if you are finding it a bit easy you can take it up to your own level because you've got the freedom'. Other students appreciated that choices mean you can 'find out what works best for you' and 'learn in different ways'.

These research findings suggest that children and young people value the opportunity to make choices in the classroom because it involves them directly in lessons and they have more control over what they do – choice makes them feel happier, empowered and agentic. However, other studies point to the fact that choice per se is not necessarily a good thing; it can sometimes be demotivating (Katz and Assor, 2006). Teachers need to ensure that the choices offered are relevant to the students' own goals and interests, that they are not too easy or too difficult, and that the classroom culture is one which embraces individuality rather than collectiveness (ibid.).

Experiences of assessment, ability groups/sets and labelling

Assessment: tests and exams

Primary and secondary schools in all regions and nations of the UK use various types of tests and exams to evaluate the progress of their pupils, although this varies considerably across the UK. Pupils in England, for example, must sit national tests and the school is ranked in league tables based on pupils' achievements. Although so-called 'high-stakes testing' has been criticised for causing high levels of stress in children and young people, Bevan and Wilson (2013) point to the value of league tables. These researchers found that performance in Welsh schools deteriorated when league tables were abolished some years ago. They argued that this was because public 'naming and shaming' is an effective motivator for *schools* to achieve. Schools therefore aspire to a high ranking in the league tables and many focus a significant amount of their teaching on supporting their pupils' test and exam performance. Amanda Spielman, HM Chief Inspector of Education in 2019, acknowledged in a press release that 'In the worst cases, teaching to the test, rather than teaching the full curriculum, leaves a pupil with a hollowed-out and flimsy understanding' (Sellgren, 2019). But what do children and young people think?

Many children and young people in England think that tests and exams are an important and valid method of assessment (Lord and Jones, 2006) which can help them learn more and help them realise how much they have improved, or need to improve further (Robinson, 2014). Others, however, are more sceptical. When asked about what kind of school she would like, Miriam (aged 15 years) describes how she would like her school to stop thinking of students as 'useless vessels waiting in disciplined conditions to be filled with our quota of information, just so we can regurgitate it all in exams so that our school looks good' and instead appreciate that schools are populated with individuals with 'different personalities and gifts' (Burke and Grosvenor, 2003, p. 63).

Some children and young people report feelings of anxiety and stress not only about their performance in tests and exams but also about how others will perceive them if they do not do well. They also worry about where they will be placed in class and school rankings (Lord and Jones, 2006). For young people at secondary school there is the added fear of being perceived to be afraid (Jackson, 2010) so that 'young people have come to understand that to be truly successful one must be able to "handle pressure" and hide fear' (Hargreaves, 2015, p. 618). Exams and testing can also play a significant role in the labels children and young people use to describe themselves and others in terms of academic 'ability' and achievement (Lord and Jones, 2006).

Ability groups and sets

UK schools have often differentiated children and young people into 'ability' groups (within a class) and sets (whole classes of children considered to be of the same ability) for many years (Boaler *et al.*, 2000; Hargreaves, 2015) with the expectation that this will promote learning. Children and young people have very little choice over the ability group or set in which they find themselves; it is decided by the teacher, often based on how well a child or young person performs in tests and/or exams. However, when asked how they prefer to work, many children and young people express a preference for working in mixed-ability groups, particularly if they identify as being in a lower attaining group. This is partly because 'since there's different abilities,

Figure 7.3 Many children and young people prefer to work in mixed-ability groups.

you can help some people and some other people can help you in return' (this quote is from a young female attending secondary school in England) (*Tereshchenko et al.*, 2018, p. 11).

There is abundant evidence that shows how low-ability groups are more likely to be populated by children from working-class families, and high-ability groups are more likely to consist of children and young people from middle-class families (Boaler *et al.*, 2000; Reay, 2006). Reay (2006) gives an overview of research she conducted with colleagues between 1999 and 2002 in primary and secondary schools in England. She found that all the pupils in the bottom sets were working class and that most pupils in the top set were middle class. She argues that this results in the 'fixing of failure in the working classes' (p. 299). In interviews, young people in the bottom set described themselves as being 'rubbish', 'no good' or 'a nothing' (p. 300) and as having low aspirations: 'I might not have a good life in front of me' (p. 300). This was in comparison to how the children described a middle-class boy in the top set who will 'get a six' (i.e. a top grade) and who is 'heading for a good job' (p. 300). One boy said that his teacher thinks pupils in his bottom set are 'stupid'. Boaler *et al.* (2000) report similar findings in schools in London where young people in a bottom maths set described how they had experienced several changes of teacher because 'they don't think they have to bother with us … they think they can give us anybody', including a PE teacher (p. 637). Another young person in a bottom set described how their teacher 'treats us like we're babies, puts us down, makes us copy stuff off the board, puts up all the answers like we don't know anything' (p. 638).

The young people in Boaler *et al.*'s (2000) study who had been allocated to a maths set described at length how lessons were conducted as if all the young people in a set were identical; they were seen to be of the same ability and were expected to work at the same level and the same pace. This was problematic for some young people who described how 'the people who work fast have to wait for the people at the end to catch up' (p. 640), so they might find that they have nothing to do while they wait. On the other hand, 'people who are slow they don't never get the chance to finish' (p. 640). Boaler *et al.* (2000) argue that 'the placing of students into "ability" groups creates a set of expectations for teachers that overrides their awareness of individual capabilities' (p. 641). This homogenisation of children and young people – described above by a young person in another study in terms of being treated like 'herds of an identical animal' (Burke and Grosvenor, 2003, p. 94) – can have the effect of making individuals invisible, silencing their voices and preventing them from having a say in how their classes are populated and taught.

Feeling afraid in school

There are several potential sources of fear in the classroom, including bullying from other pupils. This section focuses specifically on children's and young people's fear of teachers and school systems. In a relatively recent study into this under-researched area, Hargreaves (2015) worked with 60 children in years 3 (7–8 years old) and 6 (10–11 years old) in a primary school in Surrey to ascertain their first-hand experiences. She found that, despite teachers going to great lengths to reduce fear, the children described times when they were afraid. The children described being afraid of various punishments such as getting a 'mean look' (p. 627) from the teacher or being moved away from sitting with their friends. Other children described how they were afraid of upsetting the teacher, or of answering a teacher's question and getting it wrong: 'Shall I answer? And if I get it wrong, what am I going to do?' (p. 627). Some of the children were so afraid to speak out in class for fear of other children branding them as 'geeky', weak, stupid or wrong that they avoided putting up their hand to respond to the teacher's questions (Hargreaves, 2015, p. 627).

Hargreaves (2015) reports also that some children talked about how some teachers imposed order by instilling fear in pupils. The children also described how they were scared by the teacher in the room next door shouting at another class so loudly that they could hear her through the wall. Boys in year 6 described the deputy head teacher as 'scary' and 'terrifying' (p. 627) while another pupil said that he is 'Like a tiger – you have to keep eye contact with it, otherwise it pounces on you' (p. 627). Children in year 3 said they are scared of the head teacher who 'really freaks me out ... when she shouts down the corridor' (p. 627). Hargreaves (2015) reports that nearly all the children interviewed advised that teachers should not shout because they find it scary. This wish was echoed in research reported by Burke and Grosvenor (2003) which asked children and young people about the type of school they would like. One young person wrote:

Figure 7.4 Some children report feeling afraid in the classroom.

> You know what it's like to be a child in secondary school so please next time you nag, shout or embarrass a child or pupil think back to your days at school and appreciate how we cope.

This comment by an anonymous young person refers implicitly to the relative power-lessness of the pupils in this class because all they can do is 'cope' with these types of teacher behaviours.

Low family income and participation in school

One of the main reasons children and young people often give for enjoying school is the opportunity to socialise with their friends. They describe friendships as being a source of fun and in terms of their value for social and emotional support. Being able to 'fit in' and 'join in' are important aspects of social life at school (Ridge, 2002). However, some children can find this aspect of school life challenging if they are part of a family in receipt of a low income (ibid.). State education in the UK is free but it can cost caregivers around £800 to £1000 a year to send a child to school (Meredith, 2017). The costs include those for school uniform, sportswear, school clubs, trips, lunches and snacks, a water bottle, equipment (including pens, books and technology) and transport. Some children describe how they feel excluded or marginalised from the school community and school activities because caregivers cannot afford the costs involved. Horgan (2007) found that primary schoolchildren from low-income families in Northern Ireland are acutely aware of their disadvantage from around 7 years of age when they start to notice that their circumstances are different to those of their peers.

In an interesting study which investigated the perspectives of young people from low-income families, 16 12- to 19-year-olds worked with The Children's Society and carried out 13 in-depth interviews about the effects of low income on school life (Holloway *et al.*, 2014). They report that 20 per cent of children in families who describe themselves as 'not well off at all' had been unable to attend a school trip alongside their friends due to the expense. One of the participants described their experience of having to miss a school trip as follows:

> There was a history trip to the Big Pit in Wales, I didn't go on that. It was too expensive to go, Mum couldn't afford it at the time, it was twenty-something pound.... It felt bad when everyone come back and said how much an amazing time they had.
>
> (Holloway *et al.*, 2014, p. 11)

Horgan (2007) reports that children from low-income families sometimes conceal the real reason that they cannot afford to go on school trips behind claims that they 'couldn't be bothered' (p. 44) to go. This can lead to missing out and 'the people left behind in school are the people that are looked down on (Andy, 16 years, two-parent family)' (Ridge, 2002).

In both of these examples, the children and young people describe how they found themselves excluded from joining in activities with their friends. In addition to this, some children and young people find that they cannot participate in studying particular subjects at school because of the need to buy specialised materials (Holloway *et al.*, 2014), and they may decide to stop asking their caregivers for money:

> When I first got into secondary school, it got progressively more tough because of the requirements. We needed to pay for things like my sketchbooks for Art and Tech.... The money was being stretched quite far, and, like, I started realising then that I couldn't keep asking for those things.
>
> (Holloway *et al.*, 2014, p. 42)

The research discussed here suggests that many children and young people from low-income families can be marginalised from school life, suggesting not only that their right to an education might be compromised but also that their voices are less likely to be heard because they cannot participate fully in life at school.

A way forward

In 1967, the *Observer* newspaper received almost 1000 entries to their competition which asked children and young people across the UK to describe the school they would like (Blishen, 1973). A similar competition was run by the *Guardian* newspaper 34 years later, in 2001, and received entries from over 1500 schools (Burke and Grosvenor, 2003). Reflecting upon the similarities between the children and young people's views across these two competitions and centuries, Burke and Grosvenor (2003) note that 'a passionate desire to be heard and a remarkable capacity of resistance to the total culture of school stands as a powerful link between the voices recorded' (p. 6). There were also many similarities in the changes that children and young people wanted to see in their schools, suggesting that some grievances are long-standing. The children and young people who took part in the 2001 competition suggested many changes to their schools, including the following (Burke and Grosvenor, 2003):

> We as people who have spent almost every year of our lives being told what to do by teachers, governors, etc. should have some say in how our school's run.
>
> (Angela, 15, Croydon,. p. 7)

> I would like more time to eat my dinner. I sometimes don't finish it and I seem to get thinner.
>
> (Rachel, 9, Swanwick, p. 37)

> The classrooms wouldn't be cramped and there would be fans in the corners of every room so that in summer we wouldn't be so hot! There would be comfortable chairs that don't stick to your backside when you stand up.
>
> (Hannah, 13, Ammanford, p. 113)

> I would like an interactive computer wall in the classroom so we could link up with other schools. We could even have lessons from teachers around the world.
>
> (Jeremy, 6, Orpington, p. 144)

> I would like a few teachers who listen and understand my point of view. I would also like teachers who are calm.
>
> (Emily, 11, Birmingham, p. 89)

> There would be soft bean bags to sit on and there would be lovely soft carpet on the floor.
>
> (Greta, 8, Leeds, p. 144)

In recent years, the UK government has strongly encouraged UK state schools to pay more attention to 'pupil voice' (DfE, 2014). One way in which schools have responded is by having a school council which includes pupil representatives (in Wales a school council is mandatory). School councils can be an effective way of listening to children and young people, although research suggests that children's and young people's involvement is often limited to their opinions on issues surrounding participation in school rather than issues about teaching and the curriculum (Hulme *et al.*, 2011). On some occasions the presence of children and young people can be tokenistic, which can result in pupils becoming disillusioned and disengaged (ibid.).

More recently, The United Nations Children's Fund (UNICEF) has developed a 'rights respecting schools' award which encourages schools to engage with the children's rights of the UNCRC (UNICEF). Schools are encouraged to make children's rights central to the school's ethos, their approaches to teaching, and the attitudes and behaviours of staff and pupils. Where schools adopt a children's rights approach, teachers and pupils are more likely to view their relationships as collaborative and supportive, and pupils are more likely to believe that the staff have a genuine concern for their well-being (Sebba and Robinson, 2010; UNICEF). Pupils also report that they feel more valued and listened to; in some schools they work with teachers on devising lesson plans and interviewing job applicants for teaching posts (Sebba and Robinson, 2010; UNICEF). To date, thousands of schools across the UK are working towards, or have achieved, a 'rights respecting schools' award from UNICEF.

Concluding thoughts

This chapter has discussed children's and young people's perspectives on their experiences of life in the classroom from a children's rights perspective. It is apparent that attempts have been made, over the past 20 years or so, to give children and young people opportunities to voice their perspectives and to be taken seriously. However, this can be difficult to achieve on the ground where adult voices can compete with those of children and young people. Latterly, initiatives such as school councils and rights respecting schools have gone some way to address this imbalance, although much remains to be done.

References

Austin, H., Dwyer, B. and Peabody, P. (2003) *Schooling the Child*. London and New York: Routledge Falmer.

Bevan, G. and Wilson, D. (2013) The success of 'naming and shaming': league tables have a positive impact on performance of schools and hospitals. Policy Report, University of Bristol [Online]. Available at www.bristol.ac.uk/media-library/sites/policybristol/briefings-and-reports-pdfs/pre-2017-briefings-reports-pdfs/PolicyBristol_Briefing%202_2013_Wilson_league_tables.pdf.

Blishen, E. (1973) *The School that I'd Like*. London: Penguin Books.

Boaler, J., Willian, D. and Brown, M. (2000) Students' experiences of ability groupings: disaffection, polarisation and the construction of failure. *British Educational Research Journal*, 26(5), 631–648.

Burke, C. and Grosvenor, I. (2003) *The School I'd Like*. London and New York: Routledge Falmer.

Chamberlain, T., Golden, S. and Bergeron, C. (2011) Children and young people's views of education policy. Office of the Children's Commissioner [Online]. Available at https://dera.ioe.ac.uk/2692/1/force_download.php%3ffp=%252Fclient_assets%252Fcp%252Fpublication%252F483%252FChildrens_and_young_peoples_views_of_education_policy.pdf.

Corsaro, W. (2011) *The Sociology of Childhood,* 3rd edn. London: Sage.

DfE (2014) Listening to and involving children and young people [Online]. Available at https://assets.publishing.service.gov.uk/government/uploads/system/uploads/attachment_data/file/437241/Listening_to_and_involving_children_and_young_people.pdf.

Fisher, H. (2011) Inside the primary classroom: examples of dissatisfaction behind a veil of compliance. *British Journal of Educational Studies*, 59(2), 121–141.

Hargreaves, E. (2015) 'I think it helps you better when you're not scared': fear and learning in the primary classroom. *Pedagogy, Culture and Society*, 23(4), 617–638.

Hargreaves, E. (2017) *Children's Experiences of Classrooms*. London: Sage.

Holloway, E., Mahony, S., Royston, S. and Mueller, D. (2014) *At What Cost? Exposing the Impact on Poverty on School Life*. UK: The Children's Society [Online]. Available at www.childrenssociety.org.uk/sites/default/files/At_What_Cost_Exposing_the_impact_of_poverty_on_school_life-Full_Report.pdf.

Horgan, G. (2007) *The Impact of Poverty on Young Children's Experience of School*. York: Joseph Rowntree Foundation [Online]. Available at www.jrf.org.uk/report/impact-poverty-young-childrens-experience-school.

House of Commons Library (2016) The school day and year (England). *Briefing Paper Number 07148* [Online]. http://researchbriefings.files.parliament.uk/documents/SN07148/SN07148.pdf (accessed 5 March 2019).

Hulme, M., McKinney, S. J., Hall, S. and Cross, B. (2011) Pupil participation in Scottish schools: how far have we come? *Improving Schools*, 14(2), 130–144. ISSN 1365-4802.

Ipsos MORI (2013) *Young People in Scotland Survey 2012: School Toilets* [Online]. Available at www.ipsos.com/sites/default/files/migrations/en-uk/files/Assets/Docs/Scotland/Scotland_School_toilets_report_190313.pdf.

Jackson, C. (2010) Fear in education. *Educational Review*, 62(1), 39–52.

Katz, I. and Assor, A. (2006) When choice motivates and when it does not. *Education Psychology Review*, 19(4), 429–442.

Lord, P. and Jones, M. (2006) *Pupils' Experiences and Perspectives of the National Curriculum and Assessment*. Slough: NFER [Online]. Available at www.nfer.ac.uk/publications/NCA01/NCA01.pdf.

Maitles, H. and Gilcrist, I. (2004) 'We're citizens now'! The development of positive values through a democratic approach to learning (PDF). Available at http://jceps.com/wp-content/uploads/PDFs/03-1-04.pdf (accessed 15 October 2019).

Mercer, N. and Littleton, K. (2007) *Dialogue and Development of Children's Thinking*. London and New York: Routledge.

Meredith, R. (2017) School costs parents £1,200 per child annually [Online]. Available at www.bbc.co.uk/news/uk-northern-ireland-41115589.

National Education Union (2017) *Child Poverty* [Online]. Available at https://neu.org.uk/policy/child-poverty.

Piaget, J. (1969) *The Psychology of the Child*. New York: Basic Books.

Reay, D. (2006) The zombie stalking English schools: social class and educational inequality. *British Journal of Educational Studies*, 54(3), 288–307. DOI: 10.1111/j.1467-8527.2006.00351.x.

Ridge, T. (2002) *Childhood Poverty and Social Exclusion: The Child's Perspective*. Bristol: Policy Press.

Saevi, T. (2015) Learning and pedagogic relations. In D. Scott and E. Hargreaves (eds) *The SAGE Handbook of Learning*. London: Sage, pp. 342–352.

Sebba, J. and Robinson, C. (2010) *Evaluating the UNICEF Rights Respecting Schools Award* [Online]. Available at www.unicef.org.uk/rights-respecting-schools/wp-content/uploads/sites/4/2014/12/RRSA_Evaluation_Report.pdf.

Sellgren, K. (2019) Teaching to the test gives 'hollow understanding' [Online]. Available at www.bbc.co.uk/news/education-41580550.

Sheehy, K. (2018) What matters in education? In V. L. Cooper, H. Montgomery and K. Sheehy (eds) *Parenting the First Twelve Years*. London:Pelican, pp. 159–185.

Sweatman, H. (2019) The grim reality of life as a pupil in a Scottish school [Online]. Available at www.scotsman.com/news/opinion/the-grim-reality-of-life-as-a-pupil-in-a-scottish-school-harriet-sweatman-1-4883211.

Tereshchenko, A., Francis, B., Archer, L., Hodgen, J., Mazenod, A., Taylor, B., Pepper, D. and Travers, M-C. (2018) Learners' attitudes to mixed attainment grouping: examining the views of students of high, middle and low attainment. *Research Papers in Education*, DOI: 10.1080/02671522.2018.1452962.

UNCRC (1989) [Online]. Available at www.cypcs.org.uk/rights/uncrc/full-uncrc.

UNICEF *Rights Respecting Schools Award* [Online]. Available at www.unicef.org.uk/rights-respecting-schools/.

UNICEF UK *Rights Respecting Schools Award: A Good Practice Review* [Online]. Available at www.unicef.org.uk/rights-respecting-schools/the-rrsa/impact-of-rrsa/rrsa-good-practice-review/.

Vygotsky, L. (1978) *Mind and Society*. Cambridge, MA: Harvard University Press.

8   Poverty, place and learning

Gavin Williams

Introduction

The effect of poverty and disadvantage on childhood development and future life chances is well documented (Bradshaw, 2002). It is reflected in governmental strategy and policy across the United Kingdom (UK) focusing on education providing a route out of poverty, through raising both aspiration and attainment (St Clair and Benjamin, 2011). Such a focus rests on the understanding that education, and specifically educational attainment, has consistently been shown to predict future economic and social success and is positively related to higher perceived quality of life and future life outcomes (Ross and Van Willigen, 1997). Much less researched, but equally important, is the role of place and space and the relationship between poverty, place and learning experiences. This chapter will focus specifically on a study I undertook in the south Wales valleys to explore the importance of place and belonging and how it shapes children's learning experiences in an underprivileged area. Using this particular case study, I argue that the effects of poverty and disadvantage are multidimensional and impact upon a variety of different indicators, including children's health, development and learning (Holmes and Kiernan, 2013). Furthermore, I argue that there is no clear, straightforward link between poverty, disadvantage and attainment (Raffo, 2009) as children's experiences are shaped by the environment in which they grow up.

Poverty, learning experiences and place

Poverty affects all areas of a child's life, including: physical health; the home environment; emotional and behavioural outcomes; and cognitive ability, with children living below the poverty threshold 1.3 times more likely to experience developmental delay and learning disabilities (Brooks-Gunn and Duncan, 1997). In a review of national longitudinal datasets to estimate the impact of family income on children's lives in the United States, Brooks-Gunn and Duncan (1997) also found that families who live in poverty are restricted in their choice of where to live and are more likely to live in areas

with higher levels of social problems (such as high levels of ill-health, high unemployment levels and crime) and fewer resources (such as play areas, health care facilities,
parks and after-school programmes) to support child development. These findings
have been corroborated more recently, and in other countries (e.g. Ridge, 2011).

Focusing on the lived experiences of low-income children in the UK, Ridge (2011)
found that poverty affects all areas of a child's life, including school, their social relationships, the home environment and access to leisure activities. It detrimentally
affects access to material goods that were identified as important for the children,
while the lack of income also restricted the children's access to social activities, which
was exacerbated by a lack of accessible and affordable out-of-school activities in their
areas (Ridge, 2011). The sense of social exclusion felt by children growing up in
poverty was revealed in an earlier study by Ridge, when one of the participants,
11-year-old Martin, compared his experiences to other children in his class:

> They go into town and go swimming and that, and they play football and they go
> to other places and I can't go ... because some of them cost money and that.
>
> (Ridge, 2002, p. 102)

To further explore the experiences of primary schoolchildren, Horgan (2009) conducted research in Northern Ireland. The experiences of children aged five to 11 were
explored through group interviews, comparing children living in the most disadvantaged and advantaged parts of Northern Ireland, with Free School Meals (FSM) used as
an indicator of poverty. Horgan used photographs of three separate houses for the
younger children, asking them what it would be like to live in a detached mansion, a
semi-detached bungalow and a terraced house on a social housing estate. The nine- to
11-year-old children were additionally given vignettes (short written scenarios) about
children living in the three houses and asked about their daily lives.

Findings indicated that children in the advantaged schools viewed school as a more
positive experience, while children from more disadvantaged backgrounds were more
likely to say that school was important for negative reasons (such as to avoid problems
when they grew up). Furthermore, awareness of social difference generally began in the
over-seven-year-olds with the idea emerging that the child living in the largest house would
be smart because they are rich and would therefore go to a 'good' school. This suggests
that children are aware from a young age of the restrictions placed on them in terms of
access to resources in comparison to others. Overall, Horgan concludes that poverty influences every aspect of a child's experience of school and this is prevalent from the earliest
years of primary education. In accordance with Horgan's findings, other studies have also
found that children and young people from disadvantaged backgrounds have access to
fewer resources and opportunities than their more affluent peers (e.g. Croll, 2008).

Research conducted by Wikeley *et al.* (2009) focused on access to and participation
in out-of-school learning activities with specific consideration of the reasons why – and
how – children and young people engage, comparing those from disadvantaged and
affluent backgrounds in England. Individual in-depth interviews with children in the
final year of primary school and the second year of secondary school were used to

compare the quality of educational relationships established through participation in out-of-school activities. It was found that those from disadvantaged families (again those identified as being in receipt of FSM) participated in fewer out-of-school activities than those from families not in receipt of FSM. This therefore affected their ability to establish and sustain effective educational relationships, which could have led to further learning and achievement, a finding supported by other analyses and research (e.g. Coldron *et al.*, 2009; Raffo, 2009).

Furthermore, a study by Jackson (2009) in the USA identified that the lower attainment of young people from poorer backgrounds is due to educational access and participation rather than to reduced expectations. This contrasts with the recent emphasis of policy in the UK, which presumes that the aspirations of children and young people and particularly those from disadvantaged backgrounds are too low, leading to low levels of educational achievement (St Clair and Benjamin, 2011). Ivinson *et al.* (2018) identify this as a typical policy discourse of a 'culture of poverty' present in both the USA and the UK. As Gorski (2012) explains, this discourse begins from a perspective of cultural deficit which suggests that children from deprived areas lack the required positive dispositions towards, and the resources and support required to perform well in, education. St Clair and Benjamin (2011) set out to investigate the aspirations of 12- and 13-year-olds in deprived areas across three cities in the UK through a large-scale empirical investigation. Findings indicated that aspirations of the young people were high, and not low as is often suggested in policy. In fact, the aspirations expressed by the young people were higher than the labour market could fulfil. The authors contend that aspirations are dynamic and arise from – and are embedded within – the social contexts in which they occur, signifying the importance of place in shaping experiences.

In a comparative study of post-16 education choices and transitions in Wales, Evans (2013) recognised the importance and influence of place on educational choices and aspirations. Comparing the experiences of 16- to 18-year-olds living in the Rhondda Valleys and Newport in south Wales, two areas with high levels of deprivation, the study revealed the significance of place in shaping experiences, opportunities and aspirations to progress on to Higher Education (HE). Evans (2013) found that several key factors influenced the decisions made by the young people. These included the more immediate concerns of the availability of educational and employment opportunities in each area for young people, but also the importance of the social and cultural history of each place in informing the aspirations and educational choices of the young people (Evans, 2013).

Research indicates that poverty and disadvantage affect far more than attainment, and shape children's experiences both within and outside of school. However – and as evidenced by Evans (2013) – specific experiences differ and are influenced by the place in which a child grows up (Dickerson and Popli, 2018). Place, according to Massey (1995), is made up of both space and time – a particular place is constructed through a build-up of social relationships over time, both within the locality and linking it to the outside world. Halfacree (2006) supported this and argued that localities are more than simply physical places; they are enduring spaces inscribed by social processes. For instance, in Evans' (2013) study, the aspirations of the young people from the Rhondda Valleys were shaped by a sense of belonging and attachment to the area due to the close proximity of friends and family, but also the lack of current labour market opportunities available to them. Exploring the importance of place in shaping experiences is therefore important.

The importance of place: exploring children's learning experiences in an underprivileged area

Here I discuss my own research on the learning experiences (both in and out of school) of children living in a deprived area in the south Wales valleys (Williams, 2019). The overarching aim of the study was to explore how the children's experiences of place affected their learning experiences and future life chances. In the first section, I provide some contextual information about the study and the area in which it took place. I then briefly discuss Pierre Bourdieu's theory of practice (1984) – one of the most extensively used theories in explaining social inequalities – which helps interpret the findings from my study, and will be further discussed in Chapter 9 in the context of inequalities in access to further and higher education. Finally, I discuss the key findings that identify the importance of place and belonging in shaping children's learning experiences.

The case

The focus of the research was a case study of the views of 19 children (ten girls and nine boys) aged 11 in their final year of primary education from three schools in the

Figure 8.1 View of the Rhondda Valley and the terraced housing.

upper Rhondda Valley, south Wales. Focus groups, individual interviews, observation and photo elicitation, where children took photographs of the things they believed affected their learning, were used to explore the children's views. The proportion of children eligible for FSM in each of the three schools ranged from 22 to 47 per cent, and ten of the children who participated in the study were eligible for FSM. Predominantly, the children came from working-class homes and only three had parents with experience of higher education.

The upper Rhondda Valley comprises ten villages and is characterised by rows of terraced housing as shown in Figure 8.1. One 'A road' links it to the lower Rhondda as well as mountain passes that link the area to other valleys.

The case: social and industrial heritage

The industrial and social history of the Rhondda Valley is important, as it shapes the area the children grow up in today. The Rhondda has a rich industrial heritage and transformed from a rural landscape with a population of 951 in 1851 to a peak of 167,000 in 1924 (Davies, 1993). A newfound ability in the mid-1800s to mine the rich seams of coal deep beneath the surface initiated a rapid expansion in the coal-mining industry (as depicted in Figure 8.2) of the Rhondda Valley that resulted in a population boom, as men seeking employment in the collieries migrated with their families to the Rhondda (Davies, 1993).

Figure 8.2 The industrial heritage of the valley.

Lewis (1975) notes how the large influx of people into the Rhondda Valley looking for work in the mines in the nineteenth century resulted in overcrowding in the area, and this in turn helped forge strong community bonds – a typical feature associated with industrial working-class communities – along with a significant role of religious nonconformity (i.e. the chapel) and sport (e.g. rugby) (Davies, 1993). The shared experiences of work in the mines, the relative isolation of the valleys and its geographic boundedness acted as a focal point around which other common interests developed, thus creating a strong community identity (Gilbert, 1992).

Baggs (1995) discusses the significant role of the chapels and Miners' Institutes for the population of the south Wales coalfield during the mid to late nineteenth and early twentieth century. The chapels and institutes, along with their reading rooms and libraries, placed an emphasis on self-development and provided educational opportunities for the population (Ross, 2005). The nonconformist Sunday Schools were especially important for the children of the coalfield, as they provided educational opportunities alongside games, religious study and occasional outings (Ross, 2005).

However, life in the south Wales coalfield was difficult. The geology of the area presented some significant challenges for coal-mining, and accidents and deaths were more prevalent in the south Wales coalfield than in other mining areas in Britain (Davies, 1993). This, alongside the Great Depression and a reduction in demand for steam coal from the Rhondda had a considerable impact on the coalfield during the second half of the twentieth century. The last mine in the Rhondda closed in 1990. The obliteration of the main industry and the role of mining as a primary focal point for community cohesion was therefore lost (Parry, 2003) and the effects of this are still evident today. Results from the most recent census show that the Rhondda is one of the most deprived areas in England and Wales. For example, 45.4 per cent of households in the constituency do not have an adult in employment

Figure 8.3 A former town hall in one of the villages in the Rhondda Valley.

Figure 8.4 A recently closed bank in the area.

– ranked third highest in England and Wales – while 37.8 per cent of those aged 16 or over have no qualifications – ranked fourth (Parliament. House of Commons, 2011).

What shapes our experiences: a focus on Bourdieu's Theory of Practice (1984)

As the previous section discussed, the industrial and social history of the Rhondda Valley as well as the current context shapes the children's experiences growing up in the area. It is important to recognise that experiences do not occur in a vacuum and are shaped by interactions at home, with the family and with wider society, which in turn influence our own dispositions and behaviours. Sociological and educational research, particularly that focusing on inequality, has extensively utilised the theories of Pierre Bourdieu (Reay, 2005), and in particular his theory of practice, shown in the following formula explained below:

$$[(habitus) + (capital)] + field = practice$$

(Bourdieu, 1984, p. 101)

Bourdieu's theory acknowledges that childhood is subject to external influences such as the school environment, family and place. It is a particularly relevant theory there-fore to explain the findings from my study (Williams, 2019), as it identifies the import-ance of external influences in shaping experience. Place has a significant impact on individuals, not only in terms of physical geography but also in shaping the social spaces in which they live. The social spaces – or *fields* – that individuals occupy are structured spaces that produce knowledge and are subject to particular rules and boundaries (Bourdieu, 1976), which can only be understood through investigation of their historical and current local and national context.

Habitus is defined as a 'system of acquired dispositions functioning on the practical level as categories of perception and assessment or as classificatory principles as well as being the organising principles of action' (Bourdieu, 1990, p. 13). It can be thought of as a person's everyday, taken-for-granted, mostly unconscious way of existing in the world. These dispositions – including, for example, attitudes, tastes, skills and habits – are rooted in an individual's lived history and so are based on the family environment and community in which each individual grew – or is growing – up, including experi-ences of education (Bourdieu, 1977).

Bourdieu (1986) identified several different forms of *capital*, including economic, cultural and social. Capital refers to resources which are valuable but unequally dis-tributed among people. Economic capital can be measured by an individual's wealth, property or income, and is directly convertible into money. Cultural capital underpins one's position in the fields we occupy and can be measured by our access to material goods and resources (such as books and engagement in cultural activities), educa-tional qualifications and individual tastes, and it is physically displayed in our accent and dialect. He notes how the acquisition of cultural capital takes time and that it can explain the unequal attainment levels among children and young people from different social classes, identifying that children from middle- and upper-class families acquire cultural capital from their parents (Bourdieu, 1977). Social capital is seen as the range of supportive resources available to individuals from within their family and community and the other networks/groups of which they may be members. Strengthening access to social capital through family and community links has been shown to be beneficial for children's and young people's educational achievement (Israel *et al.*, 2001), and doing this may serve to mitigate the effects of poverty and disadvantage. Bourdieu's theory is revisited in Chapter 9, in the context of access to further and higher education.

The importance of place and belonging in shaping children's learning experiences

This section outlines some of the key findings of the study (Williams, 2019) and explores the role of parents and family in the development of children's cultural capital. Overall, the children described a sense of belonging within the area and this can be attributed to the family unit. The support the children received from the family could be described as a 'bridging effect' that operated on three levels. This included support for formal learning, support to access opportunities within and outside the confines of the valley itself, and finally, links to the past, where family members provided activities to enhance the children's understanding of the area's history and culture.

Supporting formal learning

Each of the children who participated in the study discussed the support available from family members for schoolwork. This support was predominantly provided by those living with the children, most commonly parents and siblings. Being able to ask for help from parents and/or siblings was a common theme identified by all the children. When asked to take photographs of the things that affect their learning, all the children took photographs of their home and family members. Upon further discussion, the importance of the home and family for learning was made clear. Every child identified the positive influence of the support offered, while 14 of the children directly described how this support specifically helped them to learn. This support was reflected in the children's predominantly positive experiences of school and their high aspirations for the future.

The findings signify the importance of the family for the development of cultural capital and how this was used by the children and shaped their orientations, or habitus, towards school. This extends the findings of Brooker (2015), who recognised the importance of the family for the development of cultural capital for children in the preschool years, and shows how this continues to be of importance throughout children's primary school lives. The findings also support the notion of the children possessing an educational habitus, which has been influenced by the parents and family (Burke, 2016). The findings also extend those from previous research with younger children in the UK which has shown that regardless of socioeconomic status, parents engage in learning activities with their children and support learning at home (Hartas, 2011).

In addition to support from the immediate family, the wider family network was involved in assisting the children's learning. This was often linked to personal interests or personal histories, but intergenerational learning was a strong feature identified by the children. For example, Gwen commented, 'I like Geography too because we had some homework and I did it with my grandfather. We researched lots of places and that was really good.' As well as undertaking activities with grandparents, learning about their lives was also important for the children, as Chris described in his individual interview:

> Because my grandparents were in World War 2, I like to learn lots about it. I read about it in the house because my mother has bought me loads of books.

The support provided by family members demonstrates the value placed on formal education and could suggest an enduring influence of nonconformity and the Miners' Institute libraries on the people of the area, which has engendered an educational habitus where education and learning has significant value. This is evident in the children's predominantly positive views of formal education and in the support provided by family members. The findings also support those conducted in other areas of Wales where religious nonconformity was identified as a significant factor in educational success (e.g. Baker and Brown, 2008).

Access to informal learning: opportunities within and beyond the valley

Access to informal learning opportunities outside of the school environment has been shown to positively affect children, as it can enhance the accumulation of cultural capital (Kisida *et al.*, 2014). This section will focus on support provided by the family for children to access informal learning opportunities.

Parents encouraged engagement in learning activities both in the home, as Darcey identified: 'I like English though because I like reading and my parents say it is important to read. They read to me and my sister at home', and in the wider community. This parental engagement in supporting learning activities at home has been shown to positively influence development and achievement in school. In a meta-analysis of studies published between 2000 and 2013, Castro *et al.* (2015) found that children who received support from their parents to develop positive reading habits at home had higher academic attainment. The support provided by Darcey's parents here, and echoed by the other children, reinforces the emphasis placed on learning and education by those living in the upper Rhondda. It also further supports the notion of individuals in the area possessing an educational habitus that is imbued upon the children, corroborating Burke's (2016) assertion that the family unit is one of the most influential forces in the formation of a child's habitus.

In addition to support for activities in the home, 12 of the children discussed parental influence in their initial engagement in activities, while a further six spoke of the influence of grandparents. For example, Manon acknowledged her grandfather's role in her choosing to attend drama classes: 'It was because of my grandfather that I got involved in it. He asked me if I would like to go and I went along.' Introducing children to activities in the community and increasing their social networks could serve to increase their social capital, as demonstrated in Manon's account, and, as Israel *et al.* (2001) have shown, this can positively affect educational progress.

In addition to introducing the children to activities, parental and family support – most commonly in providing transport – was required for the children to access opportunities within and beyond the valley boundaries. The need to access activities beyond the immediacy of the upper Rhondda had been exacerbated by the closure of community facilities, increasing reliance on family support, as Lisa discussed:

> I learned to swim in the pool that was knocked down and now I have to travel further if I want to go to swim. That's really disappointing because I have to go in a car now with my mother or father where I could walk.

This reliance on parents and family for transport to activities could be seen as a form of objectified cultural capital (Bourdieu, 1986), as the parents are investing in their children's development by providing access to activities outside of the area. The finding that parents provided resources and supported access to these activities was not consistent with previous research which has shown that parental support is often low for those from disadvantaged backgrounds (Wikeley *et al.*, 2009). In contrast, the parents in the study supported access to a wide range of activities that served to broaden the horizons of their children. Support from parents and family was apparent for all the children in the study, and no distinct difference was evident when comparing individual experiences between those children eligible for FSM and those who were not.

When discussing access to opportunities outside of the valley the children focused on a wide range of activities, from those relating to their hobbies, to family holidays and cultural activities. Such activities enabled the children to access opportunities not available within the valley itself and to broaden their range of experiences, thus potentially serving to further increase their access to forms of social and cultural capital. One of the most commonly cited activities the children engaged in with family members outside the confines of the valley was museum visits and the theme of learning new things from the trips was evident. Chris commented that parents 'take you on trips to places like museums and shows so you can learn about different things' and Victoria also spoke about learning when discussing her visits to the museum. This finding is important, as research has shown that children's exposure to cultural institutions such as museums can motivate them to acquire new cultural capital (Kisida *et al.*, 2014), while it also shows the value placed on such trips by the children. It also enabled the children to access a wider range of enrichening experiences that are not available in the valley where they live.

Links to the past: a collective history

The importance of the children learning about the history of the area was apparent in the support provided by family members. The natural environment and freedom this provided for the children afforded them the opportunity to spend time with family and to learn about the area and its industrial heritage. Jess demonstrated this in a photograph taken while out walking with her father and explained more in the photo-elicitation interview:

> If you can see over there [points to photograph] ... well my granddad used to work there. There used to be a coal-mine there but it's closed now ... I often go walking there with my family.

Jess explained that she learned about her grandfather's role as a coal-miner, and parents or grandparents sharing information about the area and its coal-mining past was spoken about by a majority of the children. Zac, for example, spoke of learning about the history of the area with his family and how it had prompted him to undertake further research in the local library.

Figure 8.5 A former coal-mine in the upper Rhondda.

This focus on the history of the area identified its importance for the people living there and how the families wanted the children to be aware of their history and culture. This reflects the influential role of the family in shaping habitus (Burke, 2016) and provides another example of the emphasis placed on learning and education in the valley.

It also created a sense of belonging for the children. This, alongside the close physical proximity of the predominantly terraced houses, played an important role in the social landscape of the valley, as Tom described:

> You get to know a lot of people here because they are really friendly. A lot of people stand out on their doorsteps and say hello. Because they live in terraced housing the houses are linked so people are quite close to one another so they get to know each other.

The focus was not solely on mining in the area, however, and the schools also forged community links through their activities. Creating these social networks and links with the community can aid the development of social capital and attachment to a place (Knight, 2015), and serve to further embed the young people in their communities. The importance of creating such links and learning about the history of the area was a strong feature of the discussions with the head teachers of each school. The head teacher of Riverside, Mrs Rowlands, also spoke about the importance of learning about the history of the area and how the children should be proud of where they come from:

> There's also the history in terms of coal production and the impact that had around the world. So it's children being proud of living and coming from the upper Rhondda. It's not about getting the children out of the valley, it's about the children being proud of coming from the Rhondda Valley.

This notion of 'getting out 'to 'get on' – the idea that in order to succeed, children must leave their places of origin for more affluent towns or cities – is a common feature of research with people from working-class backgrounds living in deprived areas (e.g. Redmond, 2009). However, Mrs Rowlands' account presents a different narrative. She suggests that it is important to ensure people are proud of where they come from rather than them thinking they have to move out to get on. This was also demonstrated in the children's accounts. While they all had high aspirations (14 of the 19 aimed to go to university) and recognised the need to move beyond the confines of the valley to achieve their aspirations, it created a dilemma for them; they wanted to be able to continue to live in the area. This emphasises the importance of belonging and place in shaping not only their experiences but also aspirations for the future.

Concluding thoughts

As this chapter has discussed, it is undeniable that poverty influences lived experiences, attainment and future life chances. However, the findings from my study reveal the limitations in using poverty as a sole explanatory factor of children's educational and learning experiences and perceived future life chances. They signify the importance of place as a lens to focus on lived experiences, including the role of heritage, geographical landscape, local opportunities and familial support in fostering a sense of belonging.

Furthermore, the findings offer an alternative narrative to that of the typical policy discourse of a 'culture of poverty' (Ivinson *et al.*, 2018). As Ivinson *et al.* (2018, p. 141) identify, the key challenge for researchers is to help policy-makers understand lived experiences so it can 'get us out of the narrow deficit discourses that blame families and teachers for low educational achievement'. This focus on the lived experience of children and young people is paramount, as it can help policy-makers understand the importance of place in shaping experiences which in turn can aid the development of localised targeted approaches to tackle the specific issues caused by poverty and disadvantage.

References

Baggs, C. M. (1995) *The Miners' Libraries of South Wales from the 1860s to 1939*. PhD Thesis, Aberystwyth, University of Wales.

Baker, S. and Brown, B. (2008) Habitus and homeland: educational aspirations, family life and culture in autobiographical narratives of educational experience in rural Wales. *Sociologica Ruralis*, 28(1), 57–72.

Bourdieu, P. (1976) Marriage strategies as strategies of social reproduction. In R. Forster and P. Ranum, P. (eds) *Family and Society, Selections from the Annales*. Baltimore, MD: Johns Hopkins University Press, pp. 117–144.

Bourdieu, P. (1977) *Outline of a Theory of Practice*. Cambridge: Cambridge University Press.

Bourdieu, P. (1984) *Distinction. A Social Critique of the Judgement of Taste*. London: Routledge and Kegan Paul.

Bourdieu, P. (1986) The forms of capital. In J. Richardson (ed.) *Handbook of Theory and Research for the Sociology of Education*. New York: Greenwood Press, pp. 241–258.

Bourdieu, P. (1990) *The Logic of Practice*. Cambridge: Polity Press.

Bradshaw, J. (2002) Child poverty and child outcomes. *Children and Society*, 16(2), 131–140.

Brooker, L. (2015) Cultural capital in the preschool years: can the state 'compensate' for the family? In L. Alanen, L. Brooker and B. Mayall(eds) *Childhood with Bourdieu*. London: Palgrave Macmillan, pp. 34–57.

Brooks-Gunn, J. and Duncan, G. J. (1997) The effects of poverty on children. *The Future of Children*, 7(2), 55–71.

Burke, C. (2016) Bourdieu's theory of practice: maintaining the role of capital. In J. Thatcher, N. Ingram, C. Burke and J. Abrahams (eds) *Bourdieu: The Next Generation. The Development of Bourdieu's Intellectual Heritage in Contemporary UK Sociology*. Abingdon: Routledge, pp. 8–25.

Castro, M., Exposito-Casas, E., Lopez-Martin, E., Lizasoain, L. and Navarro-Asencio, Gaviria, J. L. (2015) Parental involvement on student academic achievement: a meta-analysis. *Educational Research Review*, 14, 33–46.

Coldron, J., Willis, B. and Wolstenholme, C. (2009) Selection by attainment and aptitude in English secondary schools. *British Journal of Educational Studies*, 57(3), 254–264.

Croll, P. (2008) Occupational choice, socio-economic status and educational attainment: a study of the occupational choices and destinations of young people in the British Household Panel Survey. *Research Papers in Education*, 23(3), 243–268.

Davies, J. (1993) *A History of Wales*. London: Penguin.

Dickerson, A. and Popli, G. (2018) The many dimensions of child poverty: evidence from the UK Millennium Cohort Study. *Fiscal Studies*, 39(2), 265–298.

Evans, C. (2013) *Young People in Transition in Local Contexts: An Exploration of how Place and Time Frame Young People's Educational Aspirations, Decisions and Anticipated Transitions*. PhD Thesis, Cardiff University.

Gilbert, D. (1992) *Class, Community and Collective Action. Social Changes in Two British Coalfields, 1850–1926*. Oxford: Clarendon Press.

Gorski, P. C. (2012) Perceiving the problem of poverty and schooling: deconstructing the class stereotypes that mis-shape education practice and policy. *Equity & Excellence in Education*, 45, 302–319.

Halfacree, K. H. (2006) Rural space: constructing a three-fold architecture. In P. Cloke, T. Marsden and P. Mooney (eds) *Handbook of Rural Studies*. London: Sage, pp. 44–62.

Hartas, D. (2011) Families' social backgrounds matter: socio-economic factors, home learning and young children's language, literacy and social outcomes. *British Educational Research Journal*, 37(6), 893–914.

Holmes, J. and Kiernan, K. (2013) Persistent poverty and children's development in the early years of childhood. *Policy and Politics*, 41(1), 19–42.

Horgan, G. (2009) 'That child is smart because he's rich': the impact of poverty on young children's experiences of school. *International Journal of Inclusive Education*, 13(4), 359–376.

Israel, G. D., Beaulieu, L. J. and Hartless, G. (2001) The influence of family and community social capital on educational achievement. *Rural Sociology*, 66(1), 43–68.

Ivinson, G., Thompson, I., Beckett, L., Egan, D., Leitch, R. and McKinney, S. (2018) Learning the price of poverty across the UK. *Policy Futures in Education*, 16(2), 130–143.

Jackson, M. I. (2009) Understanding links between adolescent health and educational attainment. *Demography*, 46(4), 671–694.

Kisida, B., Greene, J. P. and Bowen, D. H. (2014) Creating cultural consumers. *Sociology of Education*, 87(4), 281–295.

Knight, A. (2015) 'A fish in water?' Social lives and local connections: the case of young people who travel outside their local areas to secondary school. In L. Alanen, L. Brooker and B. Mayall (eds) *Childhood with Bourdieu*. London: Palgrave Macmillan, pp. 99–120.

Lewis, E. D. (1975) Population changes and social life. 1860–1914. In K. S. Hopkins (ed.) *Rhondda Past and Future*. Rhondda Borough Council, pp. 110–128.

Massey, D. (1995) Places and their pasts. *History Workshop Journal*, 39, 182–192.

Parliament. House of Commons (2011) *Census Data for Parliamentary Constituencies in England and Wales, Rhondda.*

Parry, J. (2003) The changing meaning of work: restructuring in the former coalmining communities of the South Wales Valleys. *Work, Employment and Society*, 17(2), 227–246.

Raffo, C. (2009) Interrogating poverty, social exclusion and New Labour's programme of priority educational policies in England. *Critical Studies in Education*, 50(1), 65–78.

Reay, D. (2005) Mothers' involvement in their children's schooling: social reproduction in action? In G. Crozier and D. Reay (eds) *Activating Participation: Parents and Teachers Working Towards Partnership*. Stoke on Trent: Trentham Books, pp. 23–39.

Redmond, G. (2009) Children as actors: how does the child perspectives literature treat agency in the context of poverty? *Social Policy & Society*, 8(4), 541–550.

Ridge, T. (2002) *Childhood Poverty and Social Exclusion: From a Child's Perspective*. Bristol: Policy Press.

Ridge, T. (2011) The everyday costs of poverty in childhood: a review of qualitative research exploring the lives and experiences of low-income children in the UK. *Children and Society*, 25(1), 73–84.

Ross, C. and Van Willigen, M. (1997) Education and the subjective quality of life. *Journal of Health and Social Behavior*, 38(3), 275–297.

Ross, D. (2005) *Wales: History of a Nation*. Edinburgh: Geddes and Grosset.

St Clair, R. and Benjamin, A. (2011) Performing desires: the dilemma of aspirations and educational attainment. *British Educational Research Journal*, 37(3), 501–517.

Wikeley, F., Bullock, K., Muschamp, Y. and Ridge, T. (2009) Educational relationships and their impact on poverty. *International Journal of Inclusive Education*, 13(4), 377–393.

Williams, G. (2019) *Boundedness, Belonging and Becoming: Primary School Children's Perspectives of Education and Learning in the South Wales Valleys*. EdD Thesis, The Open University.

9 Inequalities in access to further and higher education

Fiona Reeve

Introduction

This chapter will explore how young people make transitions from compulsory schooling into work, or increasingly, into education and training. The focus will be on young people in industrialised societies in the Global North, where opportunities for further study are growing and becoming more diverse. For many young people further study is both an aspirational and achievable choice. At the same time post-school qualifications are now often viewed as necessary for 'a good job' and seen as a key means of developing career aspirations. The reverse assumption suggests that not participating in further study may reduce a young person's chances of accessing secure employment, leading to more precarious work. Viewed in this way the post-school options available to young people in these societies can be both appealing and a source of anxiety. In this context, what are the study choices available to young people? How do young people weigh up their choices, and what influences them? Why do some young people transition seamlessly into higher education while others do not consider this as a possible future?

These are largely sociological questions, and this is the perspective within childhood and youth studies which will be explored in this chapter. Although transitions from school are often framed in terms of individual choice and aspiration, evidence of inequalities in post-school outcomes suggests that society continues to shape the prospects for young people. This chapter will explore the outcomes for young people and how these relate to their economic position, ethnicity and gender.

Moving on or staying on?

The age at which young people are able to leave compulsory education has been shifting over the past century. Within the UK it has risen incrementally from 14 at the start of the twentieth century until by 1973 it stood at 16 in all of the four nations. In England it has risen further, now defined as the 'participation age', reaching 18 in

2015. Under the 2008 Education and Skills Act young people in England must either participate in full-time education, undertake an apprenticeship or preparatory traineeship, or participate in part-time education or training while working for no more than 20 hours per week. The English policy was positioned as a response to a decline in unskilled jobs that early school leavers could take up, and a concern about rising numbers of unemployed young people. With or without a formal requirement, participation rates beyond 16 years have risen in all of the four UK nations. For example, in Scotland 89 per cent of young people stay on at school after the year in which they turn 16 (Scottish Government, 2019). Of those who do leave at 16 the majority go into further education or training. In Wales figures from 2017 indicate that 88 per cent stayed in full-time education and training after 16 (Careers Wales, 2018). Here the UK reflects trends elsewhere with most European states setting a school-leaving age of 16 or 18. The trend to leave school at a later age begins to unsettle understandings of childhood and youth, and when adulthood begins, leading to perhaps disconcerting anomalies. For example, in Scotland you can get married or enter a civil partnership at 16 without your parents' consent, and 16-year-olds are allowed to vote in the Scottish Parliament and local elections. Yet, at the same age, young people are more likely to be in school – a context more associated with dependence and formation (as will be explored further in Chapter 6) than with independence.

The notion of extending the transition to adulthood can be pushed further by examining the options young people take up upon finally leaving school. Whereas in the 1970s within industrialised societies the majority of school leavers would have gone straight into work, the majority now transition to a higher level of education or training. Within the UK the proportion who go directly into work after school is now less than a

Figure 9.1 The age at which young people leave formal education has increased.

quarter of the cohort in each of the nations (Careers Wales, 2018; DfE, 2018; Scottish Government, 2019; Department of Education, 2018). Instead, young people are opting for higher education, further education, or to a lesser extent apprenticeships and other forms of employment-based training. Why has there been such a shift in the routes young people take? Arguably this can be linked to both changes in the nature of work and in how these changes are interpreted by policy-makers.

A knowledge economy?

In the late 1990s and the first decade of the twenty-first century, key global bodies argued that modern economies were undergoing a transformation. The Organisation for Economic Co-operation and Development, for example, claimed that 'knowledge is now recognised as the driver of productivity and economic growth' (OECD, 1996, p. 3). They argued that there was evidence of a shift from industrial to post-industrial 'knowledge-based economies' where 'productivity and growth are largely determined by the rate of technical progress and the accumulation of knowledge' (p. 18). They argued that this shift would reduce demand for unskilled workers while increasing the need for those with knowledge and skills, particularly where these related to new technologies. The implications taken from this by national policy-makers were that increasing the proportion of workers with higher level skills and knowledge should be a priority, both in terms of new entrants to the labour force and existing employees. For school leavers this meant new opportunities for vocational training, and a considerable expansion in places within higher education.

Within the UK, concerns that skills levels were falling behind those in other countries were expressed in a number of reviews, including the Leitch Review of Skills 2006 (Leitch, 2006) and in the Sainsbury report on technical education in England (Department for Business, Innovation and Skills, 2016). These led to some reorganisation of the vocational options available within further education colleges and other providers. In Scotland, the system of Higher National Certificates and Higher National Diplomas offered by colleges were maintained but adjusted. In England, a series of competing changes resulted, with the latest move being to simplify the system into a new set of technology-focused qualifications within a limited number of vocational pathways. It is proposed that these pathways will extend to higher levels (equivalent to one or two years of full-time post-school study). There have also been significant moves to reignite the apprenticeship system by encouraging employers to expand the number of places, and by creating a new option of higher level apprenticeships. In these reviews the intention has been to reform vocational education in order to address what is perceived to be a key problem within the UK system – lack of parity of esteem between vocational and academic pathways. The concern is that well-qualified young people are not choosing vocational options because of the perceived lower status of these routes, and that they are missing out on fulfilling employment (with a loss to the state of their expertise).

Those concerned with the options available for young people often look to European comparisons where vocational routes have higher status and are well resourced. In particular, comparisons are made with the German system where numbers following an academic pathway have traditionally been smaller than those following a vocational option, though the balance has recently shifted towards higher academic entrants (Deissinger, 2019). For those not pursuing university the most popular route is a form of apprenticeship within the 'dual system' which combines workplace learning and college. The dual system is built on a tradition of 'public responsibility' which incorporates the trade unions and employer organisations, drawing upon its history in the ancient guild system (ibid.). This is perhaps a reflection of a more cooperative culture. The stability of the system, its inclusion of a range of social partners and the strong commitment by employers (leading to subsequent employment) make it a relatively attractive route for young people, and one respected by parents and advisers. Some recent concerns have emerged including lack of flexibility in the system and early choice of pathway, resulting in the creation of opportunities to switch pathways, including to higher education (ibid.). Nevertheless, the status of the dual system remains high, and it is often identified in research as a model of effective vocational training.

Despite aiming for parity of esteem between different study routes in UK policy, this has proved hard to achieve in practice: again a reflection of national cultures and the role of social class in UK society. As the then prime minster Theresa May noted in 2018, 'there remains a perception that going to university is really the only desirable route, while going into training is something for other people's children' (May, 2018). As we will see, at the same time that changes have been made to vocational options,

Figure 9.2 Vocational education prepares young people to work in a particular occupation.

the higher education sector has expanded; this increase has been driven by demand from young people, facilitated by removing limits on the numbers universities could recruit, linked to changing funding arrangements (excepting Scotland). Despite the espoused wish of policy-makers, young people, parents and teachers often continue to see greater value in gaining a university degree. Even where learners start on a vocational path, if the opportunity to progress to a degree is available, they do so in large numbers such is the lure of the degree (Reeve and Gallacher, 2019). Work by the Sutton Trust in England (a charity in the United Kingdom focused on addressing educational disadvantage) suggested that 65 per cent of teachers polled would rarely or never advise a student to take an apprenticeship if they had the grades for university (2014).

How are inequalities reflected in post-school outcomes and entry to higher education?

In this context where parity of esteem between different educational pathways is not yet achieved, it is important to ask which students access different options. Data on the destinations of school leavers in England who leave at age 18, from state-funded institutions, indicates that 51 per cent of students enter higher education – outstripping work (22%), further education (7%), sustained apprenticeship (7%), other education (3%) and unknown or not sustained outcomes (10%) (DfE, 2018). Students whose low family income led to free school meals were highlighted in the data as a means of identifying the impact of economic disadvantage. These students were less likely to enter higher education (46%) and more likely to enter further education (10%) than the average student. Some variation according to ethnicity can also be observed, with white students slightly more likely to go into sustained employment (25%) or an apprenticeship (8%) and less likely to enter higher education (47%) than students of other ethnicities. Here there may be a link to regional differences with the more diverse urban areas such as London having higher university participation (59%). Gender differences can be noted in the data, with more female (53%) than male (48%) students entering higher education, whereas more males were in sustained apprenticeships (8%) than females (5%) (DfE, 2018), reflecting gender imbalances in work where apprenticeships are currently available. Similar patterns can be found in other nations in the UK, with higher education being the most significant destination in Wales (Careers Wales, 2018), Northern Ireland (Department of Education, 2018) and Scotland (Scottish Government, 2018), while in Scotland there are significant numbers of higher education learners within further education colleges.

The proportion of young people now entering higher education in the UK reflects experience in other high-income countries in the Global North, and this trend is spreading within middle- and even some low-income countries in the Global South (Marginson, 2016). In predicting this move to 'mass higher education', sociologist Martin Trow identified the key driver as the aspirations of families and young people to improve their social position (Trow, 1973). He argued that as access to higher education increases, those with more privileged positions see participation as necessary to maintaining their advantage. Furthermore, within an expanded mass system, elite institutions would continue to flourish, providing a route through which advantage could be maintained by the privileged. The UK system of 136 universities has indeed become stratified, with distinctions between the new universities (established after 1992) and the old universities (pre-1992) which are often described as more prestigious. Within the latter the Russell Group of 24 universities position themselves as leading research-intensive universities, and they tend to dominate the league tables of universities which are produced annually in the UK by newspapers and specialist guides. Thus our question becomes: What parts of a stratified higher education system do different young people access?

Vicky Boliver has researched the extent to which access to the Russell Group of universities is 'fair', by which she means that similarly qualified students have an equal rate of making applications to, and receiving an offer of admission from, these universities (Boliver, 2013). Analysing statistics from UCAS (Universities and Colleges Admission Service), the central UK system for higher education applications used by young people, she found clear inequalities. Those from lower socioeconomic groups were less likely to apply in the first place. When she examined those who had applied, she found that some ethnic groups – Black, Pakistani and Bangladeshi young people – were less likely to receive an offer. Finally, when she looked at the larger set of pupils from state schools, she found that unfair access seemed to stem from both application and admission processes. Her study was important in establishing statistical evidence of inequalities and prompting further scrutiny. Further work by Shiner and Noden (2015) explored the likelihood of application to higher, middle and lower ranking universities by attainment, social class, school type, gender and ethnicity. They concluded that attainment was a strong factor in predicting where young people would apply, but that this sits alongside (and is highly related to) school type, where private and selective schools produced higher rates of application to the elite universities. In their analysis, social class, unlike ethnicity, has a direct influence on where people apply. The influence of ethnicity is filtered through school type:

> While some minority groups, most notably the Chinese, appear to be using selective schooling to create pathways into elite higher education, candidates from other minority groups, particularly black groups, and those from less privileged social class backgrounds are concentrated in non-selective schools and colleges, which orientate them towards a broader range of universities.
>
> (Shiner and Noden, 2015, p. 1188)

More recent UCAS statistics reveal that entry to the top third of universities (which they determined by the average entry requirement) is still unequally distributed in ways that mirror earlier findings (UCAS, 2019). Growing awareness of the persistent inequalities in higher education has fuelled news headlines, particularly when they concern Oxford and Cambridge, the universities perceived to be at the very top of the 'stratified system'. For example, there was widespread reporting of the Sutton Trust finding that eight schools (mainly private) had sent more pupils to Oxford and

Cambridge than 2894 state schools; that is, about three-quarters of UK schools and colleges (Montacute and Cullinane, 2018). The MP David Lammy has drawn attention to the failure of one in four Oxford colleges to admit a single black British student in each year between 2015 and 2017 (*Guardian*, 2018). The quantitative statistical research discussed in this section helps us identify the inequalities in accessing different parts of the higher education system, and it suggests that inequality arises from a combination of where different students apply and how likely they are to receive an offer. Other forms of sociological research can help us understand what influences young people within these processes.

Understanding young people's decision-making about higher education

Research that gathers qualitative evidence of young people's perceptions of higher education can help us understand their decision-making. A number of such studies have explored the extent to which these perceptions differ according to different factors, notably social class and ethnicity. Many of the studies make use of concepts developed by Pierre Bourdieu to understand how social inequalities are reproduced across generations, which were introduced in Chapter 8.

To summarise, Bourdieu argued that one's social position is not only about the economic capital, or wealth, that one can access but also involves recognition of one's social capital (networks and social connections) and cultural capital (including educational credentials and cultural goods such as books and pictures. While cultural capital can take many different forms, in a given field some forms are considered more legitimate than others, for example, within a school a novel may be viewed as more valuable than a comic. The level of economic capital a family can access will influence the type and extent of social and cultural capital a young person can build up, for example, by paying for attendance at an elite school or going to the theatre. Bourdieu argues that although social and cultural capital are dependent on economic capital, they are not reducible to it. In this view, social class is more than just an economic status; it involves also social and cultural capital, and these together position people in a social setting as more or less advantaged than others. The value of this model lies in part in providing tools to think about and notice these other forms of capital, and to consider how they are passed on across generations.

A study by Ann Marie Bathmaker and colleagues made use of Bourdieu's ideas to investigate the experience of working-class and middle-class students at two universities in the same city: the University of Bristol and the University of the West of England (Bathmaker *et al.*, 2016). These institutions were chosen because they are located in different positions in the stratified system of higher education in the UK, with the former within the more prestigious Russell Group and the latter a 'new' university. In each university they selected a group of working-class and middle-class participants, from within the same subject areas and roughly equally spilt by gender. They assigned participating students to the working- or middle-class group on the basis of both parents' occupation, and also took other factors into account such as home neighbourhood (postcode); parents' experience of higher education; type of school (state/private); and the individual's own perception. They acknowledge that allocating individuals into just two broad categories of working and middle class is a simplified picture, as it masks differences within categories, and some young people proved difficult to categorise. They undertook a series of interviews with participants during their studies. They suggest that in analysing the interviews social class backgrounds became increasingly apparent; they were reflecting different experiences. For our purposes we are particularly interested in what they found out about the process of applying to university.

Bathmaker *et al.* drew upon Bourdieu's concept of 'habitus' to explore these experiences. As introduced in Chapter 8, habitus refers to the dispositions, the manners of being, seeing, acting, thinking, a person uses in a social context. It involves ways of speaking and being that do not need to be consciously called upon because they are embodied within the person; they appear the natural way to be. But rather than arising naturally from the individual these dispositions are influenced by their experiences over time, and in particular their cultural capital. Habitus can also take on a collective aspect as similar experiences give rise to common ways of being. Bathmaker *et al.* use this idea, and the work of others influenced by Bourdieu, to examine the extent of alignment of the different class groups to the social field of higher education. Bourdieu's theory implies that moving into a new context is experienced differently depending on the fit between existing habitus and the new social world (or field). If habitus and field align well, an individual will feel comfortable – like a 'fish in water' (Bourdieu and Wacquant, 1992, p. 127). Lack of fit produces the opposite and can lead to internal conflict. As young people consider higher education they are considering a move into a new context, and in part this is about the extent to which they think this will be a comfortable fit.

Within the project it was striking that going to university was a taken-for-granted part of middle-class life, whereas for the working-class students university generally emerged as a possibility at the later stages of secondary education (Bathmaker *et al.*, 2016). A quote from a middle-class student illustrates the taken-for-granted nature of the move:

> It sounds weird but I never thought of doing anything other than going to university. I think for most people in my school, it's more or less the standard thing to do.... I wasn't forced into it, it's just what happens.
>
> (Bathmaker *et al.*, 2016, p. 56)

As the researchers note, such is the power of the middle-class habitus, acquired in part through school, that the decision, such as it was, is made almost at an unconscious level. Other perspectives from the middle-class students illustrate how efficiently the expectation of going to university is established, with parents who were the first in their family to attend nevertheless passing on an expectation to their own children of attending. In contrast, in analysing the reflections from working-class students they note a theme of applying to university as a way of escaping limited job prospects.

Figures 9.3a and 9.3b Bristol University and UWE, two contrasting universities in one city.

For some of these students the impetus was experiencing some success in school education. Most of the young people in the working-class group were the first in their family to apply, with one tentatively describing herself as 'the first person to test it out' (p. 56). Some were clearly going against the grain of expectations amongst their peers: as one student explained, 'I sort of put my head down and tried to get on with it, despite the distractions around me from other people' (p. 147). The researchers suggest that this required independence and resilience, a finding which reflects other research on the experience of working-class students at elite universities (Reay *et al*.,2009). The working-class students received considerable emotional support from their parents in the decision to apply, but it did not appear that parents were influential in deciding where to apply.

When it came to the application process itself, clear differences were again identified by the researchers. Understanding of the stratification in higher education is part of the middle-class students' habitus, and the researchers quote this example of how natural this hierarchy seems and how much parents will invest in this aspiration:

> Everyone knows that obviously Oxbridge is the pinnacle but underneath that you've got a layer of the Bristols, the Durhams, the 3 London universities, and maybe somewhere like Warwick as well. So I had to make a lot of sacrifices for that, to be here, so did my mum and dad, to the tune of nigh on £100,000 and a lot of time and effort.
>
> (Bathmaker *et al*., 2016, p. 86)

The natural 'fit' with these universities was suggested by another middle-class student who did not feel the need to visit universities before applying; for him it was purely about reputation since he knew what to expect from universities (p. 85). Middle-class children received support from parents and school staff in understanding how to maximise their chances of going to a high-status institution, which would have high entry requirements. For example, they note one student whose grades made an application to the University of Bristol an 'outside chance', yet they were encouraged to include it on the application form, and ultimately gained a place. These students reported help from teachers, including information sessions, assistance with the UCAS form, and help with the 'personal statement' section through which prospective students demonstrate their alignment with the chosen subject area or course. The researchers note how parents, who know the logic of the education game, can step in to overcome setbacks. Here they cite the experience of middle-class students who have not achieved the requirements for their chosen university but who have been supported by their parents to secure a place at an alternative university. The family's educational habitus, their 'feel for the game', comes into play to ensure a place somewhere in higher education. In this situation, participation in higher education is viewed as an important marker of maintaining advantage.

In contrast, the working-class students could not draw upon the experience of their parents in navigating the application process. Instead, it is suggested, they have to play the game more independently. Their schools also had more limited experience of students applying to university. The researchers found cases where schools had not provided advice on which A-level subjects to study in order to apply for a particular degree, cutting off some desired options. A small number of the participants had accessed schemes which provide information and support on the application process for young people from under-represented groups, and the researchers argue for the expansion of this type of support. However, in the research most working-class students had to rely on individual effort and investigation when applying. In doing so they exercise considerable agency, with those that persist demonstrating tenacity through the application process. Research by the the Sutton Trust highlights the inclusion of a 'personal statement' within the application form as a barrier to disadvantaged students (Wyness, 2017). Two problems are identified: first, advantaged and disadvantaged students experienced differences in support for this process (echoing the earlier findings); and second, the range of work and life experiences they could write about differed greatly, resulting from the differences in economic, social and cultural capital they could draw upon. Ultimately the researchers suggest that the lack of transparency in the system, and the variation in the weight put on grades or contextual factors by different universities, makes it harder for some students (those with less access to advice) to understand 'the rules of the game' (Bathmaker *et al.*, 2016, p. 4).

Interestingly, this research by Bathmaker *et al.* (2016) reveals how these inequalities persist during university as students position themselves for graduate work. The researchers suggest that middle-class students engage in the 'hypermobilisation of capital', using family contacts within professional networks to secure opportunities for work experience and internships, often unpaid, and thus build further social and cultural capital that could lead to the right job offers. It is clear from their study that the kinds of capital devoted to this process are beyond many students, and particularly so for those who are the first in their families to attend. For these students the process of securing graduate employment requires yet more independence and individual effort. The inequalities in seeking graduate work again raise questions for the role of higher education in providing opportunities for young people.

How policy frames the problem of inequality

The ways in which inequalities in higher education are framed by policy have shifted over the past decades, from the need to 'widen access' to the sector, to emphasising its role in ensuring 'social mobility'. The former referred to the need to widen the social groups that participate in higher education, including young people from lower socioeconomic groups, ethnic minorities, those with disabilities and those with experience of care. The policy also sought to widen access to vocational and work-based learners, those learning part-time or mature learners. This breadth encompassed *communities* of learners, and it emphasised partnerships involving different public and educational organisations to reach and support learners (Moore *et al.*, 2013). The more recent frame of social mobility focuses on enabling *individuals* from disadvantaged backgrounds to improve their social and economic position, in this case through participating in higher education and securing employment. Waller *et al.* argue that this moves the focus from the many to 'a very select (and generally more capable) few' (Waller *et al.*, 2015, p. 619). Here social mobility is associated with a more individualising aim of enabling the brightest of the disadvantaged to enter a top university. Bathmaker and colleagues echo this concern, noting that 'opening access to those deemed to have "talent" is quite compatible with increasing social inequality' (Bathmaker *et al.*, 2016, p. 151). Although sympathetic to universities who are supporting young people through outreach projects and contextual offers they also point to more radical options, such as universities setting aside a number of scholarships for pupils from low-achieving local schools and policies to reduce stratification, calling ultimately for a comprehensive higher education system. Blackman echoes this call, arguing for the introduction of open access or basic matriculation quotas in all higher education institutions, with the use of financial levers to encourage institutions to address imbalances in their recruitment (Blackman, 2017).

Another way of framing the problem is to promote alternatives, and the increased focus on apprenticeships can be seen in this light. In an effort to establish 'parity of esteem' for vocational routes, higher level apprenticeships have been introduced. Yet, in extending the system, the approach of policy-makers has been to incorporate higher education qualifications within the higher level apprenticeships; as the Office for Students notes, this imbues the new route with the prestige of the 'conventional route' (OfS, 2019, p. 1). Thus we have Higher or Degree Apprenticeships in England, Wales and Northern Ireland and Graduate Apprenticeships in Scotland. These programmes are promoted as the best of both worlds; the learner is primarily an employee gaining experience while also studying part-time for a higher education qualification. They not only gain a modest salary but avoid the costs of tuition fees (where these apply). Young people concerned about the financial implications of university might well be attracted to such an option. The government has asked the Office for Students to encourage the growth of degree apprenticeships as a means of widening access to higher education for under-represented groups (OfS, 2019). Yet initial research indicates that the higher the level of apprenticeship, the fewer disadvantaged learners are recruited. Looking at degree apprenticeships, the numbers of disadvantaged young learners are only marginally higher than on conventional higher education courses, and the intake is less ethnically diverse and contains fewer students with disabilities (OfS, 2019). Arguably, apprenticeships at the higher levels are in danger of becoming another vehicle for middle-class students, and at this early point they are not yet making a significant contribution to addressing inequality. The problem with this is not only that the new system is failing to achieve one of its policy goals, but that focusing on apprenticeships leaves the remaining vocational options within further education underfunded.

Concluding thoughts: Where does this leave young people?

Young people are increasingly encouraged to make the most of their talents. Yet, as we have seen, the 'playing field' is far from level. When most young people leave school, they now transition not to work but to more education or training, all with the expectation of a better job. The incentive for staying on is increasing as job requirements rise. In the UK, the post-school options available to young people have become both more extensive with the shift to mass higher education, and more differentiated with universities of different status and offering different types of programmes. In addition, new vocational options are being developed, and attempts to simplify the vocational system have not yet succeeded. It is in navigating this differentiated system that disadvantaged students face problems not encountered by their more advantaged peers. Their families and schools may have limited experience of the university system, and it is suggested that they may lack the forms of 'capital' that can ease the process of applying. They have to exercise agency, substantial effort and considerable independence in making their application. In contrast, middle-class young people can often call upon knowledge built up within family or social networks, and this is reinforced by the resources of the schools they attend. These students absorb how to 'play the game' to maximise their chances of a place at a high-status university. These processes go some way towards explaining the current inequalities in access to universities and the slow pace of change. Arguably, recent efforts to increase the numbers of talented individuals making it through these barriers divert attention away from wider problems, towards tinkering at the edges of the admissions processes at elite universities. A more wide-ranging approach would involve a greater investment in further education, the commitment of employers to look beyond a limited range of high-status universities in their recruitment, and more effective advice and guidance across all schools. It would also involve valuing and supporting the different routes young people take after school, where value is not only seen in economic terms but in the contribution to society and personal understanding that participation in education and training can bring.

References

Bathmaker, A., Bradley, H., Hoare, A., Ingram, N., Waller, R. and Abrahams, J. (2016) *Higher Education, Social Class and Social Mobility: The Degree Generation*. London: Palgrave Macmillan.
Blackman, T. (2017) *The Comprehensive University: An Alternative to Social Stratification by Academic Selection* (Occasional paper 17), Higher Education Policy Institute [Online]. Available at www.hepi.ac.uk/wp-content/uploads/2017/07/Hepi-The-Comprehensive-University_Occasional-Paper-17-11_07_17.pdf (accessed 11 April 2019).

Boliver, V. (2013) How fair is access to more prestigious UK universities? *The British Journal of Sociology*, 64(2), 344–364.

Bourdieu, P. (1997) The forms of capital. In H. Halsey, H. Lauder, P. Brown and A. Stuart Wells (eds) *Education: Culture, Economy and Society*). Oxford: Oxford University Press, pp. 46–58.

Bourdieu, P. and Wacquant, L. (1992) *An Invitation to Reflexive Sociology*. Chicago, IL: University of Chicago Press.

Careers Wales (2018) *Pupil Destinations from Schools in Wales 2017*. Careers Wales [Online]. Available at http://destinations.careerswales.com/index.html (accessed 11 April 2019).

Deissinger, T. (2019) Problems and challenges of full-time and school-based VET in Germany. In J. Gallacher and F. Reeve (eds) *New Frontiers for College Education: International Perspectives*. Abingdon: Routledge.

Department for Business, Innovation and Skills (BIS) (2016) *Report of the Independent Panel on Technical Education* (The Sainsbury Report) [Online]. Available at https://assets.publishing.service.gov.uk/government/uploads/system/uploads/attachment_data/file/536046/Report_of_the_Independent_Panel_on_Technical_Education.pdf (accessed 11 April 2019).

Department for Education (DfE) (2018) *Destinations of Key Stage 4 and Key Stage 5 Students, England, 2016/17*. Department for Education [Online]. Available at https://assets.publishing.service.gov.uk/government/uploads/system/uploads/attachment_data/file/748199/Destinations_Main_Text_2017.pdf.

Department of Education (2018) *Statistical Bulletin 4/2018: Qualifications and Destinations of Northern Ireland School Leavers 2016/17*. Department of Education, Northern Ireland [Online]. Available at www.education-ni.gov.uk/sites/default/files/publications/education/qualifications-and-destinations-of-northern-ireland-school-leavers-20161._.pdf (accessed 11 April 2019).

Guardian (2018) Oxford faces anger over failure to improve diversity among students. *Guardian* [Online]. Available at www.theguardian.com/education/2018/may/23/oxford-faces-anger-over-failure-to-improve-diversity-among-students (accessed 11 April 2019).

Leitch Review of Skills (2006) *Prosperity for All in the Global Economy – World Class Skills*. HM Treasury.

Marginson, S. (2016) The worldwide trend to high participation higher education: dynamics of social stratification in inclusive systems. *Higher Education*, 72, 413–434.

May, T. (2018) PM Speech: The right choice for everyone [Online]. Available from www.gov.uk/government/speeches/pm-the-right-education-for-everyone (accessed 27 April 2019).

Montacute, R. and Cullinane, C. (2018) Access to advantage: the influence of schools and place on admissions to top universities. The Sutton Trust [Online]. Available at www.suttontrust.com/wp-content/uploads/2018/12/AccesstoAdvantage-2018.pdf (accessed 11 April 2019).

Moore, J., Sanders, J. and Higham, L. (2013) *Literature Review of Research into Widening Participation to Higher Education*. HEFCE [Online]. Available at https://webarchive.nationalarchives.gov.uk/20180319114530/www.hefce.ac.uk/pubs/rereports/year/2013/wplitreview/ (accessed 16 April 2019).

OECD (1996) *The Knowledge-based Economy*. Paris: OECD.

OfS (2019) Degree apprenticeships: A viable alternative? Office for Students [Online]. Available at www.officeforstudents.org.uk/media/c791216f-a1f1-4196-83c4-1449dbd013f0/insight-2-degree-apprenticeships.pdf (accessed 19 April 2019).

Reay, D., Crozier, G. and Clayton, J. (2009) 'Strangers in paradise'? Working-class stundets in elite universities. Sociology, vol 43, no. 6, pp. 1103–1121.

Reeve, F. and Gallacher, J. (2019) Is there a higher level skills gap that colleges can fill? In J. Gallacher and F. Reeve (eds) *New Frontiers for College Education: International Perspectives*. Abingdon: Routledge.

Scottish Government (2018) *Initial Destinations of Senior Phase School Leavers, No. 2: 2018 Edition*. Scottish Government [Online]. Available at www2.gov.scot/Resource/0053/00531988.pdf (accessed 11 April 2019).

Scottish Government (2019) School leaver attainment and initial destinations: statistics. Scottish Government [Online]. Available at www.gov.scot/publications/summary-statistics-attainment-initial-leaver-destinations-1-2019-edition/pages/4/ (accessed 22 April 2019).

Shiner, M. and Noden, P. (2015) 'Why are you applying there?': 'race', class and the construction of higher education 'choice' in the United Kingdom. *British Journal of Sociology of Education*, 36(8), 1170–1191. DOI: 10.1080/01425692.2014.902299.

Sutton Trust (2014) *Higher Ambitions Summit Rapporteur Report.* Sutton Trust [Online]. Available at www.suttontrust.com/research-paper/higher-ambitions/ (accessed 11 April 2019).

Trow, M. (1973) *Problems in the Transition from Elite to Mass Higher Education.* Berkeley, CA: Carnegie Commission on Higher Education.

UCAS (2019) End of cycle report 2018: Patterns of equality in England. UCAS [Online]. Available at www.ucas.com/file/212841/download?token=fR1vSwMY (accessed 11 April 2019).

Waller, R., Holford, J., Jarvis, P., Milana, M. and Webb, S. (2015) Neo-liberalism and the shifting discourse of 'educational fairness'. *International Journal of Lifelong Education,* 34(6), 619–622. DOI: 10.1080/02601370.2015.1114237.

Wyness, G. (2017) Rules of the game: disadvantaged students and the university admissions process. Sutton Trust [Online]. Available at www.suttontrust.com/wp-content/uploads/2017/12/Rules-of-the-Game.pdf (accessed 16 April 2019).

10 Normal ways for normal days

Building our practice upon the exploration of people's preferences

Jonathan Rix

Introduction

Good morning

The author is faced with an everyday problem. He has to write a book chapter which helps readers question the everyday, providing insights which enrich an understanding of childhood and which challenge their assumptions. Such a problem may not seem an everyday one for many people (everydayness is always relative), but for the author who has been writing for over 40 years, its normality is exemplified by his having RSI (repetitive strain injury) in his arms and shoulders. The challenge for the author, with the deadline date for 6000 words rapidly approaching, is to find a way to write this many words, in this short amount of time, without adding to his pain and discomfort.

The established approach would be to type up the words using a keyboard. This, however, is at the root of the author's pain. It would be possible to go back to a previously established approach, in particular handwriting the chapter, but this would not be an acceptable solution for modern-day publishers. The author is therefore relying on more recently emerged technologies, in particular voice-recognition software. However, this is the first time that the author has ever dictated an entire chapter. And it comes with a range of new challenges. First, it has altered the balance between the way in which the author engages with the words on the page. He is struggling with both speaking and looking at the screen, in a way he never did when typing. This has resulted in him having to stand up and look out of the window while he is dictating, so that he can better hold the words in his head. As a consequence, this approach feels less like writing and more like public speaking. The author is feeling a shift in his sense of himself as a writer. He is also wondering if telling the readers this is changing their perceptions about their relationship with him, and how they engage with his words. He is quite pleased with how it is going so far though; his arms aren't aching and he has managed to capture in words the idea with which he began. And he feels he is establishing another way of working. A preference.

The purpose of this introduction is partly to exemplify our need to engage with new opportunities to overcome commonplace challenges. It shows how this is disorientating, but it also aims to underline:

- The physicality of being
- The mutability (changing nature) of personal practices
- The socially situated nature of impairment and disability (though a very minor example)
- Our identity constantly being established through participation within social relations (whatever our age, whether as adults or as children)
- Our understanding of any role as a shifting relationship
- Our need as practitioners to be constantly reflecting upon our relationship with those we support and the means of that relationship.

These are the issues this chapter aims to raise, through an exploration of how practitioners engage with the people they support, drawing upon the author's research experiences. Although the chapter has a focus on practice with children and young people, it speaks to all readers in terms of reflection upon how our attitudes shape the way we behave, encouraging different ways of thinking. It considers three examples of the everyday: paperwork, attitudes and practices. It considers how an array of everyday (socially situated) responses disable and enable, with particular reference to people who are frequently identified by educational or impairment labels.

Let's try to agree something to start with ...

In 2011, I was part of a team that undertook a study of special educational needs in 50 countries for the National Council for Special Education (NCSE) in Ireland (Rix *et al.*, 2013). When we explored understandings of special education within policy, survey data and interviews, it was evident that only two concepts were universally agreed upon. 'Special' involves *additional time* and *additional space*. This generally referred to having more time or extra time to undertake an activity or more time spent practising something; it tended to include being in a space away from peers, or some peers being grouped together or having a space people could go to should they need to. Very few people mentioned a special pedagogy or a special curriculum; a few more mentioned special categories of people and quite a few more mentioned special funding and assessment, but what universally defined special was its additionality.

How we make the *additional* everyday

In all matters of support, there is a tension between individual and collective perspectives. In the context of special education and inclusion, this tension is frequently characterised as being between a 'medical model' view focused on the individual (which sees difficulties a person faces as resulting from something different about the person) and a 'social model' view focused on the collective (which sees difficulties as situated in society's response to people's differences).

This tension between the individual and collective is also evidenced more widely in the ways we allocate and deliver all kinds of institutional, personal and economic support. For example:

- Our funding streams and policies talk of *universal* and *personalised* services – such as those associated with Education, Health and Care Plans and the NHS Long Term Plan.
- Within the vast majority of classrooms, children are mostly taught together but evaluated separately. As they grow up, they move from a broad education to an increasingly selective one.
- In matters of health, education and social care it is commonplace to think about preventive and wide-scale activity leading to increasingly intensive and individual-ised support. This is frequently 'matched' to a category (for instance, across 50 countries in the NCSE study:
  - the notion of a 'continuum' was evident wherever we looked, and
  - we identified 60 different categories of special education).

This tension between the collective and the individual seems a very matter-of-fact thing; we are separate biological entities who only exist because we are social entities; surely it makes sense that any practical response needs to take both into considera-tion? In this context, everyday support has become universal and wide scale, while the additional support has become individualised and personalised.

However, there are numerous examples of individualised practices going to extremes which seem counterproductive and ethically dubious – isolating and control-ling children who are considered difficult.

- Just put 'Autism Cage' into a search engine to see what some schools (from all around the world) have created. The name accurately describes what they are: cages built inside a classroom, where an autistic child is confined.
- Or consider the isolation booths in 'consequence rooms' or 'inclusion units' in England (and beyond), where children are sent for behaviour which schools find unacceptable. Here children are frequently expected to sit in silence all day, often facing the wall, with no teaching. In 2017/2018, one child was kept in one of these rooms for 35 days, allowed to the toilet for five-minute breaks three times a day (Perraudin, 2018). In 2017/2018, in one English academy chain,[1] in just 14 of their 31 schools, students were sent to these rooms 31,000 times. Over two-thirds of academy chains responding to a freedom of information request confirmed using these rooms (Staufenberg, 2018).
- Or consider the building of a hut as a classroom for a child with Down's syndrome which a former-teacher in Norway described to me as well positioned, because the

child could look out and see the other children playing. This, in a country which is seen as being a leader in inclusion – but this child is excluded from playing with their peers, expected instead to watch them enjoying activities with each other.

Even in its less extreme forms, this tightened focus on the individual and their (dis)ability can have a profound impact on an individual's identity. In their case study of Adam, Ray McDermott and Hervé Varenne (1995) outlined how learning difficulties were created by the educational context. They explored how there was much that one young person, Adam, could do outside of school, but how his identity as learning disabled emerged through all aspects of the education system; and through the involvement of the whole educational community. This arose not just because of people's conscious actions but also because of the numerous activities in which we are all involved at a systemic and personal level, for example, sitting exams, putting people in sets, choosing our friends, undertaking research. Such identities can even be created by what might appear to be the most benign of motives. Laura Méndez and colleagues, for example, describe how teachers' determination to convey knowledge contained within printed material served to constrain a student, creating 'a zone of incapacity' (Méndez *et al.*, 2008, p. 67), and positioning her as incapable, rather than understanding the strategies she used in daily life for learning and understanding in a more 'real-life' context.

So let us consider three ways through which we can contribute to the creation of a child's identity.

Attitudes

I was recently talking to a mother about her children's experiences in school. Becky described how her son, Kieron, became overwhelmed by moving into a new teacher's class, how he had begun to wet himself because of a teacher 'who couldn't say one positive thing' about him. This profound impact of the social upon the child echoes a study which described a supportive school where staff shared concerns and strategies (Fox *et al.*, 2004). In this setting a child with Down's syndrome was viewed as a full class member in one year, with support staff and the class teacher regularly meeting to discuss work, but the following year he was seen as separate from his peers. His

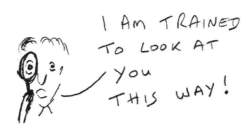

Figure 10.1 Cartoons throughout this chapter are by the author.

new teacher, a former Special Educational Needs Coordinator, saw this child's plan-ning and support as being the responsibility of support staff. As a result, in the second year he was moved to the margins, both physically and in terms of his relations with the others around him.

During research in Norway (Rix *et al.*, 2013) I visited a strengthened (special) school. The students each had an individual room, off a long corridor, where they worked with one or more practitioners at a time. The Principal of the school told me that all the walls between the rooms slid back, and that he asked teaching staff to do this since learning is a social activity; but regretfully, he told me, the teachers pre-ferred to keep the walls in place, because this suited their ways of working. On that same trip to Norway, I met a young man who had profound and multiple difficulties of many kinds. He also had an individualised curriculum which included regular skiing, cycling, mountain climbing and swimming, which he carried out entirely apart from his peers. His one-to-one supporters and the school specialists explained that the young man did things on his own because the other children wouldn't want to be with him and wouldn't have time for him. I, for one, would have leapt at the chance to do things like that when I was at school; I feel sure the company would have just made things more interesting to me. Of course, such a choice had been taken away from the young man's peers by the presumptions of the specialists.

It is perhaps unsurprising that a practitioner's beliefs about ability, disability and learning appear to affect who they see as their responsibility; nor is it surprising that it affects how they subsequently work with those for whom they are responsible. As part of extensive research into teachers and their classroom interactions, Jordan and Stanovich (2001) and Jordan *et al.* (2010) noted that effective teachers maximised instructional time through their preparation of lessons, clearly communicating expec-tations that all students will be engaged in learning to a high standard. This contrasted with teachers who did not have the same expectations. Their interactions with children who were identified as having difficulties focused primarily on non-academic, organisa-tional issues; or they offered space for closed, short responses of the yes/no variety. However, those teachers identified as effective had routines which allowed them to instruct individuals and small groups for large parts of the teaching time. They worked with all pupils. They engaged in interactions intended to foster student understanding and development of thinking skills. In particular, they engaged in prolonged inter-actions with pupils with special educational needs and used most of the available time to offer learners the opportunity to problem-solve, to discuss and describe their ideas and to make connections with their own experiences and prior understandings.

We can do something about our expectations; we can reflect upon our beliefs. Rather than think of people as *characteristics* we can approach them as *experiences*. We may think of both as socially situated, but the latter is something which we can do more about, more readily. Consider, for example, moving to the use of 'Labels of Opportunity' – rather than of diagnoses – which might 'encourage those who hear them to engage with possibilities' (Rix, 2007, p. 28).

This recognition that changing labels can redirect attitudes was evident in a research project I was fortunate enough to be involved in from 2016 to 2019. Four participatory research groups in the United Kingdom, Spain and Austria were brought together as part of ARCHES, a project involving heritage and technology partners across Europe, with the aim to enhance museum accessibility. These research groups involved participants who had a diverse range of access preferences. These preferences are frequently associated with the labels of sensory impairments and intellectual impairments, but many participants did not wish to be defined by such labels, nor by the labels in the original bid document, nor by those being requested by external assessors. There was a collective agreement early on in the project to subsequently refer to us as having access preferences, and it was these which we included in the collection of demographic data. Categories included:

- Blue badge parking
- Braille text
- British Sign Language
- Captioning
- Different language (please specify)
- Easy read
- Guide dog
- Guiding support
- Induction loops
- Large guides
- Magnifying glasses
- Makaton or signalong
- One-to-one support
- Pictures, symbols or easy read
- Raised line floor plan
- Scanning pen
- Screen-reader software
- Simplified information
- Sound-enhancement equipment
- Step-free access
- Gallery stools
- Tactile books
- Torches
- Walking frame
- Wheelchair

Such categories can far more effectively enable people working in museums (and elsewhere) to consider possibilities and the solutions for visitors, rather than having to make presumptions based on a generalised diagnostic label. Similarly, teachers would be better prepared by a label which enabled them to envision practice; for example, a 'person supported by signing and visual communication' is of more practical use than 'a person with Down's Syndrome'. The latter may be useful in a medical context or as a matter of pride, but within an education/social care/everyday

Figure 10.2 Are we really all in this together?

situation it fails as a description of people who may have a whole range of different access preferences.

The view of the participants within the ARCHES project was that if the language of opportunity was adopted within a setting it would encourage a shift in thinking about practice.

Paperwork

The reduction to individualisation, rather than a focus on social structures, is also firmly embedded in practitioners' ways of recording, assessing and planning for all children in diverse formal and informal roles. We resist using our records to encourage holistic responses or to change our structures. Teachers, for example, are expected to have lesson plans for the class, while for learners who are struggling there are individual versions of various kinds. The consequence is evident in a Swedish study involving content analysis of 51 Individual Education Plans (IEPs). Only two of the reports recognised in some way a challenge or opportunity as a wider school issue, while all the others required an individualised action focused on the individual child (Isaksson *et al.*, 2007).

In a study with Alice Matthews (Rix and Matthews, 2014), we identified the difference between people's formal and informal ways of representing disabled children, in particular how people involved in the child's life considered them in a social context. These representations were sought in documentation produced by the formal processes associated with education, health and care. This documentation came from the first nine years of life for one young boy with Special Educational Needs. They were contrasted with representations emerging from interviews with the professional network around two very young disabled children. Within interviews and discussions, parents and practitioners talked of the child within context, mentioning multiple influencing factors. However, from the hundreds of pages of documentation, there were only three or four mentions of contextual opportunities or complicating practical or relational issues. Within the documentation the child was viewed nearly entirely in isolation, while in the interviews the child was situated in a rich web of relationships.

This everyday recording of children's lives does not simply occur because of individual choices made by the people producing the paperwork. The systems used to record information socialise practitioners into a 'thought world' that integrates top-down criteria into day-to-day practice (Bowker and Leigh Star, 1999, p. 272). The ways in which we record our actions, views and intentions are constrained by how we are expected to say something; we have to adapt 'the particulars of the world so that they fit within the general schemas of the organization' (Brown and Duguid, 2000, p. 108). As Ina Wagner (1993) showed, changing the paperwork *can* change the nature of the response, so that, for example, the focus can shift between quality of care and administrative prerogatives.

And there are alternatives. There is a long history of people using assessment tools such as portfolios and 'passports' to record and to evidence learning; this encourages learning within a wider project-based framework (though they are somewhat out of favour in the UK at the time of writing). New ways of evaluating and supporting this learning continue to emerge, often focused on 'twenty-first-century skills' and sociocultural understandings which see the individual's learning as fundamentally linked to participation in social activity. Such approaches to evidencing learning can go beyond setting personal targets or individual goals. They can support people to consider both the collective and the individual. They can, for example, help them create bottom-up, collectively owned aspirations which can be verified by anyone and everyone in that context (Twining *et al.*, 2016).

These options may feel beyond the control of many individual practitioners, but (as we will discuss below) it is possible to change the way we plan, record our thoughts and approach challenging, everyday situations.

Practices

As practitioners, we frequently find ourselves working in ways that we feel will support people, but which can so easily be counterproductive. There is a strong research history, for example, which points to the use of a multi-modal approach to learning[2] (Rix *et al.*, 2009). Children, young people and adults learn by engaging (in objects,

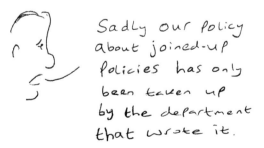

Figure 10.3 Joined-up policies.

subjects, experiences) in ways which are meaningful to them. They are agents in this. Our role as practitioners and supporters is to stretch and enrich their experiences. Most practitioners recognise the importance of the environment with access to diverse tools and resources.

However, when push comes to shove many of them fall back upon traditional approaches; for example, those regular structures and rules that have organised the work of instruction, such as single teachers, ability grouping and standard tests (Rix, 2009). As the Rector of one of very few Special Schools in Italy told us (as part of the NCSE study mentioned earlier), teachers tend to think of tools when they look for solutions, when the issue is fundamentally about communication. He recognised that it was time spent fully engaged with a diverse student community which taught this reality. In nearly all the other interviews in Italy, people talked about the need to use many strategies when working with children with special educational needs and to recognise that what worked for one group was a benefit for another.

> Special pedagogy is special for SEN children but for children who haven't got this special needs, it's just pedagogy.
> (Interview site 9, in discussion with professional development and academic staff)

However, as most of us are only too aware, there is frequently a considerable distance between our aspirations and our practice. This distance became evident to John Parry and me when we began to deliver training on In-the-Picture in 2017 (Rix *et al.*, 2020). In-the-Picture is a tool for reflecting upon the interests of very young children, derived from a qualitative research method that sought to enable the researcher to consider the perspective of toddlers with Down's syndrome. It is something we have shared in response to practitioner interest. In interviews, following up from this training, practitioners talked about the child and family-centred values underpinning In-the-Picture. These values equated to their own, as well as to those they had experienced in training and which they recognised in policy. Yet the overwhelming sense from these practitioners was that in some way they felt constrained in putting these values into practice. They talked about how undertaking In-the-Picture just for short periods allowed them to step back ... to create a space ... to hand over control; something which the established working practices discouraged. As one participant said:

> (We need) permission to do it ... from, well from ourselves ... to say I can do this, it's justified, it's legitimate, I can take X minutes out for this. And while you're doing it the parents know you're doing this, and housing can be set aside for a moment, and the fact that they haven't got speech therapy yet can be set aside for a moment. And everything stops, and it's all about the child. This is what we're doing.
>
> (Participant G1 Focus Group 3)

Evidently the pressure of process constrains people from acting upon their knowledge of best practice and perhaps working in ways that they might wish to. In our research in Italy (Rix *et al.*, 2013; Rix, 2015), one Principal of a secondary school suggested during a discussion (with a number of teaching and in-school staff present) that only 20 to 30 per cent of teachers in the school were planning and teaching collaboratively as he would like. The rest of the staff concurred. At another secondary school in a discussion about inclusive practice, staff noted:

> The other 50, 60 per cent [of teachers] they are struggling [with collaboration]. The 30, 40 per cent [who collaborate inclusively] doesn't count the working hours.

Practitioners tend to be time-poor. They prioritise. They too have preferences. As a consequence, something which is seen as additional may be also be regarded as a matter of goodwill. This reliance upon goodwill has been one of my profound frustrations as the parent of a child who has been the recipient of one-to-one support for pretty much the whole of his school career. I have known of the power of very simple approaches to affect a whole range of learning opportunities for my son Robbie; and I have watched them not being used for any number of reasons. This has been particularly evident in relation to the everyday use of cameras, wikis, YouTube, social media and telephone apps. As a family we have managed to support Robbie through the use of photographs and home video to learn to ski, to ride a bicycle, to play frisbee and to swim butterfly. WhatsApp has encouraged reading, telling stories and communicating with friends and family. Cheap cameras have been an everyday part of his learning life. But their absence has been evident at school.

We have tried to encourage the educators to use cameras and videos. We have discussed with them how we use online videos to help Robbie understand the most 'complex' concepts, or PowerPoints and wikis to support narrative and his use of words. We have produced videos of him carrying out a range of activities at home as well as of him making choices for annual reviews. We have communicated through photos and short films about holidays and weekends, and for homework. At primary school, when Robbie entered the school science project, it was reported via a dozen photographs showing him undertaking two experiments: one related to shadows and the other to the melting of ice.

The problem has always arisen when these modes of communication have entered the academic realm. In judging the science competition, the head teacher did not believe that Robbie understood what he had been doing in the photographs, and called him into her office to test that knowledge. He passed and won the school prize. Yet despite such opportunities, we have had virtually no films coming back from school. Beyond the involvement of one or two of his many committed teaching assistants, the use of photography – where it has happened – has been almost entirely about recording his learning rather than developing it. YouTube and the internet have generally been banned or unavailable; taking photographs has been a safeguarding issue; and the use of a tablet when others are not using one has been a matter of equity or has been seen tas a practice which might encourage negative behaviours.

As a consequence, just like so many other children, my son has been (inadvertently?) denied meaningful access to the majority of concepts underpinning everyone else's everyday curriculum. He has largely had to rely on the traditional grammars of schooling (Tyack and William, 1994), and the presumptions about his limitations have led to a future defined by 'life-skills'.

Institutions seem unable to respond with the everyday flexibility that is expected beyond their boundaries, reflecting not only the availability of resources but also their underlying goals (and perhaps those of our political institutions). I often find myself drawn to the notion of Slow Inclusion (Bates, 2005), in which people are given time to explore the complexity of policy and practice, professional and personal values, going 'on a journey in which attitudes gradually change through accepting relationships' (p. 4):

> People committed to slow inclusion know that there are problems to overcome and arrange time, skills, finances and risks to get the best for everyone. We aim for flexibility with stability. Since the task is complex, our understanding is poor and our theoretical models are weak, we need to keep on learning. This means that we have to accept chaos sometimes and abandon the myth of control.

In our everyday lives, perhaps working with young children, our actions are our simplest way of communicating. These actions may involve the use of words or tools, but they are always physical, embodied, human moments (even if hidden behind the click of a mouse). The physicality of the space is one of the primary reasons for adopting multi-modal practices. Through them, the opportunities to communicate are multiplied. However, this takes time. It requires a different kind of planning; one which recognises the social and relational nature of what is going on; that does not seek a linear learning objective but considers the collaborative learning opportunities on the way; one that enables participants to lead and to be lead; one that takes advantage of all the senses, and allows children to grasp the personal and collective relevance of an experience. It requires planning for the unexpected and being flexible to where relationships/interactions might take you. All of us can plan for such moments. They might even be perfectly normal.

Concluding thoughts

Seeking the normal

You are faced with an everyday problem. We are faced with an everyday problem. We can continue in much the same way, largely repeating patterns from our past or we can take advantage of opportunities that have been around for just as long.

The author we met at the start does not need to keep on typing.

Other options are available.

Much of what is required is at a scale beyond most of our means. Our point of engagement is local, it is personal, it is complex and full of contradictions. However, should we wish, there are things we can do in relation to our own personal attitudes, paperwork and practices. We can recognise that we are not just responsible for one

Figure 10.4 Social care?

child or some children but that we have a collective duty to support all our learning. We can seek and take advantage of multi-modal opportunities. We can record, plan and encourage social interactions, seeing the child or young person within context. We can focus upon the things people need to feel supported, upon their communication and access preferences. We can voice them. And we can consider how these small changes make us view ourselves and our relationships with others.

The voice-recognition user is sat down now, looking out of the window. It is a very beautiful sunset this evening.

He wonders what tomorrow will bring …

Acknowledgement

This work was performed within the framework of the H2020 project ARCHES (www. arches-project.eu), which has received funding from the European Union's Horizon 2020 research and innovation programme under grant agreement No. 693229.

Notes

1 Most secondary schools in England are currently academies – schools which are funded by the state but independent of local authority control. Many are part of partnerships, forming 'academy chains' of several schools with shared strategies.
2 Multi-modal approaches use a wide variety of modes for exploring learning opportunities – these may be textual, aural, linguistic, spatial, digital and visual resources. They often also encourage a creative element.

References

Bates, P. (2005) In praise of slow inclusion [Online]. Available at http://peterbates.org.uk/wp-content/uploads/2017/04/inpraiseofslowinclusion.pdf (accessed 10 May 2019).

Bowker, G. and Leigh Star, S. (1999) *Sorting Things Out*. Cambridge, MA: MIT Press.

Brown, J. and Duguid, P. (2000) *The Social Life of Information*. Boston, MA: Harvard Business School Press.

Fox, S., Farrell, P. and Davis, P. (2004) Factors associated with the effective inclusion of primary-aged pupils with Down's syndrome. *British Journal of Special Education*, 31(4), 184–190.

Isaksson, J., Lindqvist, R. and Bergström, E. (2007) School problems or individual shortcomings? *European Journal of Special Needs Education*, 22, 1, 75–91.

Jordan, A. and Stanovich, P. (2001) Patterns of teacher–student interaction in inclusive elementary classrooms and correlates with student self-concept. *International Journal of Disability, Development and Education*, 48, 1, 33–52.

Jordan, A., Glenn, C. and McGhie-Richmond, D. (2010) The Supporting Effective Teaching (SET) project. *Teaching and Teacher Education*, 26(2), 259–266.

McDermott, R. and Varenne, H. (1995) Culture as disability. *Anthropology & Education Quarterly*, 26, 3, 324–348.

Méndez, L., Lacasa, P. and Matusov, E (2008) Transcending the zone of learning disability. *European Journal of Special Needs Education*, 23(1), 63–73.

Perraudin, F. (2018) Pupil brings legal action against school's isolation policy. *The Guardian*, 11 December 2018 [Online]. Available at www.theguardian.com/education/2018/dec/11/pupil-brings-legal-action-against-schools-isolation-booths-outwood-grange-academies-trust (accessed 13 May 2019).

Rix, J. (2007) Labels of opportunity – a response to Carson and Rowley. *Ethical Space: The International Journal of Communication Ethics*, 4(3), 25–28.

Rix, J. (2009) A model of simplification: the ways in which teachers simplify learning materials. *Educational Studies*, 35(2), 95–106.

Rix, J. (2015) *Must Inclusion Be Special – Rethinking Educational Support within a Community of Provision*. Abingdon: Routledge.

Rix, J. and Matthews, A. (2014) Viewing the child as a participant within context. *Disability & Society ahead-of-print*, 1–15.

Rix, J. and Parry, J. and Pinchbeck, M. (2020) 'Building a better picture' – practitioners' views of using a listening approach with young disabled children. *Journal of Early Childhood Research*, 18(1), 3–17.

Rix, J., Hall, K., Nind, M., Sheehy, K. and Wearmouth, J. (2009) What pedagogical approaches can effectively include children with special educational needs in mainstream classrooms? A systematic literature review. *Support for Learning*, 24 (2), 86–94.

Rix, J., Sheehy, K., Fletcher-Campbell, F., Crisp, M. and Harper, A. (2013) Exploring provision for children identified with special educational needs: an international review of policy and practice. *European Journal of Special Needs Education*, 28(4), 375–391.

Staufenberg, J. (2018) Isolation rooms: how swathes of schools are removing pupils from their classrooms. *Schools Week*, 19 October [Online]. Available at https://schoolsweek.co.uk/isolation-rooms-how-schools-are-removing-pupils-from-classrooms/ (accessed 13 May 2019).

Twining, P., Rix, J. and Sheehy, K. (2016) Developing Point of Learning – an innovative approach to enhancing professional learning. Available at www.imagine.education/developing-point-of-learning/.

Tyack, D. and William, T. (1994) The 'grammar" of schooling: why has it been so hard to change? *American Educational Research Journal*, 31(3), 453–479.

Wagner, I. (1993) Women's voice: the case of nursing information systems. *AI and Society*, 7, 295–310.

11 Children, young people and voluntourism

Heather Montgomery

Introduction

Volunteer tourism or 'voluntourism' can be broadly defined as describing 'tourists who, for various reasons, volunteer in an organized way to undertake holidays that might involve aiding or alleviating the material poverty in some groups in society, the restoration of certain environments or research into aspects of society or environment' (Wearing, 2001, p. 1). Since the turn of the millennium it has become one of the fastest growing alternative tourist markets (Conran, 2011). Key features of this experience involve contributing to and even joining communities rather than simply watching them or 'consuming' them as tourists are perceived to do, and another feature is the way people are volunteering their time and resources (although paradoxically many pay thousands of pounds to companies that facilitate this experience). While voluntourists may be of all ages, this chapter will focus on young Westerners – often on gap years – working as volunteers in orphanages. This so-called 'orphanage tourism' is a niche form of volunteer tourism that encourages young, Western volunteers to work in short-term placements as caregivers, particularly in South East Asian and sub-Saharan African orphanages. It is one of the most visible and direct ways of illustrating the inter-cultural contacts between young Westerners and children overseas and yet there are concerns about the consequences of this contact and the impacts it has on both groups of children and young people, raising important questions about the role of good intentions in improving vulnerable children's welfare.

Gap years and voluntourism

A gap year is a period in which a young person delays further education or employment to travel, often between school and university (Lyons *et al.*, 2012). For many young people this year is a period without exams or assessment, taken as a gap between the structure and discipline of school and before university, or between university and full-time employment. The stereotype of a gap year student (in the UK at least) is of a white, middle-class, privately educated young person being funded by their parents to enjoy a year away from responsibilities. It is based on a particular class-based assumption of automatic progression from school to university: indeed, it is often mocked as a 'gap yah' (suggesting the privileged accent of a privately educated pupil 'doing' his or her gap year). In this way the gap year can be seen as a direct descendant of the eighteenth-century 'grand tour', an essential part of the education of young English gentlemen. Typically, visiting Paris, Rome, Venice, Florence and Naples, young men would spend the years between leaving school and coming into their inheritance travelling around Europe, ostensibly seeing the sights of these cities, improving their languages and their knowledge of high culture and art. It was also an opportunity for young men to 'sow their wild oats' away from England, to womanise, gamble, drink and generally misbehave in places where they could bring no shame to their families back home. It further represented the commodification of culture by the wealthy as something to be defined, visited and collected, so that certain cities and certain monuments were defined as the epitome of good taste that everyone of the right social background should enjoy and recognise as important. A gap year, although by no means still the preserve of the wealthy, does share some similar features and still involves large power imbalances and situations where relatively privileged

Figure 11.1 A young missionary playing football with an African child.

Westerners choose to visit the not-so-privileged. There are certain areas of the world which are very much on the tour (South East Asia, India and South America), while others are not – almost no one travels round the UK or Northern Europe during their gap year. Yet it is also worth remembering that contemporary gap years can take many forms and not all of them involve travel. For many young people the cost of university tuition fees means that gap years are spent saving for university, while others use it to 'temp' or intern in the sort of industry in which they wish to pursue a career.

For those who are still able to take gap years however, there has been a move away from the stereotypical year spent travelling in Asia or South America 'seeing the sights' or visiting the beaches and, since the turn of the millennium, there has been an upsurge in voluntourism, in which young people spend their time (and money) in parts of the developing world teaching English, building schools or working in orphanages (Wearing, 2001). Whole industries have sprung up to set up these placements and, for a fee, young Westerners can travel to a new country, live and work there, contribute to a less well-off community and – ideally – build relationships with local people. It is important to note the idealism behind such trips and, although this chapter will go on to analyse voluntourism quite critically, the urge to go and help others, make their lives better, and to learn more about other places is fundamentally a good one. It is far too easy to sneer at idealism or describe it as naivety but whatever criticisms this chapter makes of the consequences and impacts of volunteer tourism, it is not seeking to belittle or disdain this idealism.

Indeed, when questioned on their motivations, young volunteers focus on altruism and their desire to 'do good'. Mary Mostafanezhad (2014, p. 115) in her study of Cambodian orphanages asked young volunteers about their time working there and what their photographs of their experiences showed:

> Angie, a 26 year old English woman explained: 'I think this image shows how we as Westerners from developed countries can help children in the Third World. I want to show my friends and family that if I can do it, anyone can do it.' Similarly, Janna, a 27 year old Australian volunteer tourist commented: 'I have tons of images showing my experience with the children. They [the children] have no one else but us. It is important that we show others how we can help children in the Third World.'

The sense of giving and of building an emotional connection to the people with whom they are volunteering is central to many young people's ideals. In a study in northern Thailand Mary Conran asked young people about their most memorable experiences of volunteering with children. Lea, a 21-year-old Norwegian volunteer, told her: 'I think for me it has been holding the kids' hands and, like one of them grabbed my arm and it is just things like that that makes it worth it' (Conran, 2011, p. 1460). This comment was strikingly similar to one made by a young volunteer in Cusco, Peru called Sabrina, who told the researcher about the difference she made and the rewards she felt: 'It's their smiles', she said, smiling herself, 'it is so wonderful to see how happy they are with even just a little bit of attention'. Sabrina wanted to work here – helping truant children gain the social and academic skills to reintegrate into the national school system – in order to do 'something good' with children (Sinervo, 2011, p. 5).

For many, this emotional connection is the unique currency they bring to the project and which differentiates them from tourists who want escapism and hedonism without emotional involvement (Sinervo, 2011; Polus and Bidder, 2016). 17-year-old Chris from South Africa said:

> Like traveling you are just kind of watching it like window shopping in a way. But by volunteering ... you get to, like I am doing, go to the schools, see the children, see the villages, see the rural life and also meet the people and get involved with the people ... you actually get to participate in the children's lives.... You get to know them when they are just being themselves. And that's the real experience, that's the real nice part.
>
> (Conran, 2011, p. 1460)

For other young people working in a poorer country is also a form of political solidarity and many young people who volunteer do so not just to travel or to help others but also to challenge political injustices. As many commentators have pointed out, young volunteers 'tend to be middle and upper class, well-educated and globally conscious individuals who sympathize with popular global justice agendas such as anti-globalization, anti-neoliberalism, and anti-imperialism' (Conran, 2011, p. 1456). The young people who volunteer overseas often see themselves as global citizens more concerned with tackling international problems such as climate change or wealth inequalities than their national identity. They are ideologically committed to challenging the ways that poorer countries come off worse in trade deals and international treaties, getting blamed for their own problems and inability to pull themselves out of poverty without external support. Lyons *et al.* (2012, p. 369) claim that gap year volunteering can be a form of 'revolution' which changes political and personal identity. They quote a young Australian man who had recently returned from a gap year tutoring Hazara refugees who said: 'For the vast part of my life, I've been very proud to be Australian. Unfortunately, we have a form of government that has made me very distressed about being Australian.' Mary Conran argues that this awakening of political and social consciences may be one of the best aspects of working as a volunteer overseas and that many young people become more politically active in their home countries and become drawn into other forms of public service. She quotes Ute, a 22-year-old female German volunteer:

> By experiencing a different culture and a different way of life you can better yourself and also take it back to your own country and teach other people, get involved in other organizations.... By actually getting involved you kind of explore for yourself, get your own opinion and take it back to others, so they might be able to get a different perspective.
>
> (Conran, 2011, p. 1466)

For some young people volunteer tourism may well be life-changing, leading to new skills, new careers, new ways of interacting with people, or new ways of thinking about one's self. Jen, a 22-year-old American woman, said that Thailand is the 'land of smiles, I will miss that. When I reach America, I am going to hate it, everyone walks with their heads down, they don't look at each other. Lots of love, there is so much love here. I want to bring that back with me' (2011, p. 1460). For Jen, volunteer tourism is an acknowledgement of her privilege – she wants to give her time and commitment abroad but also to change her home society. Others come back more politically aware and committed, less materialistic, and more aware of the social and economic imbalances between and within countries (Freidus, 2017). Glynn, a 24-year-old Englishman, claimed that 'The difference … is that when you travel around and see the poverty or the underdevelopment, you kind of feel arrogant swaggering around with your backpack and throwing money and sort of carry on … it's more of wanting to put something positive there rather than walking happily and laying around there' (Conran, 2011, p. 1467).

Despite the claims of altruism or political solidarity however, some researchers have seen the voluntourist experience as more ambiguous. Many of these volunteers are also motivated not only by what they can give but also by what they get out of the experience. As Wearing (2001) has argued, volunteers usually expect a bilateral experience, hoping and desiring to be of benefit to the host community, especially to the children, but also hoping that it will contribute to their personal development. This may be through learning to speak the native language (one reason for the popularity of volunteering in South America), gaining experience of NGO work in order to boost future career prospects, developing new skills and abilities, meeting like-minded volunteers as well as the excitement and fun of travelling independently (but also safely) to an unknown place (Polus and Bidder, 2016). Many of these young people have paid large amounts, sometimes several hundreds or even thousands of pounds, for their placement and it is not unreasonable to expect a concrete return on that investment when they return in the form of better language or life skills or an edge in the employment or higher education marketplaces (Lyons *et al.*, 2012). Other academics have even seen voluntourism in orphanages as a tangential way of experiencing celebrity culture in which humanitarianism, development work and the image of celebrities have coalesced into what has been described as 'vacationing like Brangelina' (Mostafanezhad, 2014, p. 1) after the Hollywood actress Angelina Jolie's humanitarian work with children. As Becki, a 20-year-old British blogger and volunteer, put it: 'If you can't look like Angelina, be like Angelina' (Mostafanezhad, 2014, p. 114). Perhaps more troubling are sites such as the *Humanitarians of Tinder* (https://humanitariansoftinder.com/) in which people feature poor children in their dating profiles to prove their humanitarian credentials and boost their romantic chances.

What about the children?

None of this is to denigrate the motivation of often dedicated and serious young people who travel overseas wanting to contribute to other societies or to improve children's

Figure 11.2 Tourist volunteers saying their goodbyes to the children at the Dream House orphanage and children's home in Sangklaburi. Thailand.

lives. Many young voluntourists acknowledge that while their intentions may have been to give something back and do good, the experience of volunteering often has a great impact on them and confers tangible benefits, whether in the form of personal growth, professional developmental or the 'love and smiles' they receive from the children they work with. As the previous section has discussed, much work has been done on the motivations and experiences of these young people (Lyons *et al.*, 2012) but there is remarkably little work on the children who are 'volunteered with' and very few research-ers have asked children directly about their experiences and feelings of these volun-teers or about the impacts on individual children's lives (Carpenter, 2015a, 2015b).

Overall, academic assessments of the volunteer/child relationship have been largely negative but there are, or might be, some potential benefits for children. Tess Guiney in her study of Cambodian orphanages (2012) found that relatively substantial amounts of resources (both emotional and material) were available to the children who lived in these orphanages and that children's English was better in the orphanages than among those outside. Furthermore, the orphanage children's exposure to people of different cultures and languages could enable them to learn about the outside world and also give them ideas about different career opportunities. In another study of Cam-bodian orphanages Ruth Emond (2009, p. 413) found that children who had been placed in one spoke of themselves as 'lucky' and believed that being an orphan was 'something to be grateful for' because it improved opportunities for education, nutrition and friendships, and decreased work demands on them. Other children in Cambodia told researchers they considered the education they got in the orphanage a privilege. One boy said: 'I felt very happy to come live here ... [because] I would be able to study' (Carpenter, 2015b, p. 89).

When researchers have asked children why they think Westerners come to visit them, the responses seem innocent and grateful – many invoking the language of care and affection. In Cusco, children spoke about the tourist volunteers:

> 'They teach us our homework', 7 year-old Rosa explained. 'They bring us things we need', Fidela, also 7 years old, added. 'They bring us gifts', clarified 10 year-old Mariana. 'The [tourist] friends teach us English,' agreed 15 year-old Carlos and his friend, 14 year-old Adrian. 'They give us affections', emphasised Estela, 8 years old. 'They play with us', other children responded.
>
> (Sinervo, 2011, pp. 1–2)

In doing so, the children recognise the benefits of interacting with foreigners and, for some, there is a novelty and value in these encounters. However, such statements are also problematic and raise questions about whether they are a learned response, desired by the volunteers, or an accurate representation of children's feelings and experiences. In her work on orphanage tourism in South Africa, Annalise Weckesser analyses the ways that children are conditioned to respond to volunteers and to other short-term tourists, turning their status as orphans into a commodity to please visitors. Weckesser talks of arriving at one orphanage and shortly afterwards being given hand-made cards by the children saying: 'I love you Mama Anna' and 'Bless you Mama Anna' even though they hardly knew her. In contrast the local women who worked there and had done so for some years were never given cards or such messages. She writes:

> While genuine human recognition and caring between outsiders and local children is possible, even in fleeting moments, these cards were not expressions of such connections ... but a trained affect towards visitors.... While singing, dancing and 'begging' from tourists is seen as more degrading, such drawings are perceived as wholly benign and endearing, but they are on a similar continuum of young people learning various (affective) performances for charitable gifts.
>
> (Weckesser, 2011, p. 223)

Other children, regardless of their status, learn traditional dancing and singing and put on fundraising shows at orphanages in return for tourist donations as part of a supposedly 'authentic' and mutually beneficial tourist experience. In other instances children themselves are highly attuned to the need to 'present' as orphans and try to use it to their advantage when pressing a case for support, sponsorship or employment.

Children may actively try to engender longer term, ongoing relationships with Western volunteers. In Cusco, children expressed a desire to keep in touch with volunteers once they had left and still talked of particular volunteers with affection. One way of trying to solidify these relationship commitments was by asking foreign volunteers to become their godparents. This involved both material gifts such as first communion dresses but also represented an attempt to bring volunteers into a kinship framework with mutual obligations and reciprocal duties. As Sinervo puts it: 'This connection was motivated by both economics ... and by a desire to recognise a meaningful relationship with a foreigner' (2011, p. 12). Such a relationship however could be easily misunder-stood and Sinervo goes on to discuss foreigners buying the dresses or making one-off donations but then not keeping in touch, thereby fulfilling one part of the relationship but not the other, leaving the children bemused and sometimes upset.

While applauding the children's attempts to maximise their own advantages from these encounters, and to acknowledge that there is potential benefit in them, it is also undeniable that there is a large imbalance of power between the child and the volun-teer on many levels, and this can undermine all good intentions. Several children in South Africa complained to Annalise Weckesser about what they perceived as exploita-tion: tourists and volunteers who came to visit but then only gave them sweets, as if they were young children, or those who took pictures and promised to send money back but never did. For most children in these orphanages, their choices remained limited and, as in the case of Cusco, while children try to form ongoing or continuing relationships with these volunteers, they are rarely successful and have no leverage over these Westerners, who retain the choice whether to keep in touch, to return, and whether a longer term relationship is possible or desirable.

Reciprocal altruism or child exploitation?

Questions have to be asked therefore about the impacts of voluntourism. Clearly it has become a market and within this market orphanages have particular appeal. Working with orphans (especially in exotic countries) is much more popular than other forms of volunteering: teaching adults English, for example, or community empowerment and working with young people are significantly less likely to attract volunteers than crèches for vulnerable children or orphanages. Individual volunteers may not be responsible for the creation of this market, but they buy into it, choosing their experi-ence based on their preferred destination and the types of people they would like to work with rather than need. In South Africa one community leader told Weckesser about his attempts to take tourists and volunteers to a high school and projects with teenagers but was met with little interest. He told her that voluntourists want to see and work with children: 'the younger the better. And who can blame them? The little kiddies are so cute.' He then went on to say that if tourists 'want to see lions, you find lions. If they want to see orphans, you find orphans' (Weckesser, 2011, pp. 206, 218).

The orphan represents the archetypal innocent victim: depicted alone, abandoned, with no one to help, without a history and without any political, social or economic context. The orphan challenges ideals of a 'good' childhood as a safe space where chil-dren live within a protective family and the desire to help such children is presented as purely and uncomplicatedly humanitarian (Ennew and Milne, 1989; Holland, 1992; Burman, 1999). Yet critics of the ways that poor and orphaned children outside the West are depicted have argued that the image of the orphaned African or Asian child positions such children as helpless victims and simultaneously stigmatises their parents, families and communities as deficient caretakers. In doing so, such images confer upon the West the 'duty' to intervene and provide the care for these children that their own communities cannot (Burman, 1999). Weckesser argues that orphans become, like the animals the tourists want to visit on safari, 'part of a naturalised terrain of South Africa, which in effect dehistorizes and depoliticises the structural causes underlying such inequalities ... images of orphans become part of the timeless, unchanging landscape of (South) African poverty and hardships' (Weckesser, 2011, p. 219). Furthermore, 'the orphan' reinforces the complacent certainty of the superior position of the West and bolsters colonial metaphors of passive, incapable and infantilised places and people. Images of orphans demand not a critical assessment of the impacts of colonialism, historical injustices and structural inequalities but the need for Western intervention in the form of volunteers 'saving' the innocent, deserving and grateful children of Asia and Africa. As Patricia Holland (1992, p. 150) has argued in her analysis of the aid iconography:

> The wide eyes of the needy dark-skinned child look reproachfully out from the news pages and from those advertisements that solicit rather than seduce. The ragged child who is not ashamed to plead so dominates the available imagery of Africa, Latin America and the Indian subcontinent that the whole of that vast area beyond Western culture seems in itself to be a place of distress and childish subservience.

Not only do orphanages reinforce negative stereotypes of poorer children but they can also be harmful in other ways. Some of the earliest criticisms of voluntourism came from academics worried about the promotion of volunteering in orphanages, pointing out that institutionalised care had proved repeatedly to be disastrous for children in the West and that orphanages there were now non-existent, replaced by foster family care or small home settings which replicated family life as best they could. There is, it has been claimed, no such thing as a 'good orphanage' and 'even in a well-run facility, children do not develop normally' (Rosenberg, 2018; although see Rutter *et al.* (1998) for a more nuanced discussion of the long-term impact of orphanages). Knowing the detrimental effects of institutional care on young children, Linda Richter and Amy Norman have been highly critical of the promotion of orphanage tourism in South Africa, and expressed concern about the impacts on already vulnerable children of caregivers who come for short periods, shower the children with love and affection, and then vanish. This, they worried, might exacerbate early damage, and lead to disordered attachment.

> Children tend to approach all adults with the same level of sociability and affection, often clinging to caregivers, even those encountered for the first time moments before. Children in more orthodox family environments of the same age tend to be wary towards newcomers and show differential affection and trust towards their intimate caregivers. Institutionalized children will thus tend to

manifest the same indiscriminate affectionate behaviour towards volunteers. After a few days or weeks, this attachment is broken when the volunteer leaves and a new attachment forms when the next volunteer arrives.

(Richter and Norman, 2010, pp. 224–225)

Although Carpenter (2015b) has suggested that this form of psychological damage may not be the case in Cambodia where children are often older when they enter orphanages, it does raise questions about the respective vulnerabilities of volunteer and child and whose needs orphanage tourism are promoting.

Richter and Norman also condemn the way that orphanage tourism can create the very problem it sets out to alleviate. One consistent finding in the literature on children who live in the orphanages is how few of them are actually orphans and how many have one or more parent living. The United Nations Children's Fund, UNICEF, carried out a study of orphanages in Liberia in 2006 and found that 98 per cent of children there had at least one living parent, while a similar study in Sri Lanka suggested that 92 per cent of 'orphans' also had a parent still alive (Rosenberg, 2018). Discussing 'AIDS-orphans' in South Africa, Richter and Norman (2010) argue that the word 'orphan' is used to describe children with either one or both parents dead, thereby inflating the numbers and the scale of the crisis and, indeed, the 'need' for volunteers to work with these children. They estimate that more than 80 per cent of children in South Africa defined as orphans have a surviving parent. In Cambodia the number of

Figure 11.3 A young white woman with a camera, surrounded by African children.

children without living parents, and therefore in need of an orphanage, has decreased dramatically in recent years even as the number of orphanages (and orphanage tourism) has increased (Carpenter, 2015a).

Many of these children still have living parents, or extended family, who would be willing to care for them but who feel compelled to put them in an orphanage to ensure the best possible education for them. Orphanages therefore stand accused of breaking up the extended network of carers that lie at the heart of many non-Western kinship systems. Rather than providing support and help in the community which would allow children to remain within it, viewing children as abandoned or orphaned represents 'a cultural blunder [that] can lead to precarious outcomes for children as they can be taken from extended family members and placed in institutions that isolate them from their social networks. These fissures can be irreparable' (Freidus, 2017, pp. 1307–1308). Furthermore, it can destabilise families who may decide to send children to orphanages for better opportunities and to alleviate their poverty, forcing them to make judgements about whether the best interests of their children lie in educational and material resources or in remaining with their families.

Despite this, orphanages remain a popular focus for international development and it is easy to fundraise for them. As Tina Rosenberg argues (2018), few governments are willing to pay for anti-poverty programmes which could support whole families or communities, while money for orphanages appears to 'drop from the sky'. This is most apparent in the case of Haiti where 30,000 children live in orphanages which received $100 million a year in foreign donations in 2017. In that same year the entire US aid budget to Haiti was $200 million. These orphanages received five times the budget of Haiti's social affairs ministry, and 130 times the country's child protection budget, leaving some to argue that there is not an 'orphan crisis' in Haiti but an 'orphanage crisis' (Lumos, 2017, p. 4). By funnelling money into such institutions a situation is created whereby those designated as orphans become materially and educationally better off than those who stay within their communities and with their families. Weckesser describes a locally run project in South Africa with two houses, one for orphans and one for children with unemployed and struggling parents. The local pastor told her: 'You should have seen this place [the orphanage] at Christmas. Everyone wants to donate to my [orphaned] kids here. We got a soccer net, more toys than you can count ... and they all got new outfits. But next door, those kids got nothing' (2011, p. 213).

Orphanage tourism is now operated as a business, and volunteers are charged sometimes thousands of pounds for placements and are told that it will have tangible benefits for them in terms of their education and their own personal growth (Reas, 2013). Where this money goes however is controversial. In some cases it goes into the project and is used as part of the running costs, while in others it pays for food and accommodation for the volunteer. In some instances local NGOs admit that the money the volunteers bring in is much more beneficial than their labour, yet this is rejected by volunteers who feel that this undermines their sense of purpose and that their time is the real donation and their fees are simply a way of facilitating this (Sinervo, 2011). In other cases companies take large amounts of money but fail to deliver the 'experience' paid for (Richter and Norman, 2010), leading some to ask whether working at an orphanage is 'worth a $1000 dollars a day'.

It is unfair to blame individual Western volunteers for this situation. For many, their motives are simpler and come out of a desire to do good work or to make connections. In many countries, children, families and governments are impoverished and there is no, or very little, state support for vulnerable children. This makes voluntourism a potentially useful resource, although the lack of regulation, and the delegation of social welfare services to unqualified outsiders, is troubling. It can be argued that young Westerners themselves are exploited by the companies set up to facilitate their encounters: they are continually told by those who organise such placements that they are useful, valued and helping those in need – as the founder of one such charity, Ambassadors for Children, said: 'If a kid can be held for a couple of days, you're able to make a small difference' (Richter and Norman, 2010, p. 224). But this can be questioned on many levels. First, as Tricia Barnett, Director of Tourism Concern, has written: 'If you're going to work with children in an orphanage, [how will they] understand what you're trying to do when you don't speak their language and you don't stay long enough to form a relationship? … what does it mean to the child?' (Richter and Norman, 2010, p. 224). Second, the nature of volunteer work with children tends to be low skilled and volunteers need not have any particular qualifications or skills, other than an ability to speak English. Given the levels of unemployment in sub-Saharan Africa or in countries like Cambodia, it might be argued that volunteer tourists are taking jobs or training opportunities away from local young people, many of whom would appreciate the opportunity of having regular meals, decent accommodation and work experience (Richter and Norman, 2010). Yet orphanages, and indeed other forms of voluntourism, have created a situation where, if local charities and NGOs hired locals to do this work, they would stand accused of spending money, but by accepting paying Western volunteers to do it they are raising money.

Concluding thoughts

Claims of replicating the power imbalances and social inequalities of colonialism are perhaps too harsh to put on the shoulders of individual young, possibly inexperienced, volunteers who, it is apparent, seek out roles in orphanages overseas for a variety of reasons and motivations, including idealism and altruism, and also in recognition of their own privilege. At first glance, working with children in orphanages overseas might seem a straightforwardly laudable action which should be widely encouraged. Yet as this chapter has shown, it is a highly complex and even controversial area which has attracted a great deal of trenchant academic criticism, and it is clear that volunteering in orphanages has many unintended consequences for the volunteer and the children with whom they work as well as for perceptions of childhood throughout the non-Western world. It is necessary therefore to evaluate these encounters on many levels, and this chapter has argued that individual encounters and emotions, while often genuine and heartfelt, have to be looked at more critically. In an ideal world such encounters should be mutually beneficial to both orphans and volunteers, but this ignores the role of history, politics and power imbalances and may reinforce ideas of the non-Western child as passive, helpless and in need of rescue.

References

Burman, E. (1999) Appealing and appalling children. *Psychoanalytic Studies*, 1(3), 25–301.

Carpenter, K. (2015a) Childhood studies and orphanage tourism in Cambodia. *Annals of Tourism Research*, 55(4), 15–27.

Carpenter, K. (2015b) Continuity, complexity and reciprocity in a Cambodian orphanage. *Children & Society*, 29(2), 85–94.

Conran, M. (2011) 'They really love me!' Intimacy in volunteer tourism. *Annals of Tourism Research*, 38(4), 1454–1473.

Emond, R. (2009) 'I am all about the future world': Cambodian children's views on their status as orphans. *Children & Society*, 23(6), 407–417.

Ennew, J. and Milne, B. (1989) *The Next Generation. Lives of Third World Children.* London: Zed Books.

Freidus, A. L. (2017) Unanticipated outcomes of voluntourism among Malawi's orphans *Journal of Sustainable Tourism*, 25(9), 1306–1321.

Guiney, T. (2012) Orphanage tourism in Cambodia: when residential care centres become tourist attractions. *Pacific News*, 38, 9–14. Available at www.pacific-news.de/pn38/PN38_TG.pdf.

Holland, P. (1992) *What is a Child?* London: Virago.

Lyons, K., Hanley, J., Wearing, S. and Neil, J. (2012) Gap year volunteer tourism. Myths of global citizenship? *Annals of Tourism Research*, 39(1), 361–378.

Lumos (2017) *Funding Haitian Orphanages at the Cost of Children's Rights*. Available at https://lumos.contentfiles.net/media/assets/file/Funding_Haiti_Orphanages_Executive_Summary_Digital_Version.pdf.

Mostafanezhad, M. (2014) Volunteer tourism and the popular humanitarian gaze. *Geoforum*, 54, 111–118.

Polus, R. C. and Bidder, C. (2016) Volunteer tourists' motivation and satisfaction: a case of Batu Puteh Village Kinabatangan Borneo, *Procedia – Social and Behavioral Sciences*, 224, pp. 308–316.

Reas, P. J. (2013) 'Boy, have we got a vacation for you': orphanage tourism in Cambodia and the commodification and objectification of the orphanaged child. *Thammasat Review*, 16, 121–140.

Richter, L. M. and Norman, A. (2010) AIDS orphan tourism: a threat to young children in residential care. *Vulnerable Children and Youth Studies*, 5(3), 217–229.

Rosenberg, T. (2018) The business of voluntourism: do Western do-gooders actually do harm? *Guardian*, 13 September. Available from www.theguardian.com/news/2018/sep/13/the-business-of-voluntourism-do-western-do-gooders-actually-do-harm.

Rutter, M. and the ERA Research Team (1998) Developmental catch-up and deficit following adoption after severe global early privation. *Journal of Child Psychology and Psychiatry and Allied Disciplines*, 39(4), 465–476.

Sinervo, A. (2011) Connection and disillusion: the moral economy of volunteer tourism in Cusco, Peru. *Childhoods Today*, 5(2), 1–23.

Wearing, S. (2001) *Volunteer Tourism: Experiences that Make a Difference*. Wallingford, Oxon: CABI.

Weckesser, A. (2011) *Girls, Gifts and Gender – The Materiality of Care in Rural South Africa*. Unpublished PhD Thesis, School of Health and Social Studies, Warwick University.

12 Eugenics and the lives of disabled children

Kieron Sheehy

Introduction

What is eugenics, and how is it relevant today?

At the beginning of the twentieth century, a particular way of thinking about the value of children and their families established itself in society. This way of thinking was known as eugenics (with its roots in the Greek *eu*, meaning good/well, and *genic*, meaning breeding). It made judgements about the worth of children, and these judgements influenced policies about how children should be treated. This chapter will explore historical and contemporary aspects of eugenic thinking, including the role of technology. It will highlight the pervasiveness of this way of thinking and how it relates to the stigma that continues to have a profound impact on the lives of disabled children around the world. This chapter uses the term disabled children, rather than children with disabilities. This reflects a social model of disability, developed by disabled people, that highlights how people are disabled by factors in society (as discussed in Chapter 10). These factors might include physical barriers, cultural beliefs, attitudes and policies.

Eugenics was a perspective, a way of thinking, that determined how society should respond to children who were labelled as defective' or 'unfit', for example, disabled children and those with learning difficulties. As we will see, these decisions included the enforced segregation and long-term incarceration of children, involuntary sterilisation of young people, the withholding of life-saving care from infants and even, in some countries, a targeted extermination of disabled or 'defective' children (Sheehy, 2010).

It is tempting to think that this way of thinking about disabled children has long disappeared, yet its influence is still shaping the lives and experiences of many children around the world. It originated over 100 years ago, when Francis Galton promoted a vision of British society in which social progress could be accelerated by the controlled breeding of 'better' people. These eugenic marriages could 'do providentially, quickly and kindly' what nature did 'blindly, slowly and ruthlessly' (Galton (1904) cited in Porter, 2005, p. 167) by reducing the weaker elements as the supposedly better classes proliferated. Galton saw this as a way in which society could address issues such as poverty, unemployment and crime. This solution became popular because children deemed 'unfit', for example, those with learning difficulties, were believed to be born with 'inborn errors' that would inevitably lead them to have 'squalid' and 'worthless' lives (Porter, 1991, p, 167). Over 100 years later, a Director of the New Schools Network and appointee to the UK government's Office of Students (the regulator of higher education in England established in 2018) commented on how society should address similar issues in the near future through a 'soon-to-be-available' technology.

> To discover which embryos, in vitro, are likely to be very intelligent. ... I was proposing, sort of half-seriously that it should be made available on the NHS to the people at the bottom of the economic and IQ scale, so they could make sure, not compulsorily, it should be made available for free for those people who fall into this category [the poor or long term unemployed] ... so they can guarantee, should they want it, that they'll have intelligent chil-dren.... This would be the effective way to break the chain between entrenched poverty and lack of social mobility ...
> ... for people who are both poor and have a very low IQ. ...
> To make this technology available, for free, for the very poorest and the most stupid.
>
> (Young, *The Spectator*, The view from 22, 31 March 2016)

The idea here is to allow couples to fertilise numerous eggs and then select, through a genetic test, the very brightest one for implanting into their mother. As with Galton, once again there is the idea of achieving better children, for a better society, through a 'quick and kind' method that is presented as more efficient than nature alone. In recent years the development of new technologies, and beliefs about what may soon be possible, has allowed society's decision-makers to once again consider tackling social problems by avoiding particular children (such as those who are deemed less intelligent) from coming into existence. This has led some commenters to conclude that:

> So, some 130 years after Britain gave the world the idea of perfecting humanity, we are once again at the cutting edge of this troubled science. For good or ill, eugenics is back.
>
> (Nelson, 2016)

The rationale for current and near-future decisions about the lives of disabled children, and concerns about these decisions, appear to have their roots within the eugenics movement. In order to gain insights into the future that might exist for children with learning difficulties, we need to begin by looking to the past.

A brief history of eugenics

Charles Darwin's *On the Origin of Species* (1859), and his later book *The Descent of Man* (1871), inspired *Social Darwinism*. Social Darwinism took some of Darwin's biological ideas such as natural selection and applied them to understanding human society, developing the idea of 'survival of the fittest' (Paul, 1998). Francis Galton, a cousin of Darwin's and a Social Darwinist, founded what became known as *human eugenics* [from *eu* = 'good', *genos*, 'race', or stock]. A core belief was that those people who did best in society (i.e. those who were of a higher class, wealthier or in positions of power) were inherently 'fitter', so that 'eminent men were naturally superior and superior men are naturally eminent' (Miller, 1962, p. 155). From this perspective, the social hierarchies in society were a natural outcome of inherited natural ability, and to improve society we needed to encourage the better classes to thrive and not be swamped by their inferiors – the lower orders and races. Therefore, social welfare, for example, to support the poor or disabled, was misguided because it could interfere with the natural order of things and allow the unfit to multiply. The eugenics movement became influential worldwide.

Galton developed tests to measure the inborn differences between people. He used these anthropometric tests, on large numbers of people, to assess human abilities, including memory, perception and reaction time. The measurement of human abilities and their categorisation became a central feature of eugenic practices. This included developing measures of intellectual abilities and fostering discrimination, often relating these measures to an assumed hierarchy of races, gender and categories of ability. He was clear about the intellectual superiority of white races and the inferiority of women who were in 'all their capacities to be inferior to men' (The Dangerous Women Project, 2019); the rarity of their social achievement confirmed this for him. Those people who were located at the stigmatised intersection of race, class, gender and disability were particularly at risk of being deemed unfit or less worthy members of society. These measurements, categorisations and prejudices could be applied to deciding how children should be treated.

Segregating children

In America during the early 1900s, fitter families and better baby competitions became popular. These were organised by people such as Dr Florence Sherbon, an influential physician keen to promote 'good' genes. Families who did well in these competitions received a medal that read 'Yea, I have goodly heritage' (Derrell, 2014).

Conversely, babies and children who were less fit and presumably did not enter such competitors could be labelled by Dr Sherbon as 'mental defectives', employing categories of mental deficiency that became used internationally.

> Mental deficient(s) are commonly divided into three classes: idiots, who never leave infancy, ... imbeciles, who fall within a mental age range of 36 to 83 months ...; morons, or high-grade defectives, who may have a mental age of 7 to 12 years.
>
> (Derrell, 2014, p. 27)

Figure 12.1 American Fittest Families Competition.

In her popular book *The Family in Health and in Illness* (1937), Dr Sherbon stated that these 'defective strains' should be dealt with through segregation and sterilization (Sherbon (1937) cited in Derrell, 2014, p. 27). The belief that these children should be segregated from society was a popular one, illustrated by a British newspaper's commentary on the issue.

> One very important thing is that the idiot child should not be allowed to play about or mix with other children who are healthy. He cannot share their games, he cannot enjoy their companionship, and he can only feel his sense of inferiority. If he is too idiotic to feel that, then he should be kept from others because his company would be very unwholesome for the healthy-minded ones. Confinement to an asylum is the most humane and kind treatment for idiots, beyond a doubt.
>
> (*News of the World*, 23 August 1900)

Being identified as mentally deficient, or 'feebleminded', had profound consequences for disabled children. The segregation of children became an important social project in the United Kingdom, and the 1908 Royal Commission on the Feeble Minded confirmed the links between being feebleminded and criminality, promiscuity and degeneracy. As one contributor, the eminent psychiatrist Sir James Crichton Browne, stated, 'the feeble-minded are our social rubbish [who] should be swept up' (Merricks, 2014, p. 123). 'Sweeping up' these children was not always straightforward, as they might look the same as anyone else and remain a hidden danger within the community (Sarason Doni cited in Fido and Potts, 1989). Subsequently, the 1913 Mental Deficiency Act entrusted local authorities with the task of identifying children and young people who were labelled 'moral defectives', 'feebleminded', 'idiots' or 'imbeciles'. Throughout the decades that followed, young people with learning difficulties were identified and placed in large colonies, asylums and residential institutions. The names of these institutions changed from colonies and asylums to 'mental handicap' hospitals, but the notion of segregating them from society remained. For example, Evelyn King describes how, in 1951, she was given an intelligence test and classified as an imbecile. At this time special schools had begun to offer education for some children who were 'educationally subnormal' but other children were deemed 'ineducable'. This was why Evelyn was sent away, at five years of age, to a large mental handicap hospital.

[S]ometimes I were just a bit frightened because they get right strict and funny with you, you know. Just had to keep your mouth shut. But we just get punished and everything.... And I used to be scared stiff. I remember I couldn't use a knife and fork then. I can now, but I never used to. I used to use a spoon and if I spilled something, like tea.... Sometimes they would say, 'if you do this again I want to see your mothers and fathers again, I won't have this.' So we had to be careful what we say to them. I didn't like it in them days.... It used to make you upset, you know.

(Humphries and Gordon, 1992, pp. 89–90)

The practice of separating children with learning difficulties from their families persisted for many years. This separation often occurred shortly after birth and coercive techniques were developed to overcome resistance from the parents (Sheehy, 2010). At around the same time that Evelyn was being assessed, hospital doctors were following Dr Anderson Aldrich's approach (published 1947 in Sheehy, 2013) for successfully removing 'newborn Mongols' (an old term for Down's syndrome) from their family. The baby was taken from the mother for a spurious reason, and the father (once he had been convinced by the physician and possibly a clergyman) then told the mother why their infant's removal was in the best interests of the family. The separation would prevent a 'long series of family difficulties' (p. 37), and the father was told to emphasise the negative effect the child would have on the family's 'social standing' (p. 39). The mother merely had to acquiesce to arrangements the physician and her husband had put in place, and the infant was taken away to an institution (Sheehy, 2010).

These dramatic examples might be viewed as merely chilling historical events. However, they are underpinned by negative attitudes towards, and the stigmatisation of, disabled children. The term 'stigma' (Goffman, 1963) indicates a situation in which an individual is 'disqualified from full social acceptance' (Fitzpatrick, 2008, p. 24). An undesirable attribute is believed to be possessed by a child, which can result in negative responses to the child. There is extensive evidence that these attitudes continue to exist, and that the stigmatisation of disabled children and those with learning difficulties can still be found in different cultures and countries around the world, as considered earlier by Jonathan Rix (Chapter 10).

Across parts of Europe and the Baltic regions disabled children and their families experience discrimination and 'harmful stigma' (UNICEF, 2005), and long-term institutionalisation of children still occurs (UNICEF, 2015). Studies from African counties report that disabled children are stigmatised in many ways, and are the sources of children's exclusion from school and society (Nkomo, 2018). In Indonesia, the fourth largest nation in the world, stigma and prejudice against disabled children are relatively commonplace (Wibowo and Muin, 2018), often leading them to being invisible in society (Komardjaja, 2005). This stigmatisation of children can arise through beliefs in taboo or karma (Riany *et al.*, 2016), and can extend by association to the children's parents and teachers (Budiyanto *et al.*, 2019). A child's physical or intellectual impairment can be seen as retribution for the wrongs of ancestors, parental misdeeds or punishment by God (Rohwerder, 2018). These beliefs are not confined to African and Asian countries of the Global South but are found across the Global North as well. A famous example of this occurred when Glenn Hoddle, then England Football team manager, expressed his belief that

> You and I have been physically given two hands and two legs and half-decent brains. Some people have not been born like that for a reason. The karma is working from another lifetime.... What you sow, you have to reap.
>
> (Arlidge and Wintour, 1999)

So, while there is evidence that attitudes towards children with disabilities are becoming more positive in many contexts and national policies (Rix *et al.*, 2013; Walker and Scior, 2013), discriminatory beliefs towards children with learning difficulties (also known as intellectual disabilities) appear to be ongoing and ubiquitous. A study of 88 countries across Africa, Asia, Southern and Central America and in Russia found that there was an 'active desire' to segregate children with intellectual disabilities (Scior *et al.* (2015) cited in Rohwerder, 2018). As explored in Chapter 10, practice with children and young people in the UK and other Global North countries often involves separating disabled children from their peers. In Rohwerder's study, the desire for segregation reflected 'deep rooted prejudice' related to stigmatising beliefs. The consequences of these negative attitudes might be discerned in disabled children being three to four times more likely to be victims of violence than their non-disabled peers (Jones *et al.*, 2012) and the incidence of hate crimes towards disabled young people (Fyson and Kitson (2010) cited in Walker and Scior, 2013). However, societies can also respond to disabled children in ways that are more extreme than segregation or social ostracism.

Beyond segregation

Although societies have developed and progressed in many profoundly positive ways over the past century, particular ways of thinking about disabled children appear to remain. These ways of thinking continue to be expressed in social relationships and actions, and utilise the technologies and actions that are available, accessible and sanctioned at the time. For example, surgical techniques for the sterilisation of individuals developed during the nineteenth century (FPA The Sexual Health Company, 2010) and subsequently Galton advocated the use of this new technology for the compulsory sterilisation of those who were identified as 'unfit'. This eugenic perspective underpinned Winston Churchill's (1910) argument that

> the unnatural and increasingly rapid growth of the feebleminded classes, coupled with a steady restriction amongst all the thrifty, energetic and superior stocks constitutes a race danger. I feel that the source from which the stream of madness is fed should be cut off and sealed up before another year has passed.
>
> (International Churchill Society, 2011)

In 1907 compulsory sterilisation for eugenic purposes was legalised in the United States of America and the sterilisation of women and men with intellectual disabilities became a common, legal practice across Europe, the United States of America and Canada (Sheehy, 2010). In Germany in 1933, Hitler's new government enacted their Eugenics Sterilisation Law, and by 1939 approximately 300,000 compulsory sterilisations had taken place (Kevles, 1985). Compulsory, and involuntary, sterilisation was practised extensively in the USA until the 1960s and elsewhere until the 1970s (Tilley *et al.*, 2012). While sterilisation did not achieve a compulsory status in the UK, the practice did occur. For example, Tilley *et al.* (2012) give the account of 'Anita', who was sterilised without her knowledge at the age of 14 (during the early 1970s),having been told that her appendix had been removed.

Sterilisation was not the only technological solution to the social 'problem' of disabled children, and more immediate 'solutions' were discussed in Britain (Porter, 1991) and enacted elsewhere. It is estimated that between 1939 and 1945 approximately 200,000 inmates of institutions for the disabled, including children with learning disabilities, were given lethal injections, gassed or starved to death in Nazi Germany (Burleigh (1994) cited in Mackintosh, 1998). The horror of these and other atrocities led to a greatly reduced popularity for anything associated with, or labelled as, eugenics after World War II. Yet, as we have seen, negative attitudes towards disability remained and so it is perhaps not unexpected that lethal responses, as opposed to segregation, towards children with intellectual disabilities still occurred.

One way in which this happened was through withholding life-saving in special care nurseries (Duff and Campbell, 1973), which in 1975 was described as 'rapidly gaining status as "good medical practice"' (Robertson, 1975). This practice became headline news in the USA with the infamous 'Baby Doe' case, in which a child with Down's syndrome was starved, and consequently died of pneumonia and dehydration in April

Figure 12.2 'We don't stand alone', a 1930s Nazi poster promoting eugenics. The shield says, 'Law for the Prevention of Offspring with Hereditary Disease'. The other flags indicate the other countries that use (left) or are considering using (bottom and right) sterilisation of the 'unfit'.

1982 (Diamandopoulos and Green, 2018). Prosecutions for withholding medical care in these situations were rare (Evans, 1981).

Outside of hospitals and institutions, across the world the lives of stigmatised children remain at risk within their own families and communities. In some cases, the stigmatisation and shame these children are believed to bring are implicated as important factors in infanticide and 'mercy killings'. These can happen at birth or years afterwards – the rationale for these killings includes beliefs that the child will bring misfortune to the family, or that the child would be 'better off dead' (United Nations, 2005).

> Often called 'mercy killings' such murders are usually a response to societal beliefs about disability and lack of social support systems for individuals with disability and their family, not the actual physical condition of the child him or herself. In 'mercy killings' a parent or caretaker justifies withholding basic life sustaining supports (usually food, water and/or medication) or actively takes the child's life through suffocation, strangulation or some other means, with the intention of 'ending suffering'.
>
> (United Nations, 2005, p. 6)

In rural areas in Ghana, Togo, Sierra Leone, Niger and Guinea, the ritual killing of disabled children has been noted, away from the risk of detection by officials (Kassah *et al.*, 2012; Njelesani *et al.*, 2018). Some commenters have stated that these killings, often of children labelled as 'evil' and 'spirit children', is increasing (Revd Fr. Akosah (2011) cited in Kassah *et al.*, 2012). When children are not directly killed, disabled women in northern Ghana described how children can be hidden so that no one will know about them and they will eventually die through neglect (Nepveux (2004) cited in Kassah *et al.*, 2012). In many African countries disabled girls are 'doubly disadvantaged' and are much more likely than boys to be abandoned in this way or killed at birth (Rohwerder, 2018).

Compelling evidence from many countries indicates that disabled children and those with intellectual disabilities are at risk owing to stigma and negative beliefs (United Nations, 2005). The United Nations International Children's Emergency Fund (UNICEF) conducted extensive research into children's lives around the world and concluded that, currently,

> Children with disabilities are one of the most marginalized and excluded groups in society. Facing daily discrimination in the form of negative attitudes, lack of adequate policies and legislation, they are effectively barred from realizing their rights to healthcare, education, and even survival.
>
> (UNICEF, 2019)

Modern technologies and the future of disabled children

We are now in a period where technology is able to screen unborn foetuses in detailed ways, and where mapping the human genome allows for the identification of an increasing number of features of the unborn child. In Chapter 2 (this volume), Heather Montgomery explored the question of differing perspectives on the unborn, including the impact of new medical technologies. The question is raised here of whether the previously discussed, and apparently widely held, negative beliefs about disabled children and their worth in society will impact upon the use of these new technologies. Some disability activists have been concerned that these technologies might risk a resurgence of eugenics.

> Disabled people are under threat for their very existence in our modern technological societies. Medical science feels able to flex its muscles and power to abolish all life where the unborn foetus may be imperfect or impaired.
>
> (Rock, 1996, p. 121)

An example which illustrates this concern is the use of antenatal screening for Down's syndrome in Iceland. Down's syndrome is a genetic disorder in which children have three copies of chromosome 21. They are likely to experience difficulties in learning to varying degrees and, due to recent improvements in care, their general health and longevity have improved significantly (Diamandopoulos and Green, 2018). In 2005, Nuchal translucency (NT) screening that can identify foetuses with Down's syndrome was promoted to mothers in Iceland (Gottfredsdóttir and Björnsdóttir, 2010). This screening became part of a process in which 100 per cent of foetuses identified with Down's syndrome were terminated (Gottfredsdóttir and Björnsdóttir, 2010). The Chair of Iceland's National Federation for People with Disabilities stated that

> It is deplorable that every [foetus] diagnosed [with Down's syndrome] is aborted in this country. Insufficient research has been done on the individuals who live with the defect or the views of their parents. This information has to be available before a decision is made.
>
> (Chair of Throskahja'lp, 12 August, 2005 in Gottfredsdóttir and Björnsdóttir, 2010)

There appears to be a consensus that this option enhances parental free choice, is a private matter for individuals and not a political issue. Consequently, the calls for a wider debate has not been taken up (Gottfredsdóttir and Björnsdóttir, 2010). A concern has been raised that in reality the pressure to undertake screening from social and media influences is intense, and that parents develop a sense that should take responsibility for assuring their child is 'normal' (Beck-Gernsheim (2002) cited in Gottfredsdóttir and Björnsdóttir, 2010).

Elsewhere, interview data highlight how these difficult personal choices are framed by social contexts and pressures: ' – e.g., the services available, expectations, cultural attitudes toward disability, familial and other support [*and these*] – interfere with this choice being freely made' (Thomas and Rothman, 2016, p. 409). How society views disability, expressed through the services it provides for disabled children, and the stigmatisation that might or might not exist, impacts upon the choices individuals feel they are able to make. It has been argued that, within the United Kingdom, there is a social assumption that parents want an abortion in these cases and that obstetricians offer directive advice to this end (Shakespeare (1998) cited in Love, 2017). Across England and Wales, numerous European countries and Australia, termination rates following diagnosis for Down's syndrome vary between 88 and 95 per cent (see Thomas and Rothman, 2016).

Shakespeare (1999) has distinguished between 'historical eugenics' which works at the level of a population, and 'contemporary eugenics' which works at the level of individuals and families. However, this distinction, made over 20 years ago, would appear to blur somewhat in the context of Iceland, where the society in which individual choices are made impacts so profoundly upon a potential population of disabled children.

More widely, screening for gender and other characteristics occurs (Nelson, 2016); for example, in the USA increasing numbers of parents pay to screen the gender of their potential children to ensure 'family balance' (Capelouto *et al.*, 2018). This practice supports Nelson's (2016) argument that where these services can be bought, a government is no longer required to pursue eugenics – parents will do it themselves. These cumulative individual decisions appear to be disregarded in discussions of national progress. Looking at populations and countries, the Social Progress Index (SPI) ranks nations on the extent to which they provide for their citizens. The 2017 Index ranked Iceland first for 'tolerance and inclusion' (Social Progress Imperative, 2017). This might be contrasted with the conclusion that Iceland is reported to be close to becoming the first country to not have any children with Down's syndrome (Reinders *et al.*, 2019).

This elimination of potential disabled children from society is widespread; however, other options are now developing. Emerging technologies are offering the possibilities of differentially selecting and altering children. One of these is a new gene-editing technique known as CRISPR-Cas9 (Clustered Regularly Interspaced Short Palindromic Repeats), which holds the promise of fixing faulty DNA through the genetic modification of human embryos. It appears to avoid many of the issues of previous ways of 'improving' the population's children.

> There are no deaths, no sterilisations, no abortions: just a scientifically guided conception. The potential avoidance of disease, to the betterment of humanity. So who could complain?
>
> (Nelson, 2016)

It has been claimed, though not substantiated, that some CRISPR children have already been born in China, who one day after IVF conception were protected from HIV for the rest of their lives and who will now pass on their altered genes to future generations (Peters, 2019).

There seems to be a good case for using this technology 'to rid families of monstrous genetic diseases' (Miller, 2015), and many painful life-threatening and limiting diseases might hopefully be addressed. However, there is a risk that such technologies will go beyond a therapeutic intervention and be used for enhancement (Peters, 2019), to deliver new definitions of who is healthy and who is 'unfit'.

Concluding thoughts

Over a century ago the eugenics movement defined and categorised what was healthy and normal, and consequently which children were deemed 'defective' (Sheehy, 2010). This way of thinking was used to remove disabled children from society (Wilson and Pierre, 2016). Currently we live in a world where the lives of disabled children remain widely at risk through violence and mercy killing (UNICEF, 2019), and where many parents choose that potential disabled children are not born. The creation of a new technology is welcomed, as it holds the promise of 'fixing' faulty genes and addressing life-threatening diseases and conditions (Pollack, 2015). However, 'the new genetics will enable adults to control children's identities in previously unimaginable ways' (Alderson, 2002, p. 1). Indeed, the moral and technical questions about how we treat disabled children, and improve the health of children in the population, may become 'a consumer question of who can afford it' (Kevles, 2016, p. 49). It seems likely that we will become able to improve babies, perhaps in relation to their athletic or even intellectual abilities. In this 'free market eugenics' it seems probable that the wealthy will be the first customers and that the technology's use will move away from merely addressing purported and genuine biological issues and towards delivering advantages for consumers (Kevles, 2016). The lower socioeconomic classes will become the 'genpoor class' (Gouw (2018, p. 503) cited in Peters, 2019) and, as in history, the victims of eugenics will reflect the social hierarchies and prejudices of the time. This is why the ability to modify a children's genes, 'designed to order', has been seen as 'the opening of a return to the agenda of eugenics' (Pollack, 2015).

References

Alderson, P. (2002) The promise or threat of the new genetics to children. *Bulletin of Medical Ethics*.

Arlidge, J. and Wintour, P. (1999) Hoddle's future in doubt after disabled slur. *Guardian*, 30 January. Available at www.theguardian.com/football/1999/jan/30/newsstory.sport7.

Budiyanto et al. (2019) Indonesian educators' knowledge and beliefs about teaching children with autism. *Athens Journal of Education*, 10, 1–23.

Capelouto, S. M. et al. (2018) Sex selection for non-medical indications: a survey of current preimplantation genetic screening practices among U.S. ART clinics. *Journal of Assisted Reproduction and Genetics*, 35(3), 409–416. doi: 10.1007/s10815-017-1076-2.

Derrell, A. (2014) *The Women of Reform: Kansas Eugenics*. University of Missouri-Kansas City.

Diamandopoulos, K. and Green, J. (2018) Down syndrome: an integrative review. *Journal of Neonatal Nursing*. doi: 10.1016/j.jnn.2018.01.001.

Duff, C. and Campbell, A. (1973) Moral and ethical dilemmas in the special-care nursery. *New England Journal of Medicine*, 289(17), 890–894.

Evans, D. (1981) Death and mentally retarded persons. *Mid-American Review of Sociology*, 6(2), 45–60.

Fido, R. and Potts, M. (1989) 'It's not true what was written down!' Experiences of life in a mental handicap institution. *Oral History*, autumn(2), 31–34.

Fitzpatrick, M. (2008) Stigma. *British Journal of General Practice*, (April), 294. doi: 10.3399/bjgp08X280100.

FPA The Sexual Health Company (2010) *Contraception: Past, Present and Future Factsheet*. Available at www.fpa.org.uk/factsheets/contraception-past-present-future#AREW (accessed 20 September 2019).

Goffman, E. (1963) *Stigma: Notes on the Management of the Spoiled Identity*. London: Penguin.

Gottfredsdóttir, H. and Björnsdóttir, K. (2010) 'Have you had the test?' A discourse analysis of media presentation of prenatal screening in Iceland. *Scandinavian Journal of Caring Sciences*, pp. 414–421. doi: 10.1111/j.1471-6712.2009.00727.x.

Humphries, S. and Gordon, P. (1992) *Out of Sight: The Experience of Disability 1900–1950*. Plymouth: Northcote House.

International Churchill Society (2011) Leading Churchill myths: 'Churchill's campaign against the "feeble-minded" was deliberately omitted by his biographers'. *Finest Hour*, 152, autumn. Available at https://winstonchurchill.org/publications/finest-hour/finest-hour-152/leading-churchill-myths-churchills-campaign-against-the-feeble-minded-was-deliberately-omitted-by-his-biographers/.

Jones, L. *et al.* (2012) Prevalence and risk of violence against children with disabilities: a systematic review and meta-analysis of observational studies. *The Lancet*, 380(9845), 899–907. doi: 10.1016/S0140-6736(12)60692-8.

Kassah, A. K., Kassah, B. L. L. and Agbota, T. K. (2012) Abuse of disabled children in Ghana. *Disability and Society*, 27(5), 689–701. doi: 10.1080/09687599.2012.673079.

Kevles, D. (1985) *In the Name of Eugenics: Genetics and the Uses of Human Heredity*. New York: Alfred A. Knopf.

Kevles, D. J. (2016) The history of eugenics. *Issues in Science and Technology*, 32(3), 45–50.

Komardjaja, I. (2005) The place of people with intellectual disabilities in Bandung, Indonesia. *Health & Place*, 11(2), 117–120. doi: 10.1016/j.healthplace.2004.10.008.

Love, G. (2017) Contextualising abortion: a life narrative study of abortion and social class in neoliberal England. University of Sussex. Available at http://sro.sussex.ac.uk/.

Mackintosh, N. J. (1998) *IQ and Human Intelligence*. Oxford: Oxford University Press.

Merricks, P. (2014) *Should such a faith offend? Bishop Barnes and the British eugenics movement, c.1924–1953, Research Archive and Digital Asset Repository*, Oxford Brookes University. Available at https://radar.brookes.ac.uk/radar/file/c63959ce-9451-4fc8-8943-7c25dc2b4f8a/1/merricks2014should.pdf.

Miller, G. A. (1962) *Psychology: The Science of Mental Life*. Harmondsworth: Penguin.

Nelson, F. (2016) The return of eugenics. *the Spectator*. Available at www.spectator.co.uk/2016/04/the-return-of-eugenics/.

Njelesani, J. *et al.* (2018) From the day they are born: a qualitative study exploring violence against children with disabilities in West Africa. *BMC Public Health*, 18(153). Available at http://doi.org/10.1186/s12889-018-5057-x Odukoya.

Nkomo, N. (2018) Ecosystemic factors influencing the accessibility of ECD services for young children with disabilities in Zimbabwe. University of Pretoria.

Paul, D. B. (1998) The selection of the 'survival of the fittest'. *Journal of the History of Biology*, 21(3), 411–424. Available at: www.jstor.org/stable/4331067.

Peters, T. (2019) Are we closer to free market eugenics? The Crispr controversy. *Zygon*, 7–13. doi: 10.1111/zygo.12501.

Pollack, R. (2015) Eugenics lurk in the shadow of CRISPR. *Science*, 348(6237), 871 LP – 871. doi: 10.1126/science.348.6237.871-a.

Porter, D. (1991) 'Enemies of the race': biologism, environmentalism, and public health in Edwardian England. *Victorian Studies*, 34(2), 159–178.

Porter, D. (2005) *Health, Civilization and the State: A History of Public Health from Ancient to Modern Times*, *Bmj*. London: Routledge.

Reinders, J., Stainton, T. and Parmenter, T. R. (2019) The quiet progress of the new eugenics. Ending the lives of persons with intellectual and developmental disabilities for reasons of presumed poor quality of life. *Journal of Policy and Practice in Intellectual Disabilities*, 16(2), 99–112. doi: 10.1111/jppi.12298.

Riany, Y., Cuskelly, M. and Meredith, P. (2016) Cultural beliefs about autism in Indonesia. *International Journal of Disability, Development and Education*, 63, 623–640. doi: 10.1080/1034912X.2016.1142069.

Rix, J., Sheehy, K., Fletcher-Campbell, F., Crisp, M. and Harper, A. (2013) *Continuum of Education Provision for Children with Special Educational Needs: Review of International Policies and Practices.* Dublin: National Council for Special Education.

Robertson, J. A. (1975) Involuntary euthanasia of defective newborns. *Stanford Law Review*, 27(2), 213–269.

Rock, P. J. (1996) 'Eugenics and euthanasia: a cause for concern for disabled people, particularly disabled women. *Disability and Society*, 11(1), 121–127. doi: 10.1080/09687599650023399.

Rohwerder, B. (2018) Disability stigma in developing countries. *K4D Helpdesk Report*, p. 26. Available at https://assets.publishing.service.gov.uk/media/5b18fe3240f0b634aec30791/Disability_stigma_in_developing_countries.pdf.

Shakespeare, T. (1999) 'Losing the plot'? Medical and activist discourses of contemporary genetics and disability. *Sociology of Health and Illness*, 21(5), 669–688. doi: 10.1111/1467-9566.00178.

Sheehy, K. (2010) Stigmatising and removing defective children from society: the influence of eugenic thinking. In L. Brockliss and H. Montgomery (eds) *Childhood and Violence in the Western Tradition*. Childhood in Archaeology. Oxford: Oxbow Books, pp. 1–21.

Sheehy, K. (2013) *Eugenics.* New York: Oxford University Press.

Social Progress Imperative (2017) 2017 Social Progress Index overview, 1 May 2018, p. 2017. Available at www.socialprogressindex.com/overview.

The Dangerous Women Project (2019) *Eugenics and Feminism.* Available at http://dangerouswomenproject.org/2017/02/28/eugenics-and-feminism/ (accessed 1 September 2019).

Thomas, G. M. and Rothman, B. K. (2016) Keeping the backdoor to eugenics ajar? Disability and the future of prenatal screening. *American Medical Association Journal of Ethics*, 18(4), 406–415. Available at www.ncbi.nlm.nih.gov/pubmed/18733507%0Awww.pubmedcentral.nih.gov/articlerender.fcgi?artid=PMC1650661.

Tilley, E. *et al.* (2012) 'The silence is roaring': sterilization, reproductive rights and women with intellectual disabilities. *Disability and Society*, 27(3), 413–426.

UNICEF (2005) *Children and Disability in Transition in Cee/CIS and Baltic States.*

UNICEF (2015) *Situation Analysis of Children in Uganda*. Available at www.unicef.org/uganda/UNICEF_SitAn_7_2015_(Full_report).pdf (accessed 1 September 2019).

UNICEF (2019) *Introduction, Disabilities*. Available at www.unicef.org/disabilities (accessed 1 September 2019).

United Nations (2005) Violence against disabled children. UN Secretary General's *Report on Violence against Disabled Children*. Thematic Group on Violence against Disabled Children. Findings and Recommendations, pp. 1–33.

Walker, J. and Scior, K. (2013) Tackling stigma associated with intellectual disability among the general public: a study of two indirect contact interventions. *Research in Developmental Disabilities*, 34(7), 2200–2210.

Wibowo, S. B. and Muin, J. A. (2018) Inclusive education in Indonesia: equality education access for disabilities. *KnE Social Sciences*, 3(5), 484.

Wilson, R. A. and Pierre, J. S. (2016) Eugenics and disability: what was and is eugenics? In B. Mirandaa-Galarza and P. Devlieger (eds) *Rethinking Disability: World Perspectives in Culture and Society*. Antwerp, Belgium, pp. 93–112.

13 Psychiatrising children

Brenda A. LeFrançois

Introduction

Psychiatrisation is a process of diagnosing, and labelling 'mentally ill', those people who are seen to have thoughts, feelings or behaviours that are outside of what is understood socially and culturally to be the norm. Psychiatrisation is a term that was first used by adults in the service user and survivor movements to draw attention to the potentially oppressive and socially unjust process and outcomes of diagnosis and treatment within mental health services. Hence, this chapter discusses child psychiatrisation as a form of oppression against children. Using a mad studies framing it deconstructs this oppression, including providing an analysis of social injustices such as marginalisation and subjugation within mental health services. I argue that this oppression takes place through the interrelationships between adult power, professional power and systemic whiteness or racism being imposed upon children and young people. In addition, what is understood as the 'norm' in terms of acceptable thoughts, feelings and behaviours is shrinking in our society as what we consider abnormal enlarges. These issues will be considered in this chapter, along with a discussion of the role of child development in helping shape what we consider to be 'normal' and 'abnormal', through its support of psychiatric assumptions. A case study follows in order to exemplify these biomedical relations of ruling over children, young people and, to a certain extent, their carers.

Throughout this chapter, a mad studies lens is used. When I use the term 'mad' or 'mad people' in this chapter, I am using it in the same way it is used throughout the mad studies literature. 'Mad' is a derogatory term that has been reclaimed by people who have been deemed 'mad' within the mental health services. Like the reclaiming of the once derogatory term 'queer' by LGBTQ+ communities, it is a term meant to startle, to unsettle and to start politicised conversations about psychiatric oppression and sanism (discussed further below: sanism is a form of oppression that includes stereotyping, low expectations, discrimination and other forms of violence directed towards mad people), including the stigma perpetuated through the naming of certain people as abnormal and others as sane, both inside and outside the clinic. When I discuss 'mad communities', I mean any gathering of service users and psychiatric survivors who come together in person or virtually to either: (1) discuss their experiences of oppression within mental health services; (2) engage in mutual aid in relation to experiences of distress; (3) engage in social activism in relation to benefit cuts or forced treatment or other varied issues; (4) engage in mad pride celebrations; or (5) engage in mad artistic and other forms of mad cultural production.

As an umbrella approach, mad studies include critiques of psychiatry that emanate from service users and psychiatric survivors, mad people, critical psychiatrists, radical professionals, disability studies theorists, disability activists, anti-psychiatry activists and those working and theorising within the field of critical mental health. Although all these approaches differ, what they do have in common and what enables them to be part of the field is their critiques of the medical model of mental health used in Western psychiatry and that dominates mental health practice. Although certain people, both adult service users, child and adolescent service users and their carers may find the dominant biomedical model of psychiatry helpful – and, indeed some will even describe it as 'life-saving' – yet many experience such diagnosis and treatment as oppressive. This chapter is written to bring forward the issues of oppression that are usually silenced by psychiatric authority.

'But I don't want to go among mad people,' Alice remarked. 'Oh, you can't help that,' said the Cat: 'we're all mad here. I'm mad. You're mad.'
    – *Lewis Carroll*

Figure 13.1 Alice in Wonderland: We're all mad here.

What is mad studies?

Mad studies is relatively new to academia, having established itself as a field of study over the past ten years, first in Canada and increasingly in other places around the world, including in the UK. Mad studies made its first appearance within universities in Canada and Scotland through courses in mad people's history (Bain *et al.*, 2015; Reaume, 2019; Snyder *et al.*, 2019) taught from the perspective of those who have been psychiatrised. Although the field called 'mad studies' is fairly new, its origins date back over 60 years and are rooted in psychiatric survivors' movements which have a vibrant history around the world of organising grassroots social actions, creating and running alternative services as well as engaging in survivor research. The knowledge, theorising, interventions and social actions of these social movements, all developed through first-hand lived experience, remain centred within mad studies, even as it establishes itself within academia.

Defining mad studies, however, is a daunting task. In some ways it defies description, primarily because as a field of study it is ever-changing, taking up local issues that differ from place to place and that are decided collectively usually within small local mad communities rather than by individual academics or others in positions of authority who may want to impose a specific framework for mad studies upon everyone. That being said, there remains nonetheless some important work done within mad studies, such as making overtly visible the violence experienced by people deemed mad, which includes psychiatric oppression, epistemic injustice and (antiblack) sanism.

By psychiatric oppression, I am referring to several forms of oppression that may be experienced by service users. First, there is the imposing of biomedical understandings of mental distress and altered states of mind upon people deemed mad, forcing an illness narrative even when this may not fit the understandings of the person experiencing the distress. This illness narrative is forced on service users despite a lack of physical markers of 'mental illness', the lack of objective tests to determine a diagnosis of 'mental illness' and despite a generally weak scientific evidence base for this biomedical framing of people's extreme experiences (Burstow, 2015; LeFrançois and Voronka, in press). The biomedical model, as such, provides theoretical assumptions that are instead proffered as fact, including the unproven assertion that 'mental illness' is hereditary and the untenable idea that 'mental illness' is caused by chemical imbalances in the brain (for a critique of this theory, see Lacasse and Leo, 2005; Moncrieff, 2009; Pies, 2011). Second, the most often used biomedically informed treatments, such as psychiatric drugs and electroshock (ECT), also may be experienced as oppressive by service users, given the many adverse effects of both (Fabris, 2011; Healy, 2016; van Daalen-Smith *et al.*, 2014). This experience of oppression is often magnified when service users are treated against their will through sectioning in hospital or under legally binding treatment orders in the community (Warme, 2013), although even voluntary or informal treatment is often experienced as coercive by service users (Fabris and Aubrecht, 2014; LeFrançois, 2014a). Thirdly, being seen within mental health services as inherently dangerous, bad, weak or wrong – a deficit model of understanding people deemed mad – is also experienced as oppressive by many service users (Daley *et al.*, 2019; Menzies *et al.*, 2013).

By epistemic injustice or epistemicide, I am referring to the notion that some people are seen as knowledge holders and knowledge producers whereas others are not (Fricker, 2007; Santos, 2014). Epistemic injustice intersects with racism in ensuring that racialised people are not recognised as legitimate knowers. Children, disabled, mad and elderly people, whether racialised or not, are also not understood to be legitimate knowers (Mills and LeFrançois, 2018), reproducing social inequalities and a strict hierarchy of privilege, power and white (male able-bodied) supremacy. Epistemic injustice ensures that mental health service users are seen as completely lacking in credibility and are disbelieved. It also ensures that a biomedical understanding of mental illness will remain firmly imposed upon people, dismissing service users' own interpretations of their thoughts, behaviours and emotions, including social and structural causes of distress such as violence, abuse and trauma (LeBlanc and Kinsella, 2016). That is, the denial of mental health service users as having valid perspectives on their own distress, including how it might be diagnosed and treated, based on their lived experiences, is intricately tied to their being seen as 'lacking insight' and 'lacking capacity' when those understandings do not conform to biomedical understandings. In this way, epistemic injustice ensures the subjugation of mad people. Most insidious is the way in which epistemic injustice becomes deeply engrained in how mental health services relate to service users who are also from Black and minority ethnic (BME) communities and/or those who are children.

By sanism (Fabris, 2011; Meerei *et al.*, 2016; Poole *et al.*, 2011), I am referring to a form of oppression that includes stereotyping, low expectations, discrimination, and other forms of violence directed towards mad people. Sanism also takes place at the systemic and structural levels. It plays itself out within the general population and within mental health services, including within the process of diagnosis and within the laws, policies and procedures that guide practice within these services. Moreover, sanism is bolstered by racism, sexism and classism. Given the overrepresentation of BME people within coerced psychiatric treatment (Care Quality Commission, 2011) in particular, and the racism that both leads to and characterises these encounters (Kanani, 2011; Metzl, 2009), sanism is recognised as being intimately tied to and inseparable from racism both conceptually and in practice. This has led to important theorising in mad studies in relation to the overwhelming experiences of anti-black sanism (Meerei *et al.*, 2016). Furthermore, the concept of stigma is seen as a symptom of sanism (Poole *et al.*, 2011). However, the concept of stigma alone – and the ever abundant anti-stigma campaigns – is seen as limited in its abilities to shed light on sanism and to end the oppression faced by service users, as it fails to take into consideration the ways in which biomedical diagnoses and treatments perpetuate oppression and epistemic injustice (Gorman and LeFrançois, 2018).

A mad studies framing of child psychiatrisation

Like adult service users, children and young people may also experience psychiatric oppression, epistemic injustice and sanism. The act of diagnosis alone may render some children and young people abject (LeFrançois and Diamond, 2014), understanding and labelling them abnormal, deficient and sick. This process has material implications for children both as people-in-the-present and as adults-of-the-future. In this chapter, I focus on the implications of psychiatrisation for children and young people in the present, although it is important to note that this process of psychiatrisation may have lifelong negative impacts for those who have been labelled and treated within mental health services.

Child and adolescent psychiatry understand children and young people diagnosed with mental disorders to have had their 'normal' childhood developmental process gone awry (LeFrançois and Coppock, 2014; Mills and LeFrançois, 2018). Like adults, however, 'mental illness' is also understood to exist primarily within children's brains, being the result of chemical imbalances, heredity and a broken brain (Chrisjohn *et al.*, 2017). Social, political and other environmental issues are either ignored or seen as only of tangential importance, for example, where the environment may be believed to trigger a genetic predisposition. Again, these theories are proffered as fact, despite decades of scientific research not demonstrating that biogenetics or biochemistry play any role whatsoever in the distress that children and young people may experience

Figure 13.2 Who is normal?

(Breggin, 2014). This biomedical or biogenetic approach to understanding distress is critiqued within mad studies as *biological reductionism*, where all distressed or distressing thoughts, behaviours and feelings are reduced to a biological source and biological explanation. This biological reductionist thinking paves the way for biochemical treatments and gives psychiatry its legitimacy and standing as a medical profession. This biological reductionism also bars any possibilities for understanding different sources of the distress that children and young people may experience.

Paired with the biological reductionist understandings of emotional distress as 'mental illnesses' is both the shrinking concept of 'normalcy' (Davis, 1995) and the widening definition of what constitutes the 'abnormal'. That is, if we understand all children and young people's emotions, behaviour and thoughts to exist on a long continuum representing what it means to be human, psychiatric expertise chops up that continuum into a small and shrinking band of 'normality'. Theories of child development bolster this concept of what it means to be normal as that to which all children are meant to aspire. Strikingly, children who are deemed mentally ill are seen as having developed wrongly, and thus are in need of corrective psychiatric treatment. Yet, with each new edition of the *Diagnostic and Statistical Manual of Mental Disorders* (DSM) being published with more and more disorders, the concept of what it means to have abnormal thoughts, behaviours and feelings is widening (Littrell and Lacasse, 2012), at the same time that what constitutes 'normal' shrinks. An example of this shrinking concept of 'normalcy', the latest edition of the DSM, DSM-5 (American Psychiatric Association, 2013), categorises as a mental illness anyone who grieves for more than six months. Are we really to believe that a child or young person who cries and mourns the death of a parent or loved one for more than six months to be abnormal, sick, mentally ill? Others have also criticised diagnoses that have been created particularly for children (Breggin, 2001; Mills, 2014), including ADHD, oppositional defiant disorder and other so-called conduct disorders as taking behaviours that have been typically noted in childhood throughout history – but that may be very challenging and distressing for adults to witness and manage – and pathologising those typical behaviours as mental illnesses. Indeed, the question can be asked: Has the shrinking notion of the 'normal' led to the pathologisation of childhood itself?

Children's and young people's own understandings of their distressing thoughts, feelings and behaviours may be dismissed – if they are even listened to at all – when they do not conform to biomedical conceptualisations. To dismiss children's and young people's understandings in this way is an example of sanism and epistemic injustice; they are not seen as knowledge holders because of their status as 'mentally ill' and they are seen as lacking insight because their understandings are not consistent with biomedical explanations. However, this sanism is directed at children and young people in a way that intersects and is bolstered by their status as 'children' (LeFrançois, 2014b), as their age and maturity is seen (with an adult lens) to delimit their abilities to reflect upon and understand their experiences.

This denial of children's and young people's abilities to understand their distressing thoughts, feelings and behaviours means that adult/psychiatric biological reductionist thinking pervades and conceals any other possibilities, such as spiritual, cultural, political, social and environmental explanations. For example, it is not unusual for chil-dren and young people to have spiritual understandings of their experiences of hearing voices or seeing things that others do not see (Escher and Romme, 2010). In addition, BME and Indigenous children and young people, whether living in the Global South or the Global North, may hold cultural and spiritual understandings of their experiences that do not conform to or lie completely outside of Euro-Western conceptualisations, given vast differences in worldviews (Mills and Fernando, 2014). Political explanations of distress are also denied, as Rabaia *et al.* (2014) demonstrate how state-sanctioned political violence is masked when, for example, the distress resulting from living under Israeli occupation is classified as being the result of children's and young people's biology rather than the direct result of war, occupation and related hostilities. Other social and environmental sources of children's and young people's distress are also denied or masked, such as the physical, sexual and emotional abuse of children at the hands of adults, the overwhelming experience of bullying at school and the separation from parents/carers/siblings within child protection systems, juvenile justice jails or immigration detention centres. Most alarming, in this refusal to listen to and accept children's and young people's interpretations of their experiences of distress, is the reliance on harmful biomedical treatments (Breggin, 2014; Mills, 2014; van Daalen-Smith *et al.*, 2014) rather than focusing on social, environmental and political solutions to ending the distressing violence that exists in the real world. Parents and carers are also expected to accept the biological reductionist understanding of their children's distress as well as the biomedical treatment plans for them. If parents or carers ques-tion or refuse this biomedical wisdom, they are often seen as a part of the problem and may also be pathologised as mentally ill, thus solidifying biomedical dominance while exemplifying its hereditary theory of mental illness.

Case study

In order to exemplify some of the issues raised above in relation to the psychiatrisation of children and young people, the following case study is offered based on the amalga-mation and anonymisation of multiple cases that reflect the experiences of some young people and their carers:

> Anthony is currently a 24-year-old former service user of mixed heritage who entered the mental health system at age of 15 as an informally admitted inpatient. He was brought to the hospital by his mum, Moira, given some extreme behavi-oural changes in him. Anthony had told her some weeks before that he was occa-sionally seeing visions of his father, who had died seven months earlier. This both frightened and saddened him. He was also expressing a great deal of worry over his studies and his fear of failing at school. In addition, there was a situation at school two days before the admission to hospital where Anthony was heard shout-ing at a group of other students which was reported to Moira by the head teacher. This surprised Moira as she had always known her son to be gentle, kind and soft-spoken. The morning prior to the admission to hospital Anthony told his mum that

Figure 13.3 Isolation.

he felt strongly that he was in a position to save humanity. He also indicated that he was hearing the voices of spirits who would help him do so. Moira brought Anthony to his GP, who referred him to the local child and adolescent mental health services inpatient unit.

At the time he was admitted to the inpatient unit, Anthony was adamant that he did not want to be admitted at that time but instead wanted to wait until half-term so as not to overly disrupt his studies. He was in the midst of working on his GCSEs and did not want to be left behind. With this refusal, the psychiatric nurse and social worker requested to meet alone with Moira, later indicating in Anthony's medical file that he was 'too psychotic and agitated' to be involved in further discussions regarding his admission. In this meeting that took place without Anthony's consent or presence in the room, the psychiatric nurse informed Moira that her child was quite unwell and required immediate inpatient admission in order to allow the multidisciplinary team of mental health practitioners to assess him, diagnose him, determine his level of risk of harm to self or others and treat him. It was explained to Moira that it would be best to admit her son informally rather than detaining him under the Mental Health Act, and that this could be accomplished by her signing the admission to hospital form for her son. Anthony was never shown or asked to sign the admission to hospital form. Shortly after his admission, Anthony was told by the consultant psychiatrist that his admission would be for two weeks. However, in the end, Anthony spent six months in the inpatient unit. Throughout the weeks and months of his admission, the care team met regularly with Moira without Anthony's awareness, consent or presence, in order to discuss his treatment and progress. Here we see how adultism intersects with sanism, ensuring that informed consent was never sought from Anthony, and ensuring that he was seen as too incompetent to be involved in discussions regarding his treatment and care.

During the first week of admission, Moira met with the social worker who took a family history, by asking Moira several questions. Moira indicated that she was born and raised in the north of England. She met Anthony's father while on a trip to London when she was a young person. Anthony's father was a black man originally from Guyana who had immigrated to the UK as a young person in the late 1970s. He was much older than Moira when they met. They married and settled together in London soon after meeting. A year later, Anthony was born and within three months her husband left her. Their separation was not amicable, and Moira characterised him as irresponsible and 'probably mentally ill'. She returned with her baby to her hometown in the north, where they remain today. Anthony had very little face-to-face contact with his father, but Moira described frequent telephone calls between them which she characterised as consisting of emotionally abusive conversations. These telephone calls ended abruptly seven months ago, when Anthony's father was found murdered in London. They were given very little information about the incident, and the murder case remains unsolved. This information was put in Anthony's medical file but none of the issues relating to this family history were brought up or verified with Anthony by the social worker.

That being said, sometime after his admission Anthony began to speak openly with one of the psychiatric nurses. He disclosed to the nurse that he had experienced intense racism at his (mostly white) school from both other students and teachers. He described his isolation at school, the racist slurs that a small group of students taunted him with, and the way he felt stereotyped by teachers as lazy and unintelligent despite applying himself diligently to his studies. He indicated feeling that teachers did not expect him to do well academically and regularly dismissed his contributions to class discussion. He also explained that he mostly tolerated this racism from students and teachers quietly, but he did lash out verbally to the group of students once last week, as he just couldn't take it anymore. He was feeling under intense stress due to the death of his father and his fears of not succeeding in school. He also expressed the belief that he had a higher purpose in life that he must fulfil. Rather than document these traumatic and stressful experiences in his medical file as leading to his experiences of distress, the discussions were documented instead as evidence of Anthony's symptoms of paranoia and delusional beliefs. Here we see how sanism and racism intersect, ensuring that Anthony would not be believed and fulfilling a biologically reductionist understanding of his experiences of distress.

After the initial two weeks of admission, Anthony was assessed by the consultant psychiatrist and diagnosed with schizophrenia, generalised anxiety disorder and queried bipolar disorder. It was stressed that a chemical imbalance inside Anthony's brain had caused these mental disorders, without mentioning that this theory of mental illness being caused by chemical imbalances is no longer held as plausible by the psychiatric profession. Further, the consultant psychiatrist indicated to Moira that these disorders were similar conditions to those of cancer and diabetes. However, the differences between these physical illnesses and the mental disorders Anthony was diagnosed with were never explained to her, including the lack of physical markers of mental disorders and the lack of objective tests to determine diagnoses. For treatment, Anthony was put on a cocktail of psychotropic medications but was never told about the possible adverse reactions (common or rare) that he may experience from these prescribed medications. The consultant psychiatrist did explain, however, that mental illness is a hereditary illness and it was most likely passed on to Anthony genetically from his father. This was stated without acknowledging the lack of scientific evidence for the hereditary nature of mental illness and without acknowledging that Anthony's father was never diagnosed with a mental disorder but was merely understood to be so by Moira, his estranged wife. This links to the racist stereotyping of black men as mad (and dangerous) and demonstrates how anti-black sanism can be deployed even if black men manage to evade direct contact with mental health services.

During his six months in the inpatient unit, Anthony requested several times to go home. Each time he was told that he could not leave at this time but that arrangements would be made to discuss the possibility with his mum. It was documented several times by psychiatric staff in the medical records that Anthony

Figure 13.4 Racist bullying in school.

frequently requested being discharged. However, his wishes were never acted upon. Moira was informed at these times that Anthony lacked insight into his illness and his need to be in hospital. She was further informed that it would be in his best interest to remain in hospital. He was allowed periodic weekend passes to go home, but only at times when Moira agreed to take him and agreed to administer his psychiatric medications. This all occurred while he was an involuntary or informal patient; as he was never detained involuntarily under the Mental Health Act, he was free to leave at any time but was led to believe that he did not have such a choice.

In addition to requesting discharge from the inpatient unit, Anthony frequently indicated adverse reactions to the psychiatric medication he was prescribed and requested repeatedly to be taken off those drugs that were causing the harmful effects. In fact, he often stated to any practitioner who would listen to him on the ward that the medications were making him feel worse than the distress that led him to come to the inpatient unit in the first place. He complained of poor concentration, confusion, memory problems, heavy sedation, worsened anxiety, racing thoughts, numbness in his legs and head, sexual dysfunction including inability to masturbate, intrusive thoughts, increased hallucinations, stomach pains, deep sadness, fatigue, neck spasms, rigid muscles, chest pains, difficulty breathing and extreme weight gain. At times these adverse reactions were documented in Anthony's medical file, but were usually accompanied by concerns that he might stop taking the prescribed medications. At these times, pressure was put on Anthony to continue to take his medications despite his complaints of adverse effects. At one point, a psychiatric nurse indicated to him that the medications could not be causing him memory problems, for example, as they were known to help increase memory, a statement that could not possibly be ascribed to any of the drugs he was prescribed. In addition, in relation to the side effect of sexual dysfunction, a note was made in Anthony's medical records that he appears to be obsessed with masturbation, and that a diagnosis of obsessive-compulsive disorder should be considered.

Listening to her son's complaints regarding the medication and recognising that he seemed to be getting worse rather than better after three months of hospitalisation, Moira began to think that there was something wrong with this treatment and to question the care team, including the consultant psychiatrist. First, she questioned the use of medications which carried side effects and that seemed to be making him worse. Second, she demanded that her son be discharged back into her care. The more Moira began to question and make demands on behalf of her son, the less she was invited into the inpatient unit by the consultant psychiatrist to discuss Anthony's progress. Indeed, it was noted at this point in Anthony's file that the mother–son relationship appeared to be overly enmeshed, with mum being so overly involved in Anthony's life that he was being curtailed developmentally. It was further stated that Moira was impeding Anthony's progress in his mental health treatment which may be due to her own mental health issues. This new framing of Moira as problematic once she began to critique her son's treatment and care is consistent with the trend of pathologising non-compliant parents and carers, and then demonstrating how that supposed pathology is further evidence of the hereditary nature of mental illness.

Nearing the end of his time as an inpatient, Anthony began to realise that if he wanted to be discharged eventually he would need to appear to be a more compliant and docile patient. For the last month he was there, he stopped complaining about the side effects of the medications, he stopped asking to be discharged and he began to thank the various practitioners for the treatment and care he was being given, noting how much better he was feeling. As a consequence, the practitioners noted in Anthony's medical file that he was no longer 'treatment resistant', was progressing well with the current treatment and was ready for discharge. After those six months of admission, and with the school year over, Anthony returned home with his mum. He attempted to return to his GCSEs but the adverse effects of the psychiatric medications left him unable to concentrate, study or even get up early enough in the morning to attend classes on time. By the age of 16 he dropped out of school completely, giving up his earlier dreams of completing his GCSEs, then A levels and then attending a university in order to become a marine biologist. Instead, he remained under the care of the consultant psychiatrist as an outpatient and remained on psychiatric medications continuously for six years, making the decision at the age of 21 to withdraw from his medications on his own and to stop seeing any mental health practitioners. Although the withdrawal symptoms where extremely painful, Anthony stuck to his goals and came off the drugs completely within six months. At this present time, Anthony has been drug-free and completely symptom-free for three years. He has not, however, been able to regain the education path he was on prior to being admitted into the inpatient unit.

Concluding thoughts

As we see in the above case study, Anthony was able to end his career as a psychiatric patient but not without some difficulty. Although it is the case that some children and young people escape this path once entering the child and adolescent mental health system, many others remain part of a pipeline from children's mental health services to adult mental health services. The potential negative impact of being psychiatrised as a child or young person cannot be overstated. Rather than focusing on anti-stigma campaigns that reify psychiatric oppression, epistemic injustice and sanism, perhaps we should focus instead on the impact of being psychiatrised in a world that demands adherence to a shrinking notion of 'normal' behaviour, thoughts and feelings, in a world that rewards conformity and emotional sedation, in a world that punishes spirituality outside of dominant notions of religion, and in a world that denies the social and environmental causes of distress, including racism, child abuse and other forms of violence.

References

American Psychiatric Association (2013) *Diagnostic and Statistical Manual of Mental Disorders* (5th edn). Arlington, VA: American Psychiatric Association.

Bain, M., Ballantyne, E., Bell, C., Collie, S.-A. and Fullerton, L. (2015) *Doing Mad Studies: Experiences, Influences and Impacts. How Was It for Us?* Paper presented at the conference Making Sense of Mad Studies, Durham University, Durham, UK, September.

Breggin, P. R. (2001) *Talking Back to Ritalin*. Cambridge, MA: Da Capo Press.

Breggin, P. R. (2014) The rights of children and parents in regard to children receiving psychiatric diagnoses and drugs. *Children and Society*, 28(3), 231–241.

Burstow, B. (2015) *Psychiatry and the Business of Madness: An Ethical and Epistemological Accounting*. London: Palgrave Macmillan.

Care Quality Commission (2011) *Count Me In 2010: Results of the 2010 National Census of Inpatients and Patients on Supervised Community Treatment in Mental Health and Learning Disability Services in England and Wales*. London: Care Quality Commission and National Mental Health Development Unit.

Chrisjohn, R. D., Shaunessy, M., with Smith, A. O. (2017) *Dying to Please You: Indigenous Suicide in Contemporary Canada*. Penticton, B: Theytus Books.

Daley, A., Costa, L. and Beresford, P. (2019) *Madness, Violence, and Power: A Critical Collection*. Toronto: University of Toronto Press.

Davis, L. J. (1995) *Enforcing Normalcy: Disability, Deafness, and the Body*. London: Verso.

Escher, S. and Romme, M. (2010) *Young People Hearing Voices*. Ross-on-Wye, Herefordshire: PCCS Books.

Fabris, E. (2011) *Tranquil Prisons: Chemical Incarceration under Community Treatment Orders*. Toronto: University of Toronto Press.

Fabris, E. and Aubrecht, K. (2014) Chemical constraint: experiences of psychiatric coercion, restraint, and detention as carceratory techniques. In L. Ben-Moshe, C. Chapman and A. C. Carey (eds) *Disability Incarcerated: Imprisonment and Disability in the United States and Canada*. New York: Palgrave Macmillan, pp. 185–200.

Fricker, M. (2007) *Epistemic Injustice. Power and the Ethics of Knowing*. Oxford: Oxford University Press.

Gorman, R. and LeFrançois, B. A. (2018) Mad Studies. In B. M. Z. Cohen (ed.) *Routledge International Handbook of Critical Mental Health*. Abingdon: Routledge, pp. 107–114.

Healy, D. (2016) *Psychiatric Drugs Explained*. (6th edn). London: Elsevier.

Kanani, N. (2011) Race and madness: locating the experiences of racialized people with psychiatric histories in Canada and the United States. *Critical Disability Discourse*, 3, 1–14.

Lacasse, J. R. and Leo, J. (2005) Serotonin and depression: a disconnect between the advertisements and the scientific literature. *PLoS Medicine*, 2(12), n.p.

Leblanc, S. and Kinsella, E. (2016) Toward epistemic justice: a critically reflexive examination of 'sanism' and implications for knowledge generation. *Studies in Social Justice*, 10(1), 59–78.

LeFrançois, B. A. (2014a) Voluntary commitment. In A. T. Scull (ed.) *Cultural Sociology of Mental Illness*. London: Sage, pp. 947–950.

LeFrançois, B. A. (2014b) *Adultism. Encyclopedia of Critical Psychology*. Berlin Heidelberg: Springer-Verlag, pp. 47–49.

LeFrançois, B. A. and Coppock, V. (2014) Psychiatrised children and their rights: starting the conversation. *Children & Society*, 165–171.

LeFrançois, B. A. and Diamond, S. (2014) Queering the sociology of diagnosis: children and the constituting of mentally ill subjects. *CAOS: The Journal of Critical Anti-Oppressive Social Inquiry*, 1, 39–61.

LeFrançois, B. A. and Voronka, J. (in press) Mad epistemologies and the ethics of knowledge production. In T. Macias (ed.) *Un/Ethical Un/Knowing: Ethical Reflections on Methodology and Politics in Social Science Research*. Toronto: Canadian Scholars Press.

Littrell, J. and Lacasse, J. R. (2012) Controversies in psychiatry and DSM-5: the relevance for social work. *Families in Society*, 93(4), 265–270.

Meerei, S, Abdillahi, I. and Poole, J. M. (2016) An introduction to anti-black sanism. *Intersectionalities*, 5(3), 18–35.

Menzies, R., LeFrançois, B. A. and Reaume, G. (2013) Introducing mad studies. In B. A. LeFrançois, R. Menzies and G. Reaume (eds) *Mad Matters: A Critical Reader in Canadian Mad Studies.* Toronto: Canadian Scholars Press, pp. 1–22.

Metzl, J. M. (2009) *The Protest Psychosis: How Schizophrenia Became a Black Disease.* Boston, MA: Beacon Press.

Mills, C. (2014) Psychotropic childhoods: global mental health and pharmaceutical children. *Children & Society*, 28(3), 194–204.

Mills, C. and Fernando, S. (2014) Globalising mental health or pathologizing the global South? Mapping the ethics, theory and practice of global mental health. *Disability and the Global South*, 1(2), 188–202.

Mills, C. and LeFrançois, B. A. (2018) Child as metaphor: colonialism, psy-governance and epistemicide. *World Futures*, 74, 503–524.

Moncrieff, J. (2009) *The Myth of the Chemical Cure: A Critique of Psychiatric Drug Treatment.* London: Palgrave Macmillan.

Pies, R. W. (2011) Psychiatry's new brain-mind and the legend of the 'chemical imbalance. *Psychiatric Times*. Available at www.psychiatrictimes.com/blogs/couch-crisis/psychiatry-new-brain-mind-and-legend-chemical-imbalance.

Poole, J. M., Jivraj, T, Arslanian, A., Bellows, K., Chiasson, S., Hakimy, H., Pasini, J. and Reid, J. (2011) Sanism, mental health, and social work/education: a review and call to action. *Intersectionalities*, 1, 20–36.

Rabaia, Y., Saleh, M. F. and Giacaman, R. (2014) Sick or sad? Supporting Palestinian children living in conditions of chronic political violence. *Children & Society*, 28(3), 172–181.

Reaume, G. (2019) Creating mad people's history as a university credit course since 2000. *New Horizons in Adult Education and Human Resource Development*, 31(1), 22–39.

Santos, Boaventura de Sousa (2014) *Epistemologies of the South: Justice against Epistemicide.* Boulder, CO: Paradigm.

Snyder, S., Pitt, K. A., Shanouda, F., Voronka, J., Reid, J. and Landry, D. (2019) Unlearning through mad studies: disruptive pedagogical praxis. *Curriculum Inquiry,* 49(4), 485–502.

Valdivia, R. (1999) *The Implications of Culture on Developmental Delay.* Educational Resources Center, ERIC Digest, #E589.

Van Daalen-Smith, C., Adam, S., Breggin, P. and LeFrançois, B. A. (2014) The utmost discretion: how presumed prudence leaves children susceptible to electroshock. *Children & Society*, 28(3), 205–317.

Warme, G. (2013) Removing civil rights: how dare we. In B. A. LeFrançois, G. Reaume and R. Menzies (eds) *Mad Matters: A Critical Reader in Canadian Mad Studies.* Toronto: Canadian Scholars Press.

14 Children in the digital world

Privacy and autonomy in surveilled digital lives

Mimi Tatlow-Golden

Introduction

Children's and young people's lives changed dramatically in the late twentieth century. This chapter, taking a different slant to much public commentary on children's digital lives, explores privacy and surveillance in contemporary childhoods. Being a child has always entailed being surveilled in various ways, but the digital world has profoundly changed the nature and extent of surveillance and privacy that children and young people experience. Privacy matters because it is a crucial protector of autonomy. It facilitates control over information about us that is shared, and affects self-expression and how we author our own lives.

Many new childhood experiences ensue from engaging with digital technologies, including online games, media-sharing sites, social media and other applications, and these have led to extensive discussions about effects on children's and young people's well-being. Concerns in the media often focus on 'screen time' (time spent on digital devices for whatever purpose), content viewed in digital media, or contact with bullies or those seeking to harm children. There is no question that certain harms are a pressing concern, whether social media groups devoted to sharing information about self-harming, or the extent of global sexual exploitation that is being uncovered online, among others. Yet, as headlines about children's digital media activity often mirror the negative way in which novels, the radio, comics or television were received in their time, it is important to understand exactly what feature of new media is considered harmful, and why. There is currently a lack of solid evidence, for example, indicating that digital device use itself causes poor mental health in young people. It depends on what is being done with those devices and why they are being used. Evidence for the benefits and opportunities offered by digital applications also rarely makes the headlines.

Still, technology has brought many truly profound changes to childhoods in a digital world, and one of these is in the domain of surveillance. Paradoxically, digital technologies can facilitate privacy in some ways, yet imperil it in many others, leading to interrelated effects on children's and young people's autonomy and identity. Underlying these changes in twenty-first-century digital childhoods are some fundamental questions: Can children and young people expect privacy? How do privacy, autonomy and identity interact in the digital world? And what are the implications for children's developing and future selves? To consider these questions, this chapter examines practices in social media of children, young people, adults, and the social media companies themselves. Taking both micro- and macro-perspectives, it explores 'sharenting'; young people's own engagement with social media; and digital data extraction and surveillance by commercial actors in this data ecosystem.

Privacy 'is no longer a social norm'.

(Facebook founder Mark Zuckerberg, 2010 cited in Tunick, 2014)

Privacy isn't just about hiding things. It's about self-possession, autonomy, and integrity.

(Garfinkel, 2000, p. 4)

Social media: making private lives public

Children's and young people's lives were once experienced and represented almost exclusively in private domains. If parents recorded images and news of childhood events at all it was in photo albums and family letters, and most childhood experience was ephemeral – not recorded for posterity at all. With the advent of digital media and social networking sites, however, this changed. Generations are now growing up with the experience of 'deep mediatization' (Couldry and Hepp, 2017, p. 213) through which they are positioned, by others and themselves, in social worlds facilitated by media and communications practices. Digital media's technological 'affordances', or capabilities, mean that children, young people and others can create and share content widely, at a scale that was previously unimaginable and with audiences that are often not expected or even imagined.

Sharenting: do children have a right to privacy from their parents?

During childhood, indeed often beginning before or at birth, many parents post extensively in social media, on websites and blogs about their children. 'Sharenting' involves personal details about children online, including images and videos of pre-birth ultrasounds, the birth itself, the baby years, starting school, family occasions, children's milestones, selfies and everyday events.

Scholars identify sharenting as a practice that can deepen enjoyment of experience (Diehl *et al.*, 2016) but also a deliberate parental practice of self-representation (Blum-Ross and Livingstone, 2017; Lazard *et al.*, 2019). Parents use social media to 'do' mothering, often performing parental pride and identities by producing visual records of family closeness and children's activities and achievements (Lazard *et al.*, 2019). However, they also share challenges and frustrations, recording struggles with behavi-

Figure 14.1 Children and young people are growing up in an age of deep mediatisation.

oural or mental health diagnoses or severe illnesses, or engage in 'toddler-shaming', sharing videos of young children's outbursts (Sorensen, 2016; Steinberg, 2017). A University of Michigan study found that parents most frequently posted about getting children to sleep, eating, preschool, discipline and behaviour. Half shared potentially embarrassing information, half gave information that could identify children's location and a quarter posted photos that could be considered inappropriate (Steinberg, 2017).

There are many potential benefits to some forms of sharenting. It can allow parents to connect with friends and family, receive support and advice for challenges experienced, experience validation in their parenting role, and create family memories. In this process, however, as lawyer and children's rights expert Sarah Steinberg (2017) notes, parents have now become the narrators of children's public life stories. Although parents' storytelling is important to children's autobiographical memory and their developing sense of self (Nelson and Fivush, 2004), this narration in social media has a largely public character – perhaps ironically, given that parents are typically charged with playing a supervisory role for children's online engagement. Furthermore, it creates children's first digital data traces: the 'digital footprint' that will follow them throughout their lives. The practice raises a challenging question: Do children have a right to privacy in relation to parents' extensive sharing of their images and experiences (Shmueli and Blecher-Prigat, 2011; Steinberg, 2017).

How children and young people experience sharenting themselves has recently begun to be explored. In a cluster of studies in Europe and the United States they gave mixed responses, ranging from acceptance of sharing positive events to uneasiness about parental posting. Disquiet is seen not just during adolescence, when young people seek to develop a more independent identity and experienced heightened self-consciousness (Sebastian *et al.*, 2008), but also earlier in childhood, raising interesting questions about children, privacy and autonomy.

In the United States, two recent large-scale studies of parent–child pairs explored their views of sharenting and family technology practices. Carol Moser *et al.* (2017) surveyed 331 young people (aged ten to 17 years) and their parents. The young people said that their parents could share achievements or happy, positive content about sports, school, hobbies or family relationships – 'cute pictures', 'fun family pics' or 'pictures that make me look good' (p. 4). However, they wanted parents to refrain from sharing content that was too revealing, reflected negatively upon them, or from posting without permission or against their wishes. The list of things it was not acceptable for parents to share was extensive and examples given were:

> embarrassing photos, ugly pics, anything embarrassing, what [kids] are really like at home, baby photos, kids in their underwear or in the bathtub, swimming pool pictures, when I'm not dressed up and when my hair isn't fixed, when they get in trouble or do something bad, private stuff, MY BUSINESS, Status about my friends and my relationship with my boyfriends.
>
> (Young people's comments extracted from Moser *et al.*, 2017)

It is clear that young people have a strong sense of what transgresses their privacy, and one can imagine that parents and children might differ about what constitutes privacy. Indeed, studies do find that parents often hold a different set of norms. In Estonia, in interviews with pairs of mothers and their children aged nine to 13 years, Merike Lipu and Andra Siibak noted 'privacy boundary turbulence', with the children 'often frustrated' by their mothers' sharenting (2019, p. 60) and parents posting nevertheless. As an example, one mother, when asked whether she asked her child's permission to post, said:

> No I don't and he doesn't allow me to either (laughing). But I still tag him and he doesn't like when I take photos of him, but I still upload those too … he immediately says 'don't take a photo, don't do it, don't upload', but I still do. I am also in that photo, so I want to upload it, but he does not like it.
>
> ((Mother (aged 31) cited in Lipu and Siibak, 2019, p. 64)

In this excerpt it can be seen that the parent, foregrounding her preferences and setting aside her child's wish for privacy, is asserting her right to author an online identity not just for herself but also for her child. This example is by no means unusual. In the United States, Alexis Hiniker and colleagues (2016) compared 249 children's responses with those of their parents. They found that young people said that parents should not post about children without permission twice as often as parents did.

Perhaps this all seems rather trivial – passing tiffs about who decides about the content of family-focused tweets, posts and blogs. Yet sharenting provides windows into much wider ramifications of children's and young people's experience of growing up digital that touch upon questions of power, representation and voice. First, young people's responses to the public sharing of information and images of themselves highlight their strong interest in *privacy*. This directly contradicts the widespread portrayal of young people as a generation that shares so much online that they have given up on the notion of privacy (Hargittai and Marwick, 2016). Second, sharenting shines a light on the question of *construction of identity* (for discussions on identity see Chapter 1, this volume) in the digital era, and of who has the right to craft an identity online, as parents posting about children without consent may infringe the child's or young person's ability to 'create and shape their own image' (Sorensen, 2016, p. 157). Furthermore, sharenting practices also point to the broader issue of the permanent data record or *'digital footprint'* created in digital media about every child and young person. Enveloping all of these issues is the fundamental question: What kind of autonomy do children and young people have in their digital activities and in creating their identities online?

Young people's social media activities: a 'privacy paradox'?

Young people engage with digital media and online communication in many locations and for many purposes whether for social networking, gaming, creating and viewing videos on video-sharing sites and more. These sites allow them to engage in peer connections, identity exploration as well as entertainment, and they can afford young people considerable privacy from their parents and from others in facilitating peer communication on personal devices.

As surveillance scholars Valerie Steeves and Priscilla Regan (2014) note, engaging with digital media involves a complex interrelationship between apparently contradictory desires for *privacy* and *publicity*. Steeves and Regan draw upon several studies

Figure 14.2 Young people and their peers actively engage with digital media.

in Canada to conclude that young people actively engage online and expect family members to respect their self-determination by not accessing their online sites, or only doing so on invitation; they hold strong norms about who sees what they do in these media, and violation of these norms causes distress:

> From diarizing on anonymous blogging sites with no intended audience, to deepening ties to real-world friends through social networking, to posting videos on YouTube with the hope of attracting a large number of viewers ... in each of these situations, [young people] relied on a complex set of norms to govern who should and should not look and how the viewer should respond to what they see. When these norms are violated, they report a general sense of discomfort and unease.
>
> (Steeves and Regan, 2014, p. 302)

Interactions on social media involve sharing a great deal of personal information and imagery. As young people share a great deal of content online, it is assumed that they do not care for privacy – and adults often describe their behaviours as naïve, irresponsible or risky (Marwick and boyd, 2014). Yet young people do care deeply about their privacy online; this is termed the 'privacy paradox' (Barnes, 2006). Researchers have found that there are multiple reasons why people engage in this contradictory behaviour (boyd and Hargittai, 2010; Hargittai and Marwick, 2016). In some instances it is because people do not understand the risk or are unaware of how to protect their privacy. As awareness rises about privacy issues, and school-based 'e-safety' education increases, this is becoming somewhat less salient. However, young people do continue to offer up personal information to digital providers and online communities – because engaging online gives access to their friends and wider social groups as well as to activity and event information for school, university or jobs. Furthermore, the structural, design and so-called 'privacy' features of many social and other media make it complex or impossible to control the flow of information to others as well as to the companies that run these media and sell and share the data widely.

Eszter Hargittai and Alice Marwick (2016) found that young people do understand and care about the risks of sharing information online when they carried out group interviews with 40 young adult participants in the United States, half of whom were aged 19 to 21 years. Yet the young people felt that they did not have any control over this process. The privacy paradox also applies to adults, who similarly say they care about their privacy, yet share details with others in social media and elsewhere, where they can be shared widely through networks and extracted by social media platforms and other digital actors. In fact, studies in the US and the UK researching age differences in actions to protect privacy find that there is either little of a generational divide – indeed, young people engage in *more* actions to protect their privacy than do older people (Hargittai and Marwick, 2016).

Identities and contexts

Identity, although often thought of as a unitary construct, is actually performed differently in various contexts (see Chapter 1, this volume). We all adapt to the norms and cultures of the various settings in which we find ourselves, whether home, school, work or elsewhere, in a process of flexible self-presentation that sociologist Erving Goffman (1959) described as 'impression management'. Media scholars Alice Marwick and danah boyd cite a young person who describes the various ways in which he engages differently with different people, and his expectation that audiences will understand this:

> I think it's just the certain way that you talk. I will talk to my sister a different way than I'll talk to my friends at school ... I mean, I think you can figure out that I'm not talking to you if I'm talking about a certain teacher.
>
> (Hunter, 14 years old, cited in Marwick and boyd, 2014, p. 1057)

In social media and other networked digital environments, impression management is particularly difficult as there are many audiences that are invisible to users of these environments. For all users, of whatever age, this is a challenge, perhaps particularly so for young people whose identities are still in development. As social psychologist and media scholar Sonia Livingstone notes:

> Privacy is integral to the communication of identity, for identity is partly enacted through managing who knows what about us and who does not.... That which is made public to some is simultaneously kept private from others.
>
> (Livingstone, 2006, p. 154)

Indeed, it is interesting to find that, in an era when it is assumed that children and young people create their lives and selves in deep mediatised environments, they "often hold on to a feeling of an authentic self that is non-digital" (Stoilova *et al.*, 2019, p. 25). This indicates the complexity of self and identity development in multiple contexts that contemporary children and young people contend with (also discussed in Chapter 1, this volume).

Addressing the challenge of identity and self-representation in a digital, networked era, social and digital media scholar danah boyd (2014) draws upon the term 'context collapse' to describe what happens when different worlds in which we present ourselves unexpectedly come up against one another. Context collapse can happen in the physical world (for example, if you are out socialising and unexpectedly run into your work manager) but it happens more often in digital environments, where users do not have control over who shares what about them and where there are frequent fluctuations in technological contexts. In these fluid, complex, networked environments, individuals may interpret contexts differently (Marwick and boyd, 2014) and social norms about what is private are subject to change. As an example, if someone 'tags' a picture with you in social media without your permission, the image may then reach many people, showing you to them in a way that you may not have chosen. In response, a new social norm has begun to develop, namely that no one should be 'tagged' in social media without being asked first.

Young people engage in multiple strategies to manage these complex networked social environments (Marwick and boyd, 2014). Some strategies employ technological affordances of particular media, such as using multiple accounts with various names and different personal details; placing different privacy settings on specific posts to hide them from some viewers; deactivating accounts and reactivating them to view and post content at times of day when adults were less likely to be supervising; or deleting comments so that they can be less easily viewed and shared.

Other privacy-promoting strategies are based on content communication. Young people report engaging in covert communication in plain sight, for example, discussing peer issues obliquely in social media, without referring directly to the matter or person concerned, to exclude 'outsider' audiences. Alternatively, they may use shared references that adults may not grasp, as a 17-year-old explained:

> When Carmen and her boyfriend broke up, she wanted sympathy and support from her friends. Her inclination was to post sappy song lyrics that reflected her sad state of mind, but she was afraid that her mother would overreact; it had happened before. Knowing that her Argentinean mother would not recognize references to 1970s British comedy, Carmen decided to post lyrics from a movie that she had recently watched with her geeky friends. When her mom saw the update, 'Always look on the bright side of life,' she commented that it was great to see Carmen doing so well. Her friends, recognizing the lyric came from the Monty Python film Life of Brian where the main character is being crucified, immediately texted her.
>
> (Marwick and boyd, 2014, p. 1058)

Further insight into privacy attitudes among young people is yielded by Alice Marwick and colleagues' study of young people aged 17 to 27 in New York City (2017). Students of lower socioeconomic status or immigrant backgrounds demonstrated acute awareness of the longer term implications of their online engagement, strongly limiting information they shared on social media, to protect themselves from public scrutiny by future employers, government or law enforcement:

> people '[are] not entitled or obliged to state their views on every relevant matter in society ... I don't think people should be obliged to know that much about me ... I don't really take political stances in my posts and I do my best to make sure my posts, even if they may be of a funny intent, don't offend any particular demographic of people.'
>
> (Batuk, 18, in Marwick *et al.*, 2017, p. 5)

This example points to an important and often forgotten feature of digital identities: that young people's digital experiences are not unitary. They are affected by social, economic and other forms of positioning that change the ways in which they engage and craft identities online. What young people do have in common is that they seek to maintain privacy online by controlling the audiences of the content they share and limiting the ways in which they can be surveilled, by restricting how information flows or who can interpret it.

In this networked world, however, such privacy strategies are partial at best. Users have much less ability to manage the flow of personal information: they are unable to control others' posts, comments, tags and digital media engagements that then become visible to different audiences. This means that young people are experiencing quite different forms of privacy and autonomy than previous generations as they seek to navigate their identity development. Traditional, individualistic privacy models engage in personal responsibility discourses, placing the onus on young people to make 'good' decisions about information sharing. Yet these now apply much less straightforwardly in a surveillant ecosystem.

Understanding privacy in the digital era requires moving away from common, paternalistic discourses about how young people are responsible for controlling their privacy online. Instead, Marwick and colleagues argue, a new approach is needed, given the fact that digital engagement involves 'the ongoing negotiation of contexts in a networked ecosystem in which contexts regularly blur and collapse' (2017, p. 1063). Note that this new definition offers an accurate description of the flow of information in networked contexts but does not propose solutions. This is probably wise. The information scientist Helen Nissenbaum is widely cited as concluding that privacy is 'neither a right to secrecy nor a right to control, but a right to appropriate flow of personal information' (Nissenbaum, 2010, p. 3). And yet, with current designs of digital networks, it is difficult to imagine how such a right will be enacted. In any given context, who will be granted the power to define what is 'appropriate'? Young people? Their friends? Parents? Schools? Employers? Local authorities? Law enforcement? Governments? The interpersonal, social, ethical and legal challenges presented by the personal information flows facilitated by digital technologies need to be resolved, as they have profound implications for children's and young people's experience now and in their futures.

The commercial world: the hidden side of privacy and surveillance

The issues this chapter has explored thus far relate to privacy as it is personally experienced. How much control do children and young people have in creating their own images? Can they determine what others see and share about them? 'Experience-near' questions such as these are widely discussed in connection with children and young people's digital worlds. Yet if we zoom out from this micro-view to examine the deep, structural features of these digital technologies, another dimension of privacy entirely comes into focus. Understanding children's and young people's privacy, autonomy and identities in the digital era requires examining this facet of digital media as well.

Internet businesses have built a model of offering so-called 'free' services. However, these are in fact powered and paid for by a vast and extraordinarily lucrative advertising technology ('adtech') system. The adtech system functions by extracting personal data about all digital users and trading them globally in microseconds. Anyone engaging with the internet, whether using email, search, games, social media, or applications supporting every aspect of life imaginable, including health and well-being, homework, mental health, information and more, is having their personal data extracted and sold for profit, and so there is, as internet lawyer Paul Bernal describes it, now a symbiotic relationship between all those who rely on 'free' sites and services, and the businesses who extract and process personal data about these people (Bernal, 2014).

This global privacy-breaching economic model is in the service of advertising. Joseph Cannataci, UN Special Rapporteur on the right to privacy, notes that our every digital activity leaves traces that are

> capable of being aggregated into forming a very accurate profile of that individual's likes, dislikes, moods ... shopping patterns ... interest(s) and sometimes even the relevant opinions ... access to such data or exploitation of such data in a variety of ways is now one of the world's largest industries generating revenues calculated in hundreds of billions most usually in the form of targeted advertising.
>
> (Canatacci, 2016)

The 'advertising as surveillance' (Bodle, 2017) model now drives the global data economy which has been characterised as surveillance capitalism (Zuboff, 2019). Why does the vast surveillance machine that relies on exploitation of personal data by digital platforms matter? There are a number of reasons, and they affect the privacy and ultimately the autonomy of all those who use these services – including children and young people.

Data is combined across systems to craft personal profiles – called 'shadow profiles' (Quodling, 2018) or 'data doubles' (Haggerty and Ericson 2010). These profiles come to represent individuals' identities from the perspective of the companies who hold and sell them to employers, governments and others. They may or may not be accurate – but they come to represent individuals to others, disturbing our own capacities to determine our identities.

Digital platforms and advertisers take users' data and experiment with them constantly. Every form of data that can be extracted is currently being experimented with, to develop creative content and micro-target advertising, in real time, to those audiences that are most responsive to their messages. All social media content and responses (likes, shares, photos and more) contribute to building profiles for ad targeting. Geolocation data is accessed via settings on children's devices or in apps, to serve ads that are specific to users' locations in real time. Music-streaming service data is used, as music is considered to be an effective proxy for mood, and advertisers seek to target people based on their moods in the moment, and serve ads relevant to real-time emotion (Montgomery, 2015).

Data is used to target specific groups such as those with particular interests, in specified locations, or of particular ethnicities – and these forms of targeting have been found to increase young people's responsiveness. Data is even extracted from children and young people in school. Through many applications offered free to educators, whether for learning, behaviour regulation, emotion regulation, activity promotion or other practices, children's and young people's lives in education – always the subject of scrutiny – are being increasingly surveilled and datafied (Andrejevic and Selwyn, 2019; Lupton and Williamson, 2017). As digital media use rates grow globally, and companies increasingly focus efforts on lower and middle-income countries, this capacity for behaviourally targeted marketing is gaining ever wider global reach (Montgomery, 2015).

Analyses of the negative effects of this exploitation are gathering force, and they indicate that there are considerable potential implications for children's well-being and development – implications that are almost completely unseen by most users, and rarely discussed when challenges of the digital age for children and young people are raised. Not only are there significant concerns about protecting personal data and privacy but the technological capacity to extract data and target users brings several fundamental challenges to children and young people's well-being.

Limiting human autonomy: manipulation through digital technologies

At the heart of the concern about commercial digital surveillance is the influence it grants powerful actors with access to these data. The vast reach of the data gathered, its aggregation and analyses, amplify the abilities not just of advertisers but other commercial entities, employers, law enforcement and other government agencies to shape people's preferences and limit their capacity to make their own choices (Calo, 2014; Nissenbaum, 2010). Indeed, Daniel Susser and colleagues (2019) conclude that data-driven practices in digital media constitute 'manipulation' at such a scale that they represent a threat to human autonomy. They define manipulation as involving an intentional, covert attempt to influence a person's decision-making by targeting and exploiting their vulnerabilities, just as digital media catalogue individuals' preferences, interests, habits and choices, to identify and influence weaknesses and vulnerabilities. They conclude that these technologies present threats to individual autonomy, with grave implications for human agency: 'being steered or controlled, outside our conscious awareness, violates our autonomy, our capacity to understand and author our own lives' (Susser *et al.*, 2019, p. 13). This is likely to apply even more so to children and young people whose development is affected by these forms of manipulation, with long-term implications about who holds the key to children's identities and data traces online.

Figure 14.3 Children's and young people's data are extracted and used to profile them.

Is media literacy the answer?

Media literacy is often proposed as the solution to privacy and other digital media-related issues. Certainly, for deep mediatised childhoods, digital media literacy is critical. Essential to being a citizen, it is required for managing personal information online, engaging with media, and participating actively in communities and democracy. Furthermore, children and young people need to understand the incursions on their privacy and autonomy carried out by corporations, politicians, governments and others via digital media. Generally, children and young people expect small privacy-protecting tactics such as having multiple accounts or using fake names to protect them, and they underestimate how information can be extracted – for example, through online quizzes – and aggregated about them (Stoilova *et al.*, 2019). They also often assume that their personal information is of little interest to anyone outside their immediate circles. As adults accord them less attention in the world, many children see their own activities as being of little interest to others (Stoilova *et al.*, 2019). It is important to note however that this applies to adults as well. Norah Draper and Joseph Turow refer to 'digital resignation': the condition produced when people 'desire to control the information digital entities have about them but feel unable to do so' (2019, p. 1824). Indeed, indifference or resignation are understandable when digital media users are not in a position to control the flow of their information effectively and there is at present no escape from this relentless data collection and profiling of each and every user of digital media. This is a major child and human rights issue that remains to be tackled at the time of writing this chapter (Amnesty International, 2019).

Concluding thoughts: surveillance, privacy and autonomy

> Questions of adult surveillance and control of young people go to the heart of the question of what childhood and youth are and should be…. Children and young people need their own spaces, physically, imaginatively and emotionally, which are free from adult power and adult surveillance.
>
> (Steeves and Jones, 2010, p. 188)

Although children and young people have always been the objects of adult surveillance, the present generation are watched over as never before. Details of their lives are published by their parents, a wide range of seen and unseen audiences have access to their social media posting, and commercial actors extract all this information to construct profiles, predict and manipulate behaviour.

Adult surveillance of children, whether in the home, at school or in the digital world, is sometimes essential, and is often well-intentioned with the goal of providing safety, care and education. Yet as Steeves and Jones indicate, children also need spaces in which they are not subject to adult surveillance. Gillian Thomas and Gina Hocking (2003) identified adult 'colonisation' of childhoods through control and surveillance and commercialisation as key trends affecting twenty-first-century childhoods. These wider forces affect 'the child's opportunities to control his or her own relationship with time and space' (p. 23).

Privacy entails having autonomy over our personal information, and choosing what others see of us. Privacy frees us from the scrutiny of others, supporting the 'development and exercise of autonomy and freedom in thought and action' (Nissenbaum, 2010, p. 83). Without privacy in the digital world, children and young people can be seen and known by others, including many who are unknown. Furthermore, they are manipulated in their preferences and choices by those who extract their data in digital technologies and hence curtail their autonomy. This raises profound questions about how surveillance affects children's and young people's lives and identities in the twenty-first century.

References

Amnesty International (2019) *Surveillance Giants: How the Business Model of Google and Facebook Threatens Human Rights*. London: Amnesty International.

Andrejevic, M. and Selwyn, N. (2019) Facial recognition technology in schools: critical questions and concerns. *Learning, Media and Technology*, DOI: 10.1080/17439884.2020.1686014.

Barnes, S. B. (2006) A privacy paradox: social networking in the United States. *First Monday*, 11 [Online]. http://dx.doi.org/10.5210/fm.v11i9.1394.

Bernal, P. (2014) *Internet Privacy Rights: Rights to Protect Autonomy*. Cambridge: Cambridge University Press.

Blum-Ross, A. and Livingstone, S. (2017) 'Sharenting,' parent blogging, and the boundaries of the digital self. *Popular Communication*, 15(2), 115–125.

Bodle, R. (2017) A critical theory of advertising as surveillance. In J. F. Hamilton, R. Bodle and E. Korin (eds) *Explorations in Critical Studies of Advertising*. New York and Oxford: Routledge, pp. 138–154.

boyd, d. (2014) *It's Complicated. The Social Lives of Networked Teens*. New Haven, CT, and London: Yale University Press.

Calo, M. R. (2014) Digital market manipulation. *The George Washington Law Review*, 82(4), 995–1051.

Cannataci, J. A. (2016) *Report of the Special Rapporteur on the Right to Privacy* (advance unedited version), A/HRC/31/64. United Nations, 8 March.

Couldry, N. and Hepp, A. (2017) *The Mediated Construction of Reality*. Cambridge: Polity Press.

Diehl, K., Zauberman, G. and Barasch, A. (2016) How taking photos increases enjoyment of experiences. *Journal of Personality and Social Psychology*, 111(2), 119.

Draper, N. A. and Torow, J. (2019) The corporate cultivation of digital resignation. *New Media and Society*, 21(8), 1824–1839.

Garfinkel, S. (2000) *Database Nation: The Death of Privacy in the 21st Century*. Sebastopol: O'Reilly.

Goffman, E. (1959) *The Presentation of Self in Everyday Life*. Garden City, NY: Doubleday.

Haggerty, K. D. and Ericson, R. V. (2010) The surveillant assemblage. *British Journal of Sociology*,51(4), 605–622.

Hargittai, E. and Marwick, A. (2016) ' "What Can I Really Do?" Explaining the Privacy Paradox with Online Apathy'. *International Journal of Communication* 10, pp. 3737–3757.

Hiniker, A., Schoenebeck, S., Y. and Kientz, J., A. (2016) *Not at the dinner table: parents' and children's perspectives on family technology rules*. Proceedings of the ACM Conference on Computer Supported Cooperative Work 27: pp. 1376–1389.

Lazard, L., Capdevila, R., Dann, C., Locke, A. and Roper, S. (2019) 'Sharenting: Pride, affect and the day‑to‑day politics of digital mothering'. *Soc Personal Psychol Compass* e12443. https://doi.org/10.1111/spc3.12443.

Lipu, M. and Siibak, A. (2019) 'Take it down!': Estonian parents' and pre-teens' opinions and experiences with sharenting. *Media International Australia*, 170(1), 57–67.

Livingstone, S. (2006) Children's privacy online: experimenting with boundaries within and beyond the family. In R. Kraut, M. Brynin and S. Kiesler (eds) *Computers, Phones, and the Internet: Domesticating Information Technology*. Human Technology Interaction series. New York: Oxford University Press, pp. 145–167.

Lupton, D. and Williamson, B. (2017) The datafied child: the dataveillance of children and implications for their rights. *New Media and Society*, 19(5), 780–794.

Marwick, A. and boyd, d. (2014) Networked privacy: how teenagers negotiate context in social media. *New Media and Society*, 16(7), 1051–1067.

Marwick, A., Fontaine, C. and boyd, d. (2017) 'Nobody sees it, nobody gets mad': social media, privacy, and personal responsibility among low-SES youth. *Social Media and Society*, April–June, 1–14.

Montgomery, K. C. (2015) Youth and surveillance in the Facebook era: policy interventions and social implications. *Telecommunications Policy*, 39, 771–786 [Online]. http://dx.doi.org/10.1016/j.telpol.2014.12.006.

Moser, C., Chen, T. and Schoenebeck, S. (2017) Parents' and children's preferences about parents sharing about children on social media. In *Proceedings of the 2017 CHI Conference on Human Factors in Computing Systems*. Denver, CO, pp. 5221–5225. Available at https://yardi.people.si.umich.edu/pubs/Schoenebeck_ParentSharing17.pdf (accessed 10 November 2019).

Nelson, K. and Fivush, R. (2004) The emergence of autobiographical memory: a social cultural developmental theory. *Psychological Review*, 111 (2), 486–511.

Nissenbaum, H. (2010) *Privacy in Context: Technology, Policy, and the Integrity of Social Life*. Stanford, CA: Stanford University Press.

Quodling, M. (2018) Shadow profiles – Facebook knows about you, even if you're not on Facebook. *The Conversation*. Available at https://theconversation.com/shadow-profiles-facebook-knows-about-you-even-if-youre-not-on-facebook-94804 (accessed 27 November 2019).

Sebastian, C., Burnett, S. and Blakemore, S. J. (2008) Development of the self-concept during adolescence. *Trends in Cognitive Sciences*, 12(11), 441–446.

Shmueli, B. and Blecher-Prigat, A. (2011) Privacy for children. *Columbia Human Rights Law Review*, 42, 759–795.

Sorensen, S. (2016) Protecting children's right to privacy in the digital age: parents as trustees of children's rights. *Children's Legal Rights Journal*, 36(3), 156–176.

Steeves, V. and Jones, O. (2010) Surveillance, children and childhood. *Surveillance & Society*, 7(3/4), 187–191.

Steeves, V. and Regan, P. (2014) Young people online and the social value of privacy. *Journal of Information, Communication and Ethics in Society*, 12 (4), 298–313. Available at https://doi.org/10.1108/JICES-01-2014-0004.

Steinberg, S. (2017) Sharenting: children's privacy in the age of social media. *Emory Law Journal*, 66, 839–884.

Stoilova, M., Livingstone, S. and Nandagiri, R. (2019) *Children's Data and Privacy Online. Growing Up in a Digital Age*. London: Department of Media and Communications, London School of Economics and Political Science. Available at www.lse.ac.uk/my-privacy-uk/Assets/Documents/Childrens-data-and-privacy-online-report-for-web.pdf (accessed 27 November 2019).

Susser, D., Roessler, B. and Nissenbaum, H. (2019) Technology, autonomy, and manipulation. *Internet Policy Review*, 8(2). DOI: 10.14763/2019.2.1410.

Thomas, G. and Hocking, G. (2003) *Other People's Children. Why Their Quality of Life is Our Concern*. London: Demos.

Tunick, M. (2014) *Balancing Privacy and Free Speech: Unwanted Attention in the Age of Social Media*. Oxford and New York: Routledge.

Zuboff, S. (2019) *Big Other: Surveillance Capitalism and the Prospects of an Information Civilization*. London: Profile Books.

15 Changing environments

Peter Kraftl

Taubaté, São Paulo State, Brazil

Murilo[1] is a 15-year-old boy who attends High School in Taubaté. He comes from a lower middle-class family. Murilo's school has been heavily involved in a project experimenting with fairly basic, sustainable technologies for developing a school garden that could ultimately provide some food for students. The technologies are a starting point for a range of conversations with Murilo about the environment.

He talks about a 'solar irrigator' – a hand-made device that, using the sun's power, feeds water to the school garden when no one is around at the weekend to water it (Figure 15.1). The irrigator drip-feeds water to plants so that none is lost unnecessarily. Murilo points out not only the reduction in waste but the interconnection between water, energy and sustainable food cultivation: this system avoids using electricity to power the irrigator, using solar-renewable energy instead. The solar irrigator works alongside other simple devices, such as a biological filter. Importantly, as Murilo put it, 'the school garden was the incentive for the construction of other projects'. In other words, the idea of growing food to supplement that which the school has to buy in for students' lunches has spawned a range of fairly rudimentary – if ingenious – forms of technological experimentation. These experiments draw attention to the importance of apparently banal, *material* stuff in young people's relationships with the environment – just as Victoria Cooper (Chapter 1, this volume) considered the importance of such banal, material stuff for children and young people's identities.

Figure 15.1 A solar irrigator hand-made by Murilo, a 15-year-old boy in Brazil.

Murilo explains that the project and offshoot experiments have helped him and his classmates acquire a range of knowledges and skills – about energy, water, food and technology. For him, the key underpinning skills were biology (how plants grow) and a knowledge of materials (the properties of recycled plastics, metals and so forth used in constructing the irrigation technologies). The project afforded opportunities to gain information about these and other aspects of sustainable food – but also a place where, as Murilo put it, the students could 'make experience': how they could be involved in youth *action* for the environment.

Yet Murilo also looked beyond the school and the immediate implications of these experiments for knowledge and skill development. He emphasised how the project (and especially a device like the solar irrigator) brings home how resources like food, water and energy are all interconnected as a kind of *nexus* (a centre of connections between several things). Crucially, these interconnections are not separate from but are woven into young people's everyday lives and concerns – for instance, with choosing healthy food. Moreover, Murilo – like many young Brazilians – was keen to highlight how, just because these were everyday concerns, this should not mean that they are solely small-scale matters that are the responsibility of individuals. Rather, he advocated that the government could help with Brazil's ongoing challenges around social and environmental justice by 'investing in cheaper and more ecological technologies to reduce the production costs of both energy and water, and food as well'.

Introduction

One of the most pervasive assumptions in modern Minority Global North[2] contexts is the idea that children have lost their 'connectedness' with 'nature'. Herein, children have been rendered less knowledgeable about their (local) environment, the sources of their food and about environmental issues more generally, while becoming more vulnerable to manifold physiological and psychological illnesses (Louv, 2008). Indeed, this assumption sits at the heart of efforts to somehow 'reconnect' children with their environments – from Forest Schools in the UK to efforts to 'green' schoolyards in the USA, New Zealand and Australia (Freeman and Tranter, 2012). In many ways these are important and valid concerns; and each of these interventions can be tremendously beneficial, not only in terms of children's learning and health but in offering opportunities for socialisation and play (Chawla, 2015).

Nevertheless, with these assumptions in mind, the aim of this chapter is to (gently) question and to decentre these concerns. It does so in two ways, both of which are vital in order to understand the changing environmental conditions with which children are living – particularly, but not only, in relation to climate change, habitat loss and pollution derived from humans' addiction to oil-derived products, such as plastics. First, it highlights how children's relationships with the environment (or, as Kraftl *et al.* (2019) put it, 'childhoods–natures') are always more *complex* than discourses of nature disconnectedness imply. Second – and with the experiences of Murilo and other children like him in mind – it explores how children's relationships with the environment are also *otherwise* than these discourses suggest. In other words, those relationships – especially outside the Minority Global North – can look different than mainstream debates about childhoods–natures might imply.

Before moving on to discuss these kinds of complexity and otherness in more depth, it is important to understand two further ways in which academics and practitioners have framed the relationship between children and 'the environment'. Both of these relate back in some ways to the idea of nature (dis)connectedness; and both are woven through the rest of this chapter, even if the discussion that follows also offers critiques of these approaches. On the one hand, a key way of thinking about childhoods–natures is in terms of learning: Education for Sustainability (EfS) or Environmental Education. Established over many years, there exist multiple approaches to environmental education, which range from knowledge about local plant or animal species to understanding environmentally relevant behaviours, to critical debates about global environmental change (Corner *et al.*, 2015; Walker, 2017). On the other hand – and often well beyond questions of the environment – a considerable body of work has sought to explore children's experiences of, agency in, and movements through, outdoor spaces. Commonly, this strand of scholarship has been concerned with children's (independent) mobilities, and a concomitant assumption that increased levels of mobility are 'good' for children's health, learning and socialisation (Porter and Turner, 2019). Notably, these two strands of work overlap, especially as environmental educators seek to engender 'connections' of various kinds between children and environments. However, childhood scholars have increasingly sought to ask: How *else* do children relate with the environment, and with questions of sustainability (Horton *et al.*, 2015)?

Elements of (re)connection, learning and mobility are evident in the experiences of Murilo – the 15-year-old Brazilian boy whose reflections on solar irrigators and other technologies opened this chapter. For instance, Murilo emphasises how the project has spawned several forms of technological experimentation that have led to learning about resources, the affordances of different (recycled) materials and the small-scale production of food. It is therefore important to emphasise here that although this chapter seeks to add complexity and to look otherwise (and elsewhere) at children's changing environments, this does not mean that issues of (re)connection, learning and mobility are usurped by other issues. Rather, the chapter includes but extends beyond these kinds of concerns to prompt reflection upon what else matters in, and what else is constitutive of, the many ways in which childhoods–natures might relate. Indeed, as the last part of the chapter highlights, this might mean unpicking assumptions that children (and humans more generally) are separate from and therefore 'relate with' the environment.

In light of the above contexts, this chapter outlines three sets of ways for thinking about childhoods–natures. Each is at least implicit in the vignette that began this chapter (where the relevant terms are italicised). First, the chapter explores how it might be possible to consider the complexity of environmental issues through the concept of the *nexus*. The concept of the nexus focuses on ideas, materials or process – in the case of this chapter, resources like food and water – that tend usually to be thought about separately, in silos. Rather, it emphasises connections between those elements. This interconnectedness is at the heart of Murilo's reflections upon how – for instance – solar irrigators combine, at a micro-scale, questions about the interrelationships between food, water and energy. Second, the chapter looks at forms of *action* by children – contrasting forms of (globalised) protest with the apparently banal experimentation that took place at Murilo's school. Finally, it considers what it might mean to 'decentre' children to some extent (Spyrou, 2017): to focus on the non-human *materials* that constitute 'nature' and how understanding those materials is as important as listening to children's voices. Doing so might, for instance, require a closer look at the workings of things like solar irrigators. For, although the vignette at the start of this chapter is short on these kinds of detail, Murilo and his classmates will have spent *hours* deeply concerned with the material details of wires, bottles, pipes and other paraphernalia in order to get their irrigators just right. However, decentring children might also prompt a more radical rethink of what the relationships between children and their changing environments might look like, in ways that might prompt a rethink of the ethics and politics of childhoods–natures (Taylor and Pacini-Ketchabaw, 2018).

Resources, interconnectedness and nexus thinking

The city of Campos do Jordão is located on the main mountain ridge running through north-eastern São Paulo State. It is the highest city in Brazil, located around 40 kilometres north of Taubaté. It is most noteworthy for being a major tourist resort in the winter months for rich visitors from Rio de Janeiro. However, the city also gained fame for more traumatic reasons: a series of landslides in 2000 that killed at least ten people (Figure 15.2). The landslides all took place in an area of informal housing that has grown to accommodate the many people working in the tourist industry. Like many such settlements in Brazil and around the world, it experiences a range of intersecting challenges: limited access to electricity supply, often accessed via illegal hook-ups or controlled by local gangs; poor street lighting and transportation; limited access to water and sanitation; and, most evident from Figure 15.2, vulnerability to the extreme weather events that are occurring in Brazil with increasing regularity and ferocity (especially rainfall) (World Bank, 2011). Indeed, recent research on the landslides in Campos do Jordão has emphasised that their cause was complex and multiple: the siting of houses on a very steep hillslope that contains a number of springs, combined with extreme rainfall in the days running up to the landslide.

In their report about informal settlements in São Paulo and elsewhere, the World Bank (2011) highlights that marginalised groups – and especially children – are particularly vulnerable to the compound and complex challenges facing communities like the settlement in Campos do Jordão. Not only are they most at risk during and after extreme climatic events and disasters like landslides, or to the loss of food, water or energy supplies, when they are often the first to go without (UNICEF, 2019), but when combined with threats like violence, in turn perpetuated by poor public transport and street lighting, they may not be able to access regular schooling or work. What is so important here is that these challenges are multiple, complex and to some extent *intractable*. In other words, it is not always (or ever) easy to identify where to start in

Figure 15.2 An informal settlement in Campos do Jordão, Brazil, showing site of a landslide.

either analysing or attempting to 'solve' such challenges. Certainly, knowing about children's mobilities (i.e. where they go in such settlements) might help. Moreover, educating children about sustainable electricity sources, or about climatic changes that are causing heavier rainfall, might be part of the solution. However, as educators in Brazil and elsewhere have recognised, all of this work tends to take place in 'silos' that cannot fully broach the sheer complexity of the challenges that face children and their families in these places (Kraftl *et al.*, 2019). Indeed, to an extent, the same can be said of childhood and youth studies, where – often for good, practical reasons – academics have tended to study children's interactions with food, water or disasters separately (e.g. Mort *et al.*, 2018).

One response to the above challenges has been to try to reconceptualise phenomena such as food, water or energy not as separate elements but as a *nexus*. The most common nexus – exemplified in microcosm by Murilo's experiences – is the Water–Energy–Food nexus. Diverting from a consideration of children for a moment, it is worth noting how nexus scholars have attempted to draw out complex connections between these 'sectors' (for more details see Leck *et al.*, 2015). They start big: often looking at how national policies manage potential 'trade-offs' between different sectors. For instance, sticking with the same region of São Paulo State, one of the key 'trade-offs' centres on whether sugar cane – and the water used to grow it – should be used to produce sugar for food or bioethanol for energy. They look at flows: they combine analyses of water, energy and food, converting flows into complex equations or visualisations that show the combined passage of stuff into, through and out of cities. They combine disciplines: analysing such flows requires not only expertise from engineers or computer modellers but social scientists who can ascertain how policies are made and how people actually use these resources. Finally, they see nexuses as both opportunities and threats – water can be a vital resource as much as a key ingredient in a landslide.

However comprehensive these approaches might seem, they pose two problems for childhood studies scholars. One problem is scale: how to link the predominantly microscale studies of children's everyday lives and mobilities (Ansell, 2009) with the overwhelmingly large-scale (city, nation or bigger) analyses of the Water–Energy–Food nexus. The other problem, as I ask elsewhere, is of *where children are, precisely*, in attempts to analyse the nexus (Kraftl, 2020). For, despite attempts to include social scientists in studies of resource nexuses, their largely 'top-down' approaches to modelling and visualisation mean that real, fleshy people – aside from selected technical and policy experts – tend to disappear (Leck *et al.*, 2015). Moreover, marginalised groups like children – despite what we know about their heightened vulnerability to nexus threats – are notably absent from any of these analyses.

One answer to both of these problems is, as the final part of the chapter highlights, to perhaps – and not uncontroversially – decentre children from analyses of the changing environmental circumstances in which they live. Another is to attempt to (re)use notions of the nexus in ways that nevertheless enable some kind of a view of the complex ways in which children experience environmental change. Walker's (2020) analyses of children's (aged 11–14) environmental concerns in the UK and India is an important starting point. It constitutes one of the first attempts to develop a 'nexus' framework for studying the complexities of childhoods–natures while attempting to 'scale up' from the local scale. She seeks to 'explore how children and young people's everyday lives are both shaped by and have an impact upon multi-scalar processes that evidence uneven material and symbolic power' (Walker, 2020, p. 2).

Writing from the contexts of families living in the southern Indian states of Telangana and Andhra Pradesh, Walker explores vignettes (stories from children's everyday lives) relating to domestic intersections of food, water and energy. As in Campos do Jordão, environmental change operated as more than background context: rather, intensification of summer heat, combined with scheduled cuts to water and energy, played a crucial role in children's lives. In the story of Nageshwar – whose family are relatively affluent – everyday experiences highlight the scarcity of water *and* energy, and their combined effects. He recalled spending an entire day using a handheld fan to keep the house cool. He talked about how electrical load-shedding reduced water to the apartments in his block, since the water supply system operated on a powered pump. This meant, in Nageshwar's words: 'two buckets will be filled with water. We'll manage like that. Washing with the drinking water' (Walker, 2020, p. 6). This is an example of a nexus 'trade-off' that has effects across multiple scales – the coping mechanisms that Nageshwar and his family had to use, but which were vital if the load-shedding were to work (for instance, trying to start the pump or use air conditioning could overload the system, especially if many families tried to do the same thing at the same time).

However, in another example of 'scale-jumping', Nageshwar and his family were – thanks to their relative affluence – able to afford privately sourced water supplies. He was well aware of the effects of doing so, since in such conditions of scarcity buying in water privately could further divert an already scarce resource from wider public supplies and from poorer communities who could not afford to buy water privately.

In the above ways, Walker's (2020) analyses do draw attention to the ways in which children and young people learn and hold knowledges about the environment. Yet – both because of a more complex 'nexus' framework and the context of environmental change in India – the implications of these knowledges are different from the insights of Minority Global North forms of Education for Sustainability. On the one hand, these knowledges are derived informally – in a domestic setting. On the other hand, as Walker (2020) points out, these knowledges do not necessarily lead to 'virtuous' or 'responsible' forms of consumption: when combined with other families' consumption of privately sourced water or energy, Nageshwar's actions could have (and putatively *do* have) profound implications for water–energy trade-offs at the national scale.

Therefore, a nexus framework could be a key tool in developing analyses of the complex ways in which children are positioned in relation to environmental change and environmental resources, across multiple spatial scales (see also Kraftl *et al.*, 2019). As the rest of this chapter notes, it is not the only response to such intractable challenges. Nonetheless, it is an important one, since nexus policy-making and practice is taking hold at an international scale, but all-too-often ignores the voices and experiences of children like Murilo or Nageshwar. Moreover, a nexus framework perhaps operates best not as a stable 'answer' to the kinds of intractable challenges faced by a place like Campos do Jordão. Rather, it offers an opportunity to keep questioning: what are the particular combinations of environmental challenges (and opportunities) that *matter* to children, in any time and place – and where and how are children positioned in relation to them? And – as the next section explores – even if children are particularly vulnerable to environmental change, what kinds of *action* do they take in response?

Taking environmental action

You would think the media and every one of our leaders would be talking about nothing else. But they never even mention [climate change]. Nor does anyone ever mention the greenhouse gases already locked in the system. Nor that air pollution is hiding some warming; so that, when we stop burning fossil fuels, we already have an extra level of warming – perhaps as high as 0.5 to 1.1°Celsius. Furthermore, does hardly anyone speak about the fact that we are in the midst of the sixth mass extinction: With up to 200 species going extinct every single day. That the extinction rate is today between 1000 and 10,000 times higher than what is seen as normal. Nor does hardly anyone ever speak about the aspect of equity or climate justice....

In the year 2078, I will celebrate my seventy-fifth birthday. If I have children or grandchildren, maybe they will spend that day with me. Maybe they will ask me about you, the people who were around back in 2018. Maybe they will ask why you didn't do anything while there still was time to act.... So, when school started in August of this year, I decided that this was enough. I set myself down on the ground outside the Swedish parliament. I school-striked for the climate.

(Greta Thunberg, 2018)

During the year in which this chapter was written (2019), climate strikes were taking place every Friday around the world. In these strikes, children and young people left school to demonstrate about climate change and its effects. In the words of Greta Thunberg (above), who was a key protagonist in the strikes, these acts of protest were not simply designed to call attention to environmental change. Rather, they were intended as a call to listen and a call to action by big businesses and especially national governments who – as both the protestors and most climate scientists agree – had hitherto been taking rather piecemeal steps in dealing with climate change.

One of the key founding principles of social-scientific studies of childhood is that of 'agency' (Esser *et al.*, 2016). That is, a sense in which – because they are so often viewed as 'becoming adults' rather than as 'beings' in their own right – there is a need to uncover children's voices and their efficacy in the world, as human subjects. More recently, these ideas have been critiqued for overemphasising *children's* (independent) agency within wider, relational generational orderings (Punch, 2020; Abebe, 2019) and for ignoring the situatedness of children's agency within the workings of a whole world of non-human materials and processes (Kraftl, 2013; see below). If the previous and subsequent sections of this chapter offer a critique or 'decentring' (Spyrou, 2017) of

Figure 15.3 Young people taking part in climate strikes.

rather more straightforward celebrations of children's agency, this section nonetheless serves as a reminder that children can and do take *action*. As the previous section – and Nageshwar's use of privately sourced water – highlighted, the question is not so much one of reporting *on* different forms of agency but engaging in critical analyses of *how* and *why* children take action, and what the effects might be.

The climate strikes offer a notable example of youth action for several reasons. First, they are – in contrast to much writing on children's agency – noteworthy because of their global scale. Extending to thousands of cities around the world, literally millions of children took part. Second, they are remarkable because of their use of social media – like Twitter – in mobilising collective protest and then visualising those protests, via hashtags like #climatestrike. Indeed, the use of media – whether 'social media' or otherwise – has been a key element of youthful protest for many decades. From the mobilisation of young people across northern Africa and the Middle East during the 2011 Arab Spring (Jeffrey, 2012), to children's hidden-in-plain-sight popular cultures (Horton, 2010), the use of (social) media has enabled forms of subversion, protest and resistance by children and young people in ways that both transcend scales and occur below the radar of 'adult' surveillance.

Third, the climate strikes bring with them particular emotional and political overtones. Significantly, these cut against common constructions of childhood as either somehow vulnerable or innocent. Instead, the word that perhaps best characterises these strikes is *anger*. In a detailed analysis of millions of Tweets using the #climatestrike hashtag, I sought to provide a flavour of this sentiment (Kraftl, 2020). For instance, of 205,097 Tweets posted during a week in February 2019 (noting that many will have been posted by adults), a total of 20,114 (9.8%) reference the terms 'extinction', with other key terms being 'devastation' (3216), 'damage' (654), 'threat' (2458), 'crisis' (3299) or 'emergency' (6267). These terms, the anger that underpins them, and the anger in the words of Greta Thunberg and other protestors, contrasts keenly with the ways in which children are usually viewed as passive vessels for the future hopes of societies (Kraftl, 2008). Indeed, as Greta Thunberg put it:

> 'And yes, we do need hope. Of course, we do. But the one thing we need more than hope is action. Once we start to act, hope is everywhere. So instead of looking for hope, look for action. Then and only then, hope will come today.
>
> (Thunberg, 2018)

Fourth, a key point of contention around the climate strikes has been around their effectiveness, particularly in terms of the responses of powerful adults. Some responses have been engaged and positive. For instance, many cities and local authorities around the world have declared 'climate emergencies', in part as a direct result of these strikes. Others have been engaged positively but critically, pointing out that in many contexts – as is the case with other wider environmental movements – the strikes look rather white and middle class. Other adults have felt threatened: indeed, the prospect of children out of school, in public spaces, ostensibly doing nothing (or in this case demonstrating), has been perceived as a risk in many contexts (see, for instance, Langevang's (2008) analysis of young men hanging out in Accra, Ghana). In other words, 'doing nothing' can in itself be a powerful, if unexpected, form of youth social action. Others have reacted more negatively still, suggesting that children would learn more by being in school, and strongly implying that children should be 'put in their place' and do not have voices worth listening to.

Thus, actions like the climate strikes – and responses to them – should provide further fodder for critical consideration in future research on childhoods–natures. They highlight, in a different way from scholarship on the water–energy–food nexus, how children and environmental change are entangled in ways that extend beyond the local scale. They raise questions about whether and how (social) media are key tools in the doing of youthful environmental action – questions that require considerable further research (although, for starting points, see Smith and Dunkley, 2018; Land *et al.*, 2019; Kraftl, 2020). Finally, they draw attention to highly emotive and politicised discourses that surround children and their action on the environment.

Thinking materially: children, non-humans and Common Worlds

This part of the chapter discusses a final set of ways in which children's relationships with changing environments might be considered. It starts with a question, which is implicit in the rest of the chapter: What might it mean to *decentre* children from analyses of childhoods (Spyrou, 2017)? This is a question that has taken up a fair amount of discussion in childhood studies. It asks again about how children live their lives in relation to others – only in this case those others are not only other humans (i.e. adults) but *non-humans*. This means, in part, looking at how the animals, plants and materials that appear in children's lives might – in some times and places – be as important as the humans. This would, again, add complexity. Sometimes, this added complexity is required because in order to understand something that *matters* to children – a phenomenon like Murilo's solar irrigator – it might actually make most sense to start *not* by asking children but to look at how that phenomenon works, to only *then* ask what children think or how they use it. And sometimes, a decentring of children is a recognition that the boundaries between humans and non-humans are porous, unstable and blurry, and that it is virtually impossible to clearly define an individual human 'being' (Aitken, 2018).

My (Kraftl, 2020) research about plastics and other materials in the British city of Birmingham is an example of such approaches. Advocating an approach to childhood studies *after childhood*, I argue that, to better understand children's entanglements with plastics and other materials, children themselves must move in and out of focus. Take Figure 15.4: a totem pole created by 11- to15-year-old school students, in collaboration with some local artists. The totem pole represented the final in a series of workshops about plastics. Although beginning quite conventionally – along the lines of more familiar forms of environmental education – a key aim of the later workshops was to unsettle the students' understandings of and relationships with plastics. This was because although it is important to know which kinds of plastics can be reused or recycled, or what can be the effects of plastics on fish, plastics have what I call capacities for *synthesis* and *stickiness* (Kraftl, 2020). Plastics are synthetic because they can take so many forms and be melded with so many other materials: some with harmful effects, others not so. But, as they combine with other materials, plastics take on new lives – perhaps becoming entangled with other garbage in the great oceanic trash vortices that have been repeatedly shown in TV documentaries. Plastics are sticky because they will hang around for so long on earth – thousands or tens of thousands of years. We are stuck with them such that some theorists think they are a kind of indicator of a future '(en)plasticized world', in which there is no escape from plastics and their ill-effects (Ghosh, 2019, p. 277).

The idea of the totem poles, then, was to unsettle the students from their comfort zones in terms of how they knew and related to plastics. A key part of this manoeuvre was to acknowledge the 'lives' of the plastics themselves. The artists collected a wide range of plastic stuff – mannequin legs, synthetic clothing, toys, packaging, plant pots, and way more besides. This plastic stuff was sourced from charity shops, skips and other places. Most of it was deemed 'waste' – until it took on a new although rather odd value when it arrived at the school. But I also spend time considering the journeys of *those* particular plastic items to the school (Kraftl, 2020). I speculate about how some of those objects 'made it' to the pile of stuff on the classroom floor that then became the totem poles. Thereafter, the discussion turns to the creation of the totem poles themselves and interactions between the students and plastics – for instance, as in Figure 15.4, how the students found different kinds of 'value' or affordances in different plastics (the watering can for sustaining life; the helmet for safety; the rose for emotional value; and so on). Only after considering the 'lives' of some of the plastic objects, and students' interactions with them *as part of those lives*, does the analysis

Figure 15.4 A plastic totem pole created by school students in Birmingham, UK.

turn to students' verbalised responses to the task, and to the plastics themselves. This kind of focusing away from and then back on to the children themselves is one example of 'decentring' that pays closer attention to how childhoods are constituted as what Prout (2005) terms heterogeneous assemblages (complex mixtures) of humans and non-humans.

I also consider whether and how more unusual forms of interdisciplinary collabora-tion – and of methodology – might be required to engage in 'decentring' children in analyses of childhoods–natures (Kraftl, 2020). The idea here is not to be 'blinded by science' but to ask whether involving techniques from outside the social sciences (which look at non-human processes) might somehow tell us *more* about issues that matter to children. My concern is with a range of metals and other elements that circu-late around, into, through and out of children's environments and their bodies. With debates about air and other forms of pollution being of significant import, it is argu-ably not sufficient to simply ask 'what children think' or learn about these pollutants. Rather, using a range of techniques from environmental nanoscience, and working with students at the same school in Birmingham, I determined relative levels of different elements in samples of water, soil, breath and urine. I look in detail at the likely sources of some of these: aluminium, from smelting, antiperspirants and coal-fired power-stations; titanium (which will potentially be relabelled as a carcinogen in France), from food colouring, cosmetics and agricultural use.

Although the levels found in the samples were not dangerous, the challenge – as with nexus thinking – is how to analyse and visualise the tiny (micro- and nano-) and enormous (global) scales at which such elements circulate, and the fact that they only temporarily pass through children's bodies and environments in *their* lives. Critical here, I argue, is the inclusion of interdisciplinary methods. Alongside the traces of different elements I used more traditional qualitative approaches (a mobile phone app, interviews and a mapping exercise) to generate a sense of students' everyday routines and, therefore, what the likely sources of exposure were and how their interactions with plastics, metals and other stuff came about. These methods were just as vital as the bio-sampling, because it is rarely possible to be precise about the sources of elements as they appear in the environment (it turns out that one molecule of aluminium looks much like another).

The research in Birmingham is indicative of broader trends in non-representational, new materialist and posthumanist scholarship on childhood. As indicated above, all of that work seeks somehow to start elsewhere than with traditional methods for under-standing children's voices and agency, and seeks to *complicate* the picture by bringing in discussions of the vast array of non-human stuff – animate and inert – that humans live with. It emphasises how the 'line' between humans and natures is either blurred or virtually non-existent (hence the repeated use of the term 'childhoods–natures' in this chapter). Thus, 'learning about' the environment suddenly seems a rather inappropri-ate aim when we (human adults and children) *are* the environment. Instead, 'learning about' becomes replaced with modes of paying attention to and taking care of what some call the 'Common Worlds' that children, animals and others inhabit (e.g. Taylor and Pacini-Ketchabaw, 2018). Like the plastic childhoods research, these new ways of doing childhood studies constitute attempts to witness conjoined 'childhoods–natures' – with the hyphen between 'childhoods' and 'natures' representing all kinds of local, contextual, multiple relationships that cannot be captured by the rather more simplistic notion of '(re)connection' (see Kraftl *et al.* (2019) for a fuller discussion).

Concluding thoughts

This chapter has explored three key ways in which contemporary scholarship on children and changing environments has become increasingly *complex* and – at the same time – more attuned to *other contexts* beyond the Minority Global North. There are many pressing environmental challenges facing today's children – both now and into the future. These have been forcefully articulated by children themselves – through the #climatestrikes – as well as by key international agencies such as UNICEF (2019). It is important to remember that while many of these challenges are local and contextual, with effects that are patterned as much by gender, ethnicity, religion or class as by age, children around the world are often rendered vulnerable by their physical size, social standing and legal status. Thus, the development of conceptual and methodological approaches to address such complex and diverse 'childhoods–natures' remains a vital task for childhood studies.

This chapter has demonstrated that many of the key environmental challenges (and key opportunities) facing children in places like Brazil are complex and intractable. Therefore, attempts to add complexity are not merely aloof theoretical exercises: they are genuine efforts to unpick the causes and consequences of (for instance) the increasing prevalence of flooding and landslides in informal hillside communities in Campos do Jordão. Specifically, three sets of conceptual and methodological resources for broaching these kinds of complexity have been put forward in this chapter – although each should also be considered a prompt for further reflection (and, in turn, subject to critique, since none provides 'the answer'). Moreover, none of these should be viewed as a replacement for more conventional ways of thinking about children and environmental change – such as ideas of (re)connection, environmental education and/ or everyday mobilities.

First, *nexus thinking* was introduced as a way of explaining complex intersections of resources in and through children's lives – and especially water, food and energy. Doing so draws attention as much to creative attempts to deal with nexus 'threats' (such as the solar irrigator) as it does to potentially less 'virtuous' practices (such as buying in privately supplied water during conditions of drought). Second, the chapter offered a revised way to consider children's agency, with a focus on children's *actions* in the #climatestrikes of 2019 (and beyond). The strikes emphasise further the 'scaling-up' of action by children, alongside the key role of (social) media. But the strikes also draw attention – again – to competing emotions and political discourses associated with children and childhood. Finally, the impulse to 'decentre' childhoods – to render them 'out of focus', even if temporarily – was introduced as a way of articulating different, perhaps new, but certainly pressing concerns when it comes to children and changing environments. For the kinds of intractable challenges discussed elsewhere in this chapter – just like the problem of plastics – require perhaps radically interdisciplinary forms of scholarship and practice that foreground interconnections between children and more-than-human objects and processes. When combined with – rather than seen as a move away from – more traditional approaches to children's voice, agency or mobility, these three sets of resources could offer the springboard for powerful future interventions into children's manifold relationships with changing environments.

Notes

1 Murilo was a participant in my *(Re)Connect the Nexus* research project, which explored young Brazilians' experiences of, and learning about, the food–water–energy nexus (see Kraftl et al., 2019; www.foodwaterenergynexus.com/). Murilo is a pseudonym.
2 Minority Global North and Majority Global South are alternative terms for Global North and Global South, which aim to emphasise the fact that the majority of the world's population lives in the less affluent countries of the Global South.

References

Abebe, T. (2019) Reconceptualising children's agency as continuum and interdependence. *Social Sciences*, 8(3), 81.

Aitken, S. C. (2018) *Young People, Rights and Place: Erasure, Neoliberal Politics and Postchild Ethics.* Abingdon: Routledge.

Ansell, N. (2009) Childhood and the politics of scale: descaling children's geographies? *Progress in Human Geography*, 33(2), 190–209.

Chawla, L. (2015) Benefits of nature contact for children. *Journal of Planning Literature*, 30(4), 433–452.

Corner, A., Roberts, O., Chiari, S., Völler, S., Mayrhuber, E. S., Mandl, S. and Monson, K. (2015) How do young people engage with climate change? The role of knowledge, values, message framing, and trusted communicators. *Wiley Interdisciplinary Reviews: Climate Change*, 6(5), 523–534.

Esser, F., Baader, M. S., Betz, T. and Hungerland, B. (eds) (2016) *Reconceptualising Agency and Childhood: New Perspectives in Childhood Studies.* Abingdon: Routledge.

Freeman, C. and Tranter, P. (2012) *Children and Their Urban Environment: Changing Worlds.* Abingdon: Routledge.

Ghosh, R. (2019) Plastic literature. *University of Toronto Quarterly*, 88(2), 277–291.

Horton, J. (2010) 'The best thing ever': how children's popular culture matters. *Social & Cultural Geography*, 11(4), 377–398.

Horton, J. and Kraftl, P. (2018) Rats, assorted shit and 'racist groundwater': towards extra-sectional understandings of childhoods and social-material processes. *Environment and Planning D: Society and Space*, 36(5), 926–948.

Horton, J., Hadfield-Hill, S. and Kraftl, P. (2015) Children living with 'sustainable' urban architectures. *Environment and Planning A*, 47(4), 903–921.

Jeffrey, C. (2012) Geographies of children and youth II: global youth agency. *Progress in Human Geography*, 36(2), 245–253.

Kraftl, P. (2008) Young people, hope, and childhood-hope. *Space and Culture*, 11(2), 81–92.

Kraftl, P. (2013) Beyond 'voice', beyond 'agency', beyond 'politics'? Hybrid childhoods and some critical reflections on children's emotional geographies. *Emotion, Space and Society*, 9, 13–23.

Kraftl, P. (2020) *After Childhood.* Abingdon: Routledge.

Kraftl, P., Balestieri, J. A. P., Campos, A. E. M., Coles, B., Hadfield-Hill, S., Horton, J., Soares, P. V., Vilanova, M. R. N., Walker, C. and Zara, C. (2019) (Re) thinking (re) connection: young people, 'natures' and the water–energy–food nexus in São Paulo State, Brazil. *Transactions of the Institute of British Geographers*, 44(2), 299–314.

Land, N., Hamm, C., Yazbeck, S. L., Danis, I., Brown, M. and Nelson, N. (2019) Facetiming common worlds: exchanging digital place stories and crafting pedagogical contact zones. *Children's Geographies*, 1–14.

Langevang, T. (2008) Claiming place: the production of young men's street meeting places in Accra, Ghana. *Geografiska Annaler: Series B, Human Geography*, 90(3), 227–242.

Leck, H., Conway, D., Bradshaw, M. and Rees, J. (2015) Tracing the water–energy–food nexus: description, theory and practice. *Geography Compass*, 9(8), 445–460.

Louv, R. (2008) *Last Child in the Woods: Saving Our Children from Nature-deficit Disorder*. New York: Algonquin books.

Mort, M., Walker, M., Williams, A. L. and Bingley, A. (2018) From victims to actors: the role of children and young people in flood recovery and resilience. *Environment and Planning C: Politics and Space*, 36(3), 423–442.

Porter, G. and Turner, J. (2019) Meeting young people's mobility and transport needs: review and prospect. *Sustainability*, 11(22), 6193.

Prout, A. (2005) *The Future of Childhood*. London: Routledge.

Punch, S. (2020) Why have generational orderings been marginalised in the social sciences including childhood studies? *Children's Geographies*, 18(2), 128–140.

Smith, T. A. and Dunkley, R. (2018) Technology-nonhuman-child assemblages: reconceptualising rural childhood roaming. *Children's Geographies*, 16(3), 304–318.

Spyrou, S. (2017) Time to decenter childhood? *Childhood*, 24, 433–437.

Taylor, A. and Pacini-Ketchabaw, V. (2018) *The Common Worlds of Children and Animals: Relational Ethics for Entangled Lives*. Abingdon: Routledge.

Thunberg, G.. (2018) School strike for climate – save the world by changing the rules. TedX, Stockholm, 24 November. Available at https://blog.wozukunft.de/2018/12/19/greta-thunberg-tedx-2018-11-24/#201-11-24en (accessed 19 December 2019).

UNICEF (2019) *#Everychild2030: Key Asks and Principles for 2018 National Review Activities*. UNICEF.

Walker, C. (2017) Tomorrow's leaders and today's agents of change? Children, sustainability education and environmental governance. *Children & Society*, 31(1), 72–83.

Walker, C. (2020) Nexus thinking and the geographies of children, youth and families: towards an integrated research agenda. *Children's Geographies*, 18(3), 351–363.

World Bank (2011) *São Paulo Case Study Overview: Climate Change, Disaster Risk and the Urban Poor: Cities Building Resilience for a Changing World*. Available at http://siteresources.world bank.org/INTURBANDEVELOPMENT/Resources/336387-1306291319853/CS_Sao_Paulo.pdf (accessed 18 October 2019).

INDEX

Page numbers in *italics* denote figures.